D0432640

COLLINS PHOTO GUIDE TO THE

Birds of Prey

OF BRITAIN AND EUROPE,
NORTH AFRICA AND THE MIDDLE EAST

Benny Génsbøl

Illustrated by Bjarne Bertel

Translated by Dr Gwynne Vevers

Adapted for the English language edition by Dr C. J. Mead

Contents

HarperCollins*Publishers* 1992

Originally published in Britain by
William Collins Sons & Co Ltd
London • Glasgow • Sydney • Auckland
Toronto • Johannesburg

© GEC Gads Fortag 1984
© in the English translation William Collins
Sons & Co Ltd
First published in the English translation 1986
Reprinted with revisions 1987
Reprinted with revisions 1989
Reprinted 1992
ISBN 0 00 219176 8

The method of identification, all illustrations
and text matter in this book are the
copyright of the above publishers. Full
permission must be obtained to reproduce
them in any form whatsoever.

Filmset by Ace Filmsetting Ltd.
Frome, Somerset
Text printed and bound in Hong Kong
by South Sea International Press Limited.

Contents

Abbreviations

ad. – adult
imm. – immature

juv. – juvenile
w. – wingspan

Key to Distribution Maps

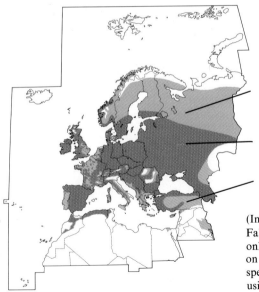

Orange: breeding range, only present in the summer

Dark orange: found throughout the year

Grey: winter distribution

(In the map for the Peregrine Falcon, the distribution is only shown in broad outline, on account of the rarity of the species. This is indicated by using a paler orange colour.)

Foreword

In the last two decades ornithologists have been particularly interested in two groups of birds: those living in wetlands and the raptors, or birds of prey. One of the reasons for this is that these groups have been badly affected by man; many waterfowl have lost their breeding and feeding places owing to drainage and reclamation schemes, and raptors have suffered from the much sited poisons, in the form of pesticides, fertilizers etc.

There continue to be numerous attacks on natural habitats of waterfowl, but at the moment it seems that the position is improving for raptors. After the catastrophic position in the 1950s and 1960s there is, at any rate in northern Europe, a clear improvement in the populations of several species. This is due to a cleaner environment, and a better appreciation of the position of raptors in the natural economy.

Fortunately it seems that man will spur himself into action when problems such as these occur, and will begin by setting in motion various forms of research. Thus, in the most recent years much information has been acquired on raptors. Very many people have undertaken projects which have helped to clarify the actual situation. Hence it was an attractive proposition to assemble some of this knowledge and to communicate certain parts of it in a form that is relatively easily accessible; with the enormous amount of information now available it has been difficult to draw a line between what must be included and what could be omitted on grounds of space. I have, as far as possible, given the population figures for the individual countries. This is a particular area where the accumulated knowledge has greatly increased in recent years.

Identification of raptors is another area in which much new information has been collected in very recent years. Thus, about ten years ago little was known about the identification of certain of the European species in flight. This is no longer so, but it remains a difficult subject.

The text for the identification section has been written in close collaboration with the book's artist Bjarne Bertel. This was especially valuable in the case of several southern and eastern species where my own experience is limited.

The numerous photographs in the book are also of great importance and considerable effort has been expended in obtaining the best available. A large number of photographers were approached and typically each has only supplied a few pictures. Pains have been taken to avoid posed photographs of birds that are tame or semi-tame.

Finally, I should like to thank the following for help in collecting information: Göran Bergmann and Kalevi Malmström (Finland), Wojtek Król (Poland), Louis Palma (Portugal) and Bernt-Ulrich Meyburg (West Germany).

In addition I am grateful to Steen Christensen for a critical perusal of the drawings for the identification sections as well as information on the appearance of some species that are rare in the Western Palearctic; to Lars Svensson for the same, and for reading through the text of the identification section and criticizing the drawings; and to Jørgen Bent Thomsen for work on the distribution maps, reading the manuscript and for information on papers from the raptor congress in Salonika, that have not yet been published.

A special and very warm thanks to Bent Pors Nielson for his particularly thorough reading of the whole manuscript.

Benny Génsbøl, May 1984

Spotted Eagle, adult in winter quarters, watching for prey in a stork colony.
Photo B. Génsbøl/Biofoto.

Introduction

Until a few years ago all the diurnal raptors were classified in a single order, the Falconiformes. Today, however, according to the list of recent Holarctic Bird Species by K. H. Voous (1977), they are classified in three orders, the Cathartiformes (New World vultures), Accipitriformes (kites, vultures, harriers, hawks, buzzards and eagles) and Falconiformes (falcons). The three orders contain about 290 species distributed throughout the world, except for Antarctica. The figure is only approximate because, in several cases, ornithologists arè not agreed on whether a population should have the status of a species or only figure as a race.

Taking the world population as a whole, the species are distributed unequally. Living conditions vary throughout the various climatic zones: the tropics have most species – about 130 breeding species and 125 visitors, with a total of about 210 regularly breeding. This corresponds to roughly 72 per cent of the world total, and they are roughly divided between savanna and rain forest. In the arctic tundra there are only four truly adapted species and four other regularly breeding raptors (scarcely three per cent of the world total). This is a reflection of the supply of prey in the two areas.

A survey of the division of species between the indifferent geographical regions shows that America and Eurasia each have roughly 100 species and Africa scarcely 90. This slightly smaller figure is possibly because

Africa has only tropical and subtropical climates. The somewhat smaller Australian region has scarcely 50 species.

Some of the species breed in more than one of these geographical regions. Most raptors are remarkable fliers, covering long distances; several of the continents are connected by land bridges, which facilitate movement from one area to another. In fact, only about 40 of the 290 species breed in more than one 'continent', and of these very few, four in all, breed in three. Only two species, the Osprey and Peregrine Falcon, are truly cosmopolitan, breeding in all four geographical regions.

Overlapping of distributions between the different parts of the world is greatest between Africa and Eurasia with roughly twenty species, and between Eurasia and Australia with about ten. It is remarkable that at least nine species breed in both the Old and the New Worlds. In addition to the two cosmopolitans these include such well-known species as the Goshawk, Rough-legged Buzzard, White-tailed Eagle, Golden Eagle, Hen Harrier, Merlin and Gyr Falcon, all birds which breed far north where the distance between the two continents is least.

The Western Palearctic has a total of 46 breeding raptor species (two, however, only irregularly) consisting of 34 of the order Accipitriformes and 12 of the Falconiformes. Of the 46 species only three belong solely to the Western Palearctic: Kite, Levant Sparrowhawk and Eleonora's Falcon. The others have a wider distribution.

7

Raptor adaptation

Golden Eagle

One of nature's characteristics is that all living organisms are adapted to their mode of life. Raptors have evolved special anatomical features designed for an existence based on continuous hunting for prey. These differ from genus to genus, as different characters are necessary to hunt lightning-fast swallows than to live on carrion.

The characters that particularly differentiate raptors from other birds are the morphology of the beak, wings, tail and eyes.

Raptor beaks
All raptors have a curved, pointed beak with the upper part longer than the lower, making it a tool for tearing flesh off prey animals. Vultures, dealing with large mammals and species

cordance between the shape of the beak and the food it takes.

For raptors, such as falcons and hawks, which catch birds it is an advantage to have a relatively short beak. Furthermore, falcons have developed a notch in the upper beak which assists in killing prey.

Peregrine Falcon

Buzzard

such as the White-tailed Eagle and Golden Eagle, which also eat carrion, require a beak of powerful dimensions: they have to be able to open up the carcass of a dead sheep or reindeer. The British ornithologist Leslie Brown studied the six vulture species in the Serengeti National Park in Tanzania and found an exact ac-

In the case of several little-known hawk species, an attempt has been made, on the basis of the form and strength of the beak, and also the shape of the feet, to estimate the type of prey they take. This method has been shown to be only approximate, and it would appear to require more detailed study.

Areas of naked skin
The naked areas on the head and neck of vultures show a high degree of specialization. Certain of the larger species stick head and neck deep into

Bearded Vulture

Black Vulture

the carcases they feed on; a cladding of feathers would become saturated in blood and gastric juices, a highly undesirable situation. Thus the parts concerned have evolved to be either naked or with small, stiff bristles. This adaptation makes it possible to tell the extent to which the individual vulture species deals with the flesh. The Egyptian Vulture only has a naked area around the head, whereas the Griffon Vulture has both head and neck down-clad. Other non-European species are almost naked on the head and neck so that without danger of fouling they can stick these parts into, for instance, the body cavity of larger mammals.

Raptor vision

Birds in general have remarkably good vision, and for raptors this is vitally important; prey has to be discerned at very long distances or under difficult conditions. It is probable that several raptors have reached the peak of what can be achieved in the field of vision; the Buzzard has about eight times the number of visual sense cells per square millimetre that humans have, indicating better vision. From a height of several kilometres vultures can discern even small items of carrion, and the Peregrine Falcon will hunt a bird which

we can only see with the help of binoculars.

Raptor eyes are so placed that they have forward binocular vision over a field of 35–50°. The monocular vision of each eye covers an angle of about 150°. Behind this there is an area of roughly 20° where the bird cannot see anything without moving its head around.

The raptor eye has a very special adaptation; there are two centres in the retina where the images are

Head of White-tailed Eagle. Note large eyes and eyebrows. *Photo A. Christiansen/Biofoto.*

formed. One of these functions mainly when the bird is using binocular vision, the other particularly in monocular vision. The eye is proportionately very large and is protected partly by the nictitating membrane, and partly (in several species) by a prominent eyebrow.

Sense of smell in raptors
Raptors have nostrils placed on the often yellow swelling or cere, of unknown function, at the base of the upper mandible. In general, the sense of smell in birds has hitherto been regarded as poor, which would also apply to raptors. However, new investigations have shown that it may play a considerably larger role than was previously thought. It has, for example, been confirmed that some of the New World vultures may be attracted to carrion by smell.

The raptor ear
In vultures with a naked head the ear can be seen as a small hole, but in general it is hidden among the feathers. In most species a sense of hearing is not essential for hunting, but it is an obvious advantage to be able to combine sight and hearing. Raptors do hear very well, and it is probable that, for example, hearing is important to Hen Harriers when flying low over open country. Their ears are placed asymmetrically; thus a mouse rustling in the vegetation can be exactly located by differences in the time that sound takes to reach the two ears.

There are, however, species in which hearing is an important/essential sense. South American forest falcons (*Micrastur*), which hunt in the twilight of the rain forests, have very large earholes and, like owls, they must use hearing when hunting.

The raptor wing
The mode of hunting of raptors extends from catching a swallow in flight to hovering for hours at a time in search of carrion. Wings for such different purposes must, by necessity, have evolved in different ways.

Raptor wings are of the same basic construction as those of other birds. There are 9–11 primary wing feathers, which are attached to the hand, but they vary in form from genus to genus. In some the outermost primaries are narrower than the remainder. Depending upon the extent of this process there are species in which the primaries are more or less free on the outermost part of the wing. When this is most marked the wings have a finger-like appearance, which is particularly characteristic of eagles and large vultures. The indented primaries function like the flaps of an aircraft wing, as regulators which adjust the up-flowing air stream. This system is, however, even finer, for each primary can be adjusted individually.

The inner part of the wing is mainly built up around the secondary wing feathers which are attached to the forearm or ulna. They may be short or long, depending upon whether the wing is narrow or broad. The number of secondaries varies much more than the number of primaries. A bird such as a Buzzard with a very moderate wing length has 10, while the large, long-winged vulture species has about 25.

In simple terms one can speak of

two types of raptor wing: the first is the soaring type, which is broad and combined with a full tail which can be unfolded as a fan, thus increasing the surface area. This is seen in its most characteristic form in the vultures (except the Bearded Vulture), eagles and buzzards and less markedly in the kites and harriers. The second type of wing is long, narrow and pointed, and thus adapted for fast flight and stooping, which is seen in the falcons. The

Rough-legged Buzzard

Golden Eagle

Goshawk

Peregrine Falcon

Montagu's Harrier

Buzzard soaring

Buzzard gliding rapidly

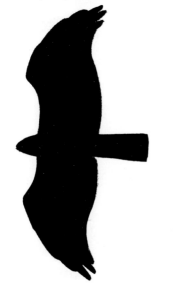

hawks, which hunt through dense vegetation with rapid turns, show an intermediate condition. Their wings are broad, short and rounded.

These different wing shapes have advantages and disadvantages. The typical soaring fliers are not fitted for long periods of active flight; their breast musculature is too slender for such a loading. These species are therefore usually airborne a little late in the day when thermals (warm air currents rising from the land) develop, helping to carry them up. When flying for long distances, as on migration, they fly over land to maximize the thermals, and do not fly over large areas of sea where there are no up-currents.

A Buzzard usually starts its migration during the morning. At this time it can find a thermal, and circles round higher and higher. The wings are spread out and so is the tail, its fan almost combining with the wings to increase the 'wing area' and thus the lift. When it reaches the top of the thermal the Buzzard begins to glide; the tail is folded, the wings curved slightly backwards and the bird glides forwards and slightly downwards. When it comes to the next valley or slope it finds the next thermal, and the process is repeated. In practice the bird can, in this way, be borne for hundreds of kilometres while using very little energy.

The species which use powered or active flight, such as the falcons and harriers, may also soar, but they do not usually rely on this method during migration. Thus they are not dependent to the same extent on the configuration of the country to produce thermals, but they may cross large areas of sea too.

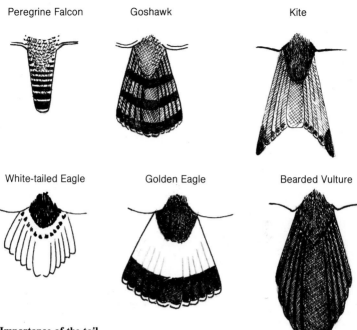

Peregrine Falcon   Goshawk   Kite

White-tailed Eagle   Golden Eagle   Bearded Vulture

Importance of the tail

There are many variations on tail-shape among the raptors: long and short, slightly forked and typically swallow-tailed, rounded and wedge-shaped. The importance of tail shape is still not entirely clear. It is, however, true that the species which need considerable manoeuvrability have a long tail, as for example the falcons, hawks and harriers. The importance of the tail as a steering mechanism is seen in the differences between tails in related species. Those that live in woodland and have to manoeuvre rapidly have longer tails than their relatives from open country.

Raptor feet

The foot of a raptor is normally adapted for killing. The prey varies considerably so it is not surprising that the feet also vary from species to species, but some general points have been established.

Short legs with very short, powerful toes suggest that the species catches its prey on the ground; a snake is best held with short, powerful toes as seen in the Short-toed Eagle. This is not an accidental development, for other

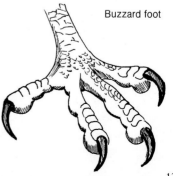

Buzzard foot

13

snake-catching species have similar feet. Long legs and long slender toes with owl-like, pointed talons are suitable for catching birds in flight. These species often have a long middle toe. If the prey does not die when struck by the raptor then the pointed talons will finish it off. This type of foot is characteristic of bird-catching hawks and falcons. A powerful back toe with a similarly shaped talon suggests that the species kills large mammals.

There are, of course, several intermediate forms to these generalisations.

There are other forms of specialization. Species which hunt on the ground have longer legs than others. This is most marked in the African snake-eating Secretary Bird which wanders about for several kilometres every day. In Europe, too, there are

species such as the Spotted Eagle and the Lesser Spotted Eagle which walk about in search of prey.

A more specialized condition is seen in the Osprey, which is equipped with toes that are adapted for holding slimy and often live fish: the underside of the toes is covered with some quite peculiar rough scales.

However, not all raptor feet are adapted for killing. Most vultures have talons that are reduced to very harmless structures which, in the course of evolution, have lost their original function.

Food

The number of species in existence today is partly a reflection on the choice of food available – species have evolved that are particularly well adapted to both common and uncommon food sources. Within the field of raptors this has led to as many as 290 different species; each of these hunts a definite type of food, for which they have become adapted, and each has also become adapted to suit different climatic conditions.

Although raptors have several food sources, there are two which are clearly dominant, namely birds and small mammals, mainly small rodents. Of the 46 raptor species in the Western Palearctic these are important prey for 38 of them. In general, secondary food sources include insects, reptiles, amphibians, fish, carrion and offal, although in some species these are primary sources. The following are different food sources, discussed in more detail.

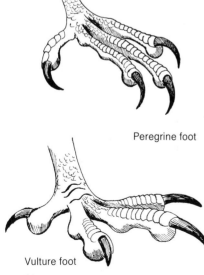

Peregrine foot

Vulture foot

'Specialities'

Some species have become specialized to take food not normally associated with raptors. These include the Egyptian Vulture which mainly eats waste material, e.g. faeces, and the Bearded Vulture which can digest bones: it has developed a special technique which involves dropping them from a great height so that they shatter.

Insects

In general, there are several species which regularly catch insects, mainly larger ones, such as grasshoppers and beetles. For species such as the Hobby, Eleanora's Falcon and Sooty Falcon, insects form an important part of the diet, but in, for example, harriers, kites, buzzards, eagles and falcons they are generally taken only as a supplement. Of the 46 species in the Western Palearctic there are only a few which do not at some time take insects.

It seems surprising that such a large raptor as a Honey Buzzard is specialized in catching insects, and to such an extent that the whole of its life cycle is centred on such prey. Thus, the species arrives late from its winter quarters and departs early in accordance with the abundance of wasps. It wakes and starts to hunt late because the prey only becomes active as the day warms up. It is less surprising, because of their small size, that species such as the Red-footed Falcon and Lesser Kestrel are also insect specialists.

Reptiles

Only one species, the Short-toed Eagle, has become a specialist in catching reptiles, mainly non-venomous snakes. However, reptiles (lizards

Red-footed Falcon, immature female with prey which it is tearing apart in the air. *Photo J. Christensen.*

in particular) are also an important food source for other raptors, such as the Booted Eagle, Dark Chanting Goshawk, Shikra and, in southern Europe, the Kestrel. Apart from these, 75 per cent of the total number of raptor species catch reptiles to a greater or lesser extent.

Amphibians

These hold a rather more restricted position as a food source. No raptor species has them as its main prey, but as in the case of reptiles most occasionally take them, and in particular frogs and small toads. Of the Western Palearctic raptors it seems to be the Lesser Spotted Eagle which particularly feeds on frogs (locally up to 42 per cent of the total prey), but frogs are also an important source of food for birds such as the larger Spotted Eagle and Marsh Harrier.

Fish

Such a commonly occurring food source as fish evidently require too much specialization to be generally taken by raptors. A single species, the Osprey, has developed a catching technique for the purpose and has fish as almost its only basic food. Fish are also very important for the White-tailed Eagle, but it can also feed on other prey if fish are not available in sufficient numbers.

Other large fish catchers are the Black Kite and Pallas's Sea Eagle. Kites and Marsh Harriers also catch fish, but not to the same extent.

Apart from these five species there are no other raptors that, generally speaking, feed to any considerable extent on fish.

Mammals

The main mammals caught by raptors are small and medium-sized rodents. There are so many species of these, from such differing habitats and in such large numbers, that many raptor species have become adapted to catch them. For species such as the Hen Harrier, Pallid Harrier, Buzzard, Rough-legged Buzzard, Long-legged Buzzard, Steppe Eagle, Imperial Eagle and Kestrel, they are simply the basis of existence. As the principal prey they very often account for over 90 per cent of the total catch in years with a good rodent population.

In addition, there are many other raptors which rely largely but not entirely on rodents. These include the Kite, Black Kite and Black-winged Kite, Marsh Harrier, Montagu's Harrier, Levant Sparrowhawk, Goshawk, Booted Eagle, Bonelli's Eagle, Golden

Pallid Harrier with a Heron. *Photo J. Pearson/Bruce Coleman.*

Eagle, Spotted and Lesser Spotted Eagle, Saker Falcon and Gyrfalcon (in lemming years).

In this last group there are a few raptors which catch game such as rabbits and hares, and thereby may come into conflict with sportsmen. These include the Goshawk, Golden Eagle, Imperial Eagle and Bonelli's Eagle.

Among the small mammals mice and lemmings are the principal prey. Larger species such as sousliks, marmots, squirrels and hamsters are also often caught. Other species taken include various shrews and moles, and less commonly small carnivores like weasels and martens; but most species, except the Golden Eagle, are just not strong enough to manage these.

Agricultural interests are not much affected by raptors, although the opposite opinion has often been expressed. It is true that from time to time a Golden Eagle will take a new-born lamb or reindeer calf, but these are usually weakened animals. The White-tailed Eagle has also been accused of killing new-born lambs, but this seldom happens. In fact, the birds are probably more interested in lambs as carrion.

Birds as prey
Falcons are especially renowned for taking birds as their principal prey; several species of different sizes hunt birds. In addition, the predators are divided geographically into the different climatic zones. In the main, falcons hunt in open country; in more enclosed terrains they leave the catching of birds to the hawks. The Sparrowhawk, for instance, is almost completely dependent upon birds for prey,

while the Goshawk is also a keen bird-catcher.

Although the falcons are in general seen as catchers of birds, they do this to varying extents. Birds form the most important prey for the Peregrine and Barbary Falcon: they generally catch nothing else. Other typical bird-catching raptors include the Gyrfalcon, Lanner Falcon, Eleanora's Falcon, Sooty Falcon, Hobby and Merlin, but locally or at certain periods of the year they may feed on other foods.

Apart from the specialists there are several raptors for which birds are a considerable but not essential food source. These species either catch birds when the occasion arises or when in good localities. This applies to the Kite, Black-winged Kite, Marsh Harrier, Montagu's Harrier, Levant Sparrowhawk, Dark Chanting Goshawk, Golden Eagle, Spotted Eagle, Bonelli's Eagle and Saker Falcon.

A number of species do not hunt birds to any great extent, even though there are local variations. These include Black Kite, Shikra, Hen Harrier, Pallid Harrier, Imperial Eagle, White-tailed Eagle, Pallas's Sea Eagle, Buzzard, Rough-legged Buzzard, Booted Eagle, Red-footed Falcon and Kestrel.

In all there are 33 raptor species which catch birds and for whom this prey is an important food source. In addition to the 33 there are other species which catch birds as a secondary source of food. Only five species, the vultures, do not catch birds, and of these there is still a possibility that the Bearded Vulture may occasionally kill living birds. In any case certain birds have learnt to recognize their raptor predators.

The birds taken range in size from a goldcrest up to a capercaillie. Most of those caught are the common species present or, for example, birds in colonies. Several of the bird-catching raptors mentioned are, however, such poor hunters that they generally only kill young birds or much weakened adults.

Raptors and sport

The fact that raptors catch birds has given rise to confrontations with the people who depend on these birds for their sport and livelihood. They felt their interests threatened and from the middle of the last century up to the middle of the present century they carried out systematic shooting of raptors.

Today we know that there are three species which share the human practice of hunting game birds: the Golden Eagle, Goshawk and Pere-grine, which mainly take wild game such as pheasants, domestic poultry or tame doves. The Goshawk, how-ever, may really cause havoc around unnaturally large pheasant stocks; but in general it is true to say that raptors do not affect *wild-living* prey to any great extent. At the most there may be moments of irritation for owners of shoots. Most raptors are only really successful with animals that are already weakened.

There may also be problems with raptors and domesticated animals; patience and goodwill are very necessary when a Goshawk visits a hen-yard. It is particularly the young Gos-hawks which go for easy prey in pheasant pens. Peregrines also arouse bitter hatred among pigeon fanciers, at any rate locally, by taking numbers of domesticated pigeons.

In former times such competition with man nearly always led to the raptor being shot. Man's attitude was

Griffon Vultures at dead sheep. *Photo G. Ziesler.*

clear: if the raptors could not keep away from what man wanted, they would be killed, regardless of the temptations put in front of their noses.

It is perhaps too optimistic to suggest that humans may now realize that the natural world around them is of value, and that it must be protected. If poultry, pheasants or pigeons are to be kept, then steps must be taken to prevent raptors reaching them, or if necessary suffer the losses. It is now occurring to more and more people that it is unreasonable that the original species should die as a result of competition with an introduced fowl from Asia.

Carrion

This is one of the more specialized food sources used by raptors. The large amount of nutritional value in carrion is reflected in the number of species which have become adapted in this field, particularly in the tropics. Vultures are normally regarded as typical consumers of carrion but of the area's five species, the Griffon Vulture, Lappet-faced Vulture, Black Vulture, Bearded Vulture and Egyptian Vulture, only the first four are typical specialists in the field of carrion. As already mentioned the Egyptian Vulture in particular feeds on offal.

Apart from the vultures, the Kite and Black Kite also eat much carrion, especially the latter. Carrion is important to the White-tailed Eagle, particularly in winter, and also to Pallas's Sea Eagle. Generally speaking several of the buzzards and eagles feed on carrion in adverse conditions, commonly in winter.

Hunting methods

Raptors use three different methods of hunting, namely searching flights, hunting from a perch and 'wandering'. Naturally these vary from species to species, and one particular species will use more than one type of hunting, depending on the prey. Searching may take place from a great height as in the Griffon Vulture, from a medium height as in the Golden Eagle or quite low over the ground as in the harriers. Soaring is used by the Long-legged Buzzard and others, active forward flight is common in the kites or hovering over the same point as in the kestrels.

Many species hunt from a perch, which is normally low, such as a branch, post or haystack, and also from a greater height as for instance an electric pylon. The prey is usually on the ground.

Some hunt on foot for prey that is of secondary importance, such as mammals, insects and frogs.

Characteristic hunting methods

Certain of the raptor families have a characteristic method of hunting. Thus, the kites search slowly from a very low height, the harriers also slowly but from a height of only a few metres with raised wings and periods of gliding. The hawks make very rapid surprise attacks, using every opportunity for concealment, while the falcons stoop on their prey.

Multiple hunting methods

Sometimes closely related species use methods that differ from their more usual hunting methods. Thus, Buzzards often hunt from a perch, the

Rough-legged Buzzard hovers and the Long-legged Buzzard soars. However, all three may diverge from the typical form, and in winter Buzzards frequently hunt like a Rough-legged Buzzard, hovering over open country.

It is remarkable how seldom ornithologists actually see a raptor hunting. This does not apply to hunting Kestrels or to Merlins and Red-footed Falcons searching for insects, but to more dramatic moments.

The reason for this is that many species only hunt when they feel secure, such as when humans are not in the vicinity; also hunting sometimes takes place in difficult terrain and it is often over in a few seconds, so that it is hard to see everything that is happening in any detail.

American investigations

Using a special camera that takes 800–1000 pictures per second the American G. E. Goslow has filmed raptors hunting; he had to use captive birds for this but it is not thought that this invalidates his findings.

He investigated two main species, Cooper's Sparrowhawk (*Accipiter cooperii*) and an American race of the Goshawk (*A. gentilis*). The two species used the same hunting technique: it began with active beats of the wings, which stopped at heights of 3.4–4.5 m and 7.5–9.0 m respectively from the prey; the actual attack took place in a glide. When quite close to the prey, hawks swing the pelvic region forwards so that it lies just under the head, brake with the tail spread and move in rapidly to seize the prey with the feet.

From his observations Goslow could see that at the moment of striking the different parts of a raptor move at different speeds. In Cooper's Sparrowhawk the bird's general speed at the head measured 4.8 m per second, while the pelvis moved at 9.5 m per second and the legs at 11.4 m per second. The result is that the prey is struck at twice the speed of the bird's normal velocity. The forward and upward movement of the spread wings and tail means that at the moment of striking the bird is almost lying on its back. The talons penetrate the prey as the bird tries to kill it, and if this does not succeed the hawk strikes it at the back of the neck after landing.

The Red-tailed Buzzard (*Buteo jamaicensis*) was also used in the investigation. In principle, the method of capture was very similar to that of the hawks, but the speed at striking was considerably less: 4.25 m per second at the head, and 6.5 m for the

Hawks swing pelvis area forwards, brake by spreading tail and strike feet forwards into the prey.

feet. For comparison a Goshawk strikes at speeds of respectively 14.0 and 22.5 m per second, so the feet strike at a speed of about 3.5 times as fast as those of the buzzard. As the power of a strike increases by a factor of four with the speed it means that the Goshawk strikes prey ten times more powerfully than the Red-tailed Buzzard, although the two birds weigh about the same (the Goshawk weighs slightly less).

Goslow's investigation, therefore, provides a logical explanation of how the Goshawk is able to strike prey that is relatively large, much larger than the Buzzard can manage.

As already mentioned Goslow used captive American raptors for his work. Free-flying birds might possibly show better form and perhaps different speeds. It is, however, likely that the technique of capturing prey is roughly the same apart from certain details, and that this would apply equally to species from the Western Palearctic.

Buzzards circling at Falsterbo. *Photo A. Christiansen/Biofoto.*

Raptor migration

The Western Palearctic area covers all four climatic zones, the principal ones being the temperate and subtropical. Only parts of Iceland and the polar islands are arctic, while only the south-western corners of the area and most of the Atlantic islands are tropical. These very different climatic conditions mean that the species have evolved a variety of overwintering patterns.

In spite of very short days, snow and intense cold, some raptors remain in their breeding area throughout the year, even quite far north on the European mainland. Thus, old Golden Eagles are reluctant to leave their territory unless hunger forces them to do so in severe winters. Gyrfalcons and Goshawks may also remain in their territory throughout the winter in the most northerly regions, but some of the Russian Gyrfalcons and the most northerly Goshawks move to more southerly parts. The three species mentioned can only remain in the breeding area because there is sufficient food for them, but large numbers of small birds migrate southwards, so leaving insufficient food for species such as the Sparrowhawk and

21

Merlin; they have to follow the small birds southwards. The Rough-legged Buzzard preys on small rodents, that remain sheltered beneath the snow, so this raptor has to leave the breeding area too. One can, therefore, consider the north European raptors, one by one, and confirm whether their food sources are close by and accessible or whether they become so reduced in numbers that the raptors have to leave their home range.

It is not only the arctic populations and those furthest north in the temperate zone which are forced away because of lack of food. Several southern species also leave their breeding grounds, such as the Short-toed and Booted Eagles, Egyptian Vultures, Eleanora's and Sooty Falcons and Lesser Kestrels. These are species which, in one way or another, are highly specialized and which are not able to find enough food in winter, even in these climatically mild regions.

Truly migratory raptors account for 24 out of the 46 breeding species in the Western Palearctic. There are some species in which the whole population migrates south or west to spend the winter in a well-defined area. In others the northern populations migrate, the southern do not, but they may disperse, and the transitional populations are partly migratory and partly non-migratory. This accounts for twelve species, including the Griffon Vulture and Imperial Eagle.

Finally, there are very stationary species in which the adults overwinter in the territory or in its vicinity. To a varying extent the young may migrate or more often disperse from where they were hatched; this differs from migration, where the birds move in a fixed direction. There are ten species which do not migrate, but may disperse, namely Tawny, Black and Bonelli's Eagle, Black-winged Kite, Dark Chanting Goshawk, Black, Lappet-faced and Bearded Vulture, Barbary and Lanner Falcon; these are all essentially southern species.

Soaring migrants

The large, broad-winged raptors such as buzzards, eagles and vultures, avoid migrating over the sea where there are no thermals. Their method of migration is based on rising air currents from the warm land. With the help of these they propel themselves up to a height of 300 metres or more and then glide forwards and downwards until they meet the next rising thermal wind. This is a particularly energy-saving form of flight; the wings are scarcely being used in active flying at all.

To avoid sea passages, and no thermals, these raptors have developed a migration pattern which takes them over land bridges, thereby crossing the sea at the narrowest points. Soaring migrants mainly fly on fixed routes, of which one of the most important is in the western Mediterranean, via Gibraltar.

Another main route to Africa passes east of the Mediterranean via the Bosporus, Turkey, the Middle East and Sinai. This is used principally by raptors from eastern Europe. A third, used mostly by Russian birds, goes through the Caucasus, along the eastern side of the Black Sea. This

Golden Eagle in winter landscape.
Photo B. Lundberg/N.

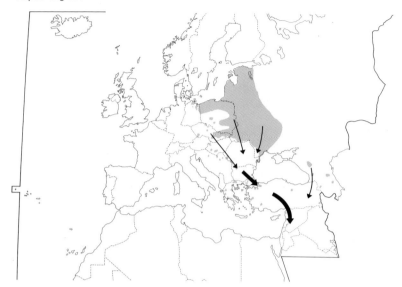

Lesser Spotted Eagle: Narrow-front migration over the land bridges. The whole population (less the Caucasus birds) passes the Bosporus in autumn.

is the most important route as regards numbers. In 1976 some 370,000 birds migrated this way, as against a typical tally of 75,000 for the Bosporus and 190,000 for Gibraltar. Other more secondary routes travel over Italy and Sicily, through Greece, Crete and Cyprus.

Active fliers

The secondary Mediterranean route is rarely used by soaring migrants, except Honey Buzzards which pass Cyprus, Sicily and Malta in large numbers. Such routes are mainly used by the active fliers, such as Ospreys, harriers and falcons which do not appear to try to avoid flying a few kilometres over the open sea. This is reflected in the fact that they

are only recorded in limited numbers at the big migration stations.

The tables on pages 26–28 show the extent of migration at the best-known places.

Spring migration routes

Most of the spring migrants pass through the principal migration stations, namely Gibraltar and the Bosporus, but quite a few, at least 40,000 in 1974 and 1975, leave Africa via Cape Bon in Tunisia. The largest concentrations in the Mediterranean are seen at Eilat in Israel (*see* table). The Scandinavian populations reach their breeding sites either through eastern Denmark and across Øresund or through Jutland, crossing the sea at Skagen.

The autumn migration routes for

three species are shown: a typical soaring migrant (p. 24), one that uses active flight (p. 25), and an intermediate form (p. 26).

A typical day of a soaring migrant

Thermals first appear when the sun has warmed up the air masses, then the warm air begins to rise. Thus the first soaring migrants are seen some hours after daybreak, from 8 to 10 a.m., and they often migrate throughout the day until about 5 p.m. The migration technique used normally carries them 25–50 km per hour, the difference in speed being related to the wind direction. It is obvious that a following wind gives greater speed than a contrary wind.

Little is known about the distances covered per day by individual raptors. It is likely, however, that Buzzards migrating over Europe cover roughly 200 km per day.

Migration of the Steppe Buzzard

It seems that some soaring migrants must travel for even longer daily stages, in order to reach their winter quarters at the time we actually know they do arrive. In his book *Birds of Prey* Leslie Brown discusses the long-distance migration of the Steppe Buzzard. From its northern breeding

Cont. on p. 28

Hobby, a raptor using active flight during migration. It flies to Africa via the land bridges over Spain, Italy and the Balkans. It may also pass the Mediterranean without using the narrowest passages. The result is a very broad-fronted migration, and the numbers of Hobby at the great migration stations are therefore restricted. The arrows only show the probable migration routes.

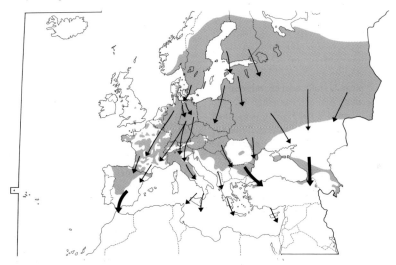

The Honey Buzzard has an intermediate form of migration. It can use soaring flight, or fly actively over long distances. The thick arrows show where migration is concentrated, while the thinner ones show secondary migration routes over large sea areas.

Number of raptors in the autumn migration at migration stations in the Mediterranean area and Caucasus:

	Gibraltar 1972 and 1974	Malta 1969–73	Bosporus selected years in period 1966–78	Arhavi/ Borcka 1976	Suez 1981
Honey Buzzard	57,600–114,000	445–824	900–23,600	137,600	79
Black Kite	24,500–39,000	7–20	1280–2730	5775	106
Kite	60–100	–	max. 10	–	–
Egyptian Vulture	2100–4000	1–7	max. 600	5	437
Griffon Vulture	420	–	max. 200	–	1284
Short-toed Eagle	4800–9000	2–11	1230–2340	243	9447
Marsh Harrier	150–350	–	max. 10	385	–
Hen Harrier	10–110	–	max. 10	–	–
Montagu's Harrier	790–1700	2–5	max. 10	124	–
Pallid Harrier	–	1	1–3	133	–
Sparrowhawk	560–950	1–2	max. 500	–	–

Levant Sparrowhawk	–	–	2800–7200	290	–
Buzzard	2700–2800	2–7	13,000–32,900	205,000	640
Long-legged Buzzard	–	–	max. 10	5	1816
Imperial Eagle	–	–	max. 20	3	556
Steppe Eagle	–	–	–	271	64,880
Lesser Spotted Eagle	–	1–2	4300–17,200	736	21,552
Spotted Eagle	–	–	max. 20	10	86
***Aquila* Species**	–	–	–	–	31,430
Booted Eagle	6870–15,140	1–2	max. 550	473	761
Osprey	40–60	7–16	max. 10	–	–
Hobby	200–220	147–233	max. 125	–	–
Red-footed Falcon	–	2–5	max. 250	–	462
Kestrel	800–1200	109–730	max. 25	–	–
Lesser Kestrel	260–550	33–80	–	–	–

Sources: Report of World Conference on Birds of Prey (Vienna, 1985). Various duplicated reports on migration at Bosporus, Beaman and Galea: The visible migration of raptors over Maltese Islands (*Ibis* 1974, 419–31). Bijlsme: The Migration of raptors near Suez, Egypt, autumn 1981, *Sandgrouse* No. 5 (1983). Cramp, S. and Simmons, K. E. L.: *Birds of the Western Palearctic* Vol II, 1979.

The spring migration at Eilat, Israel 1977, 1983, 1985 and 1986

Honey Buzzard	225,952–851,598	**Steppe Eagle**	19,288–75,053
Black Kite	24,728–28,320	**Imperial Eagle**	30–95
Egyptian Vulture	270–820	**Lesser Spotted Eagle**	40–74
Short-toed Eagle	132–345	**Spotted Eagle**	5–10
Marsh Harrier	93–371	***Aquila* species**	9083(1977)
Sparrowhawk	76–456	**Booted Eagle**	109–175
Levant Sparrowhawk	905–17,034	**Osprey**	49–130
Buzzard	142,793–465,827		
Long-legged Buzzard	28–105		
Buteo/Pernis/Milvus	149,264(1977)		

Source: Christensen, S., Lou, O., Müller, M. and Wohlmuth, H. The spring migration of raptors in Southern Israel and Sinai. *Sandgrouse* No. 3 (1981), 1–42. H. Shirihai: Eilat – an Int. Highway for Migr. Raptors. Int. Bird Watch. Center, Eilat.

grounds this raptor migrates 13,000–16,000 km to southern Africa in 6–8 weeks. So the average day's flight works out to be 240–400 km, assuming that the bird flies every day. This, however, is unlikely. The bird needs time for foraging, and the weather may not always be suitable for migration. On certain days the bird must, therefore, cover greater distances than suggested above.

Little or nothing is known about the daily flights of the active-flying migrants. It is clear that rapid-flying falcons are able to cover long distances, but whether they actually do so is not yet clear.

Foraging during migration

In his book Leslie Brown also puts forward an interesting theory. Active fliers, such as harriers, hawks and falcons, are often seen hunting for prey during pauses in migration, and they apparently catch the normal amount of food. On the other hand, soaring migrants do not seem to forage to the same extent. For a bird such as a Honey Buzzard with a long journey from Europe to Africa it would be an advantage to lose weight in the migration period. By losing 10–20 per cent of its body weight it will be lifted more rapidly by thermals and migration will become quicker. This is as yet only an attractive theory.

Migration through Northern Europe

Unfortunately for the British birdwatchers there are no good migration-watching sites in Britain for raptors. Certainly, had we the populations of long-distance soaring migrants that may have existed in the past, there would have been concentrations of birds crossing the Channel into France

Number of raptors on autumn migration at Falsterbo and Stigsnaes

	Falsterbo 1973–84	Stigsnaes 1980–83
Honey Buzzard	2670–11,200	275–2900
Black Kite	1–2	1–2
Kite	19–112	5–42
Marsh Harrier	39–150	85–231
Hen Harrier	72–221	122–202
Sparrowhawk	2290–17,042	2757–3916
Goshawk	2–36	1–15
Buzzard	5761–17,200	7680–31,286
Rough-legged Buzzard	141–1619	63–109
Osprey	55–180	37–78
Peregrine Falcon	1–8	1–5
Hobby	6–34	6–27
Merlin	79–177	46–64
Red-footed Falcon	–	1–11
Kestrel	135–513	75–217

Sources: Various annual reports from the Falsterbo Ornithological Station and the Stigsnaes Ornithological Station.

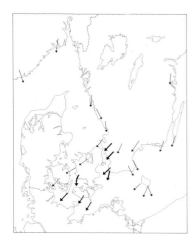

Autumn migration routes over southern Scandinavia. The main routes are shown by thick arrows. Note the preponderance of the route Scania to Zealand.

station for numbers and variety of birds. The passage is especially good if regular westerly winds set in. The numbers of birds will also depend on the species' population level and, with those raptors depending on small mammals for food, on the prey situation. Fluctuations in numbers may be three- or four-fold over just a few years. For instance high and low values, during the 1970s, for Falsterbo in autumn for three species are:

Buzzard   17,200 (1974), 5700 (1975)
Sparrow-
hawk   17,000 (1984), 2300 (1977)
Honey
Buzzard   11,000 (1974), 2700 (1978)

Of course the arrival of these birds in Denmark is nowhere near as concentrated as the departure from Sweden.

In the spring it is Denmark which

from Kent. However, since we do not now have the birds breeding with us, nor are there populations nesting north of us, all that most bird observatories are generally able to log are Kestrels and Sparrowhawks, with the occasional Hobby or Osprey.

However, the situation is very different in Scandinavia. Here there are some very healthy populations of soaring migrants and the geography of the region naturally funnels the migrants to particular sites where very large numbers can be seen. As is to be expected the points of concentration are different in the spring from the autumn. Also the prevailing winds, at the time of migration, can influence the exact route taken by the stream of birds.

During the autumn migration it is Falsterbo, the south-westernmost point in Sweden, which is the best

Spring migration routes over southern Scandinavia. The main routes are indicated by thick arrows. Eastern Denmark is the central area, but with easterly winds many birds fly up to Skagen.

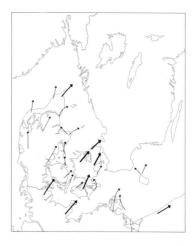

comes into its own. Unfortunately the birds are not concentrated quite as much as during the autumn and so there may be migration taking place over several of some dozens of different sites. In some years good numbers may even pass over the Copenhagen area. The one exception is the northernmost tip of Jutland, Skagen, where a really good spring migration of raptors can generally be guaranteed.

Breeding biology

Breeding is normally associated with spring. In general, this also applies to raptors, but this may not be the whole story for the breeding cycle lasts for up to eight months in some of the large species. Thus, in southern Spain, Bearded Vultures start to take an interest in nest sites as early as October, and in the same period many Eleanora's Falcons still have young in their nests. However, like other species, raptors have to rear their young when food is most readily available, so the breeding period follows the usual pattern with young in the nests in late spring and early summer.

The breeding age
There is considerable variation in the age at which different species become sexually mature, which apparently has something to do with size. Large eagles and vultures have to be roughly five years old before they start to breed. For medium-sized species three years seems to be the norm, and the smallest falcons breed when they are barely one year old.

But contrary to this, the falcons all seem to be able to breed in their first year regardless of whether they are the smallest species or the medium-sized Gyrfalcon. It should be pointed out that they can breed at this age, but the extent to which they actually do so is not known.

In many species a balanced population apparently does not allow the youngest birds to survive; there is evidently no room for them. But under extreme conditions this may not happen. After the severe winter of 1978–9, for example, there were unusually large numbers of one-year-old Goshawks among the breeding pairs in Jutland. There had not been sufficient old birds to replace those that had not survived the winter, thus giving the young birds a chance.

Losses due to a hard winter are rapidly made good in a healthy population, but unmated young of the large eagles would suggest that the population is not thriving. Most European populations of the White-tailed Eagle do not produce enough young to occupy any empty sites.

So it may be that the start of breeding does not necessarily coincide with the period at which individuals are capable of breeding.

Body size and clutch size
It may be surprising that there should be such variation in the age at which raptors attain sexual maturity, yet it is an expression of a general biological principle, that populations will only rear the number of young necessary to maintain a balance.

As already mentioned it is the large

Imperial Eagle, eastern race, landing on the nest. *Photo B-U. Meyburg.*

species, those with few or no enemies, which start breeding late, and they also produce small clutches. A very small annual production of young is sufficient for these species to survive. Such production norms became established thousands of years before man, and no allowance has been made for the depredations of this relatively late enemy. Large raptors have, therefore, been evolved to have a long life and a low annual rate of reproduction.

The situation is different with the small species. They can breed when only one year old, laying clutches of 4–6 eggs or more, and they themselves may fall prey to the larger species. The replacement is high and the average longevity correspondingly low. They have to produce numerous young for the population to survive, and thus early sexual maturity is the norm.

Non-migrants

In some species the pair remains on the territory throughout the year, and in some of these, the Golden

Eagle for example, the birds are, to a varying extent, completely tied to the home range. This is shown in their periodic visits to bring in new nest material. The sexes are frequently seen together, and at the onset of the breeding season they will have completed the various rituals which will ensure synchronization of the whole breeding process.

Migrants

It is usually the male migrant that arrives first at the breeding site. He establishes or re-establishes the territory and advertises his presence by loud screeches. If both sexes from the previous year's pairing are still alive they probably meet on the territory to carry out a new breeding season together, not through a feeling of solidarity but due to a common link with the old nesting site. In a species such as the Honey Buzzard young birds breeding for the first time may form pairs in the winter quarters. This accounts for observations of both sexes arriving at the breeding sites at the same time. As they already know each other they may have eggs in the nest about twenty days after taking up the territory.

Display flights

At the start of the breeding season all species perform some form of display. With its calls, special movements, demonstrations of plumage tracts, flight manoeuvres and so on this serves to regulate the breeding process. In many species the flight display is an impressive phenomenon. There are only a few main types, showing the close relationships, with variations from species to species.

The broad-winged soaring raptors have the most impressive displays, and two types have been observed. One is a form of undulating flight, where the bird performs a short dive with the wings more or less folded, then rises to its starting height with energetic wing beats, dives again, rises and so on. This type is used, for instance, by Ospreys, Honey Buzzards, Egyptian Vultures, Short-toed Eagles, the four harriers, Golden Eagles, and with less pronounced dives by the kites and hawks.

The second type is a very dramatic performance. The bird spirals up to a great height, folds the wings against the body and drops in a powerful dive. The fall is braked when the wings are spread out and, using the speed attained, the bird shoots up again. When it starts to slow down, but before the bird reaches the initial height, it starts a new dive. This manoeuvre may be repeated so that eventually the bird finds itself relatively low down, perhaps reaching a height of some hundred metres below the starting point. This type of display is characteristic of several buzzard and eagle species, and is very easy to see, for instance, in a Buzzard at the start of the breeding season.

In these two types, the female may take part in this fascinating performance, but she is often a very passive observer. When she does take part, the male drops towards the female who turns on her back, showing her talons; in certain cases these are seized by the male. As he is not strong enough to carry her in this way the birds fall slowly to the ground and release one another.

It is a characteristic of almost all

Goshawk in display, showing the outstretched vent feathers. *Above right*: probably its mate. *Photo K. Karel.*

forms of display flight that it commences with loud screeching.

In addition to these two distinctive forms of display the falcons have a somewhat less striking pursuit flight and the large vultures perform a mutual soaring flight.

The function of such displays is not quite clear. It seems likely that they help to synchronize the breeding process. When a male Osprey, immediately after arrival, performs his display flight, screeching loudly over the territory, it is certain that this is partly to mark the territory, and partly to attract the female. When a pair of Buzzards soar and display above the nest site, also screeching loudly, this probably helps to maintain the territory as well as providing a sexual stimulus. This interpretation is not always so easy, as in many species such display flights are also seen outside the breeding season.

Black Eagle, adult with nest material.
Photo G. Ziesler/Jacana.

Nest building

In most cases the next phase of the breeding cycle involves the building of a nest. The falcons are the only exception; they either take over the nests of other species, lay directly on cliff ledges, possibly scraping a small depression, find a small cave or even lay their eggs directly on the ground.

However, all the other Western Palearctic species build their own nests, most commonly in a tree. Certain species frequently use a cliff ledge and a few, the harriers, build on the ground.

In many cases the birds choose an old base for the year's nest. This may be the pair's own nest from the previous year, but it may have been built by another species. An individual pair may often have several nests to choose from; up to fourteen have been recorded for the Golden Eagle, but for this species there are usually 2–3, of which one is the preferred nest. In certain nests new material may be added, year after year, so they become very large, up to 6 m in height and 2 m in diameter for the large species.

The female is usually the most assidious nest builder, however, the position appears to be reversed in White-tailed Eagles. There may also be considerable differences in this respect between pairs of the same species.

Territories

As already mentioned most raptors have their own territory which protects them against others of their own species and in some cases against other competing species.

The large species, which require a daily food intake of several hundred grams, sometimes have an enormous hunting area, the extent depending upon the food potential. Thus, in southern Europe, the Golden Eagle may roam over more than 600 km². However, this may not always be necessary, for in the wilder parts of Scotland the territories in certain places may be only about 20 km², with only 10–12 km² regularly hunted.

At the other end of the scale there are species such as the Kestrel, which, in favourable localities, can do with only roughly 1 km in good years.

Colonial nesters

A few raptors nest in colonies. From a worldwide viewpoint these are primarily feeders on carrion and insects and those species which are nomadic. In the Western Palearctic the colonial nesters are the Griffon, Black and Egyptian Vulture, Black Kite, and to some extent the harriers and five falcon species: Eleanora's, Sooty and Red-footed Falcons, Kestrel and Lesser Kestrel. Many of these species may also breed solitarily; this is normal in, for instance, Marsh Harrier, Egyptian Vulture, Black Vulture and Kestrel.

It seems that colonial nesters prefer their food to be available in large quantities nearby, e.g. in the form of large carcases, offal and concentra-

Booted Eagle adult on nest with two chicks. *Photo I. Trap-Lind/Ardea.*

tions of insects, or, for Eleanora's and Sooty Falcons, small birds during their autumn migration. It is more difficult to say whether food concentrations are the reason for forming colonies in the case of the harriers; they are sometimes polygamous and this may explain their tendency to group.

Differences in hatching times

Individual eggs are normally laid at intervals of two or three days, occasionally one, four or five days. The interval is generally longest in the largest species.

In general, the female sits on the nest from the first egg. From the hatching dates of individual chicks it can, however, be seen that incubation is not normally carried out with full intensity from the start. Thus, in the Sparrowhawk a five-egg clutch can be laid in about eight days but the eggs will probably all hatch in a period of 1–3 days. There is often, however, a marked size difference between the chicks in a clutch. If there is a shortage of food during the rearing period the largest fight for what is available and the youngest die. This happens particularly during the first weeks after hatching. It is a harsh, but biologically sound principle that ensures that only the chicks that can be reared to an acceptable standard will survive.

The incubation period

Egg-laying is preceded by flying manoeuvres and the noise associated with the numerous matings and ceremonies connected with breeding, but incubation is a quiet period; there may be complete peace at the nest sites for hours on end.

Division of labour

This is typically found in raptors during the breeding season. In most species the female incubates while the male hunts and brings her the necessary food, a behaviour pattern that is continued after the chicks have hatched. Normally it is the female who divides up the food brought to the nest and guards the chicks, protecting them from the weather during the first 2–3 weeks. Only after this does she take part in hunting.

It is also normal for the male to take part, to a limited extent, in incubation, as for example while the female is tearing up the prey brought to the nest.

There are, however, variations from this pattern, particularly in the vultures where there is considerable division of labour between incubation and the provision of food for the chicks. The female appears to do most of the incubation but the male sits on the nest far longer than is purely necessary as a relief, and conversely the female plays an important part in obtaining food for the chicks.

Hatching

In some species the chick takes an amazingly long time to release itself from the egg. In the Goshawk it often takes three days from the first weak tapping sounds to the actual hatching, a process which may be completed in one day in the Honey Buzzard.

Down plumage

The chicks hatch with a silky, usually white down. At first they are scarcely able to lift their heads. For the first few days they lie for most of the time with half-closed lethargic eyes. After

Imperial Eagle, western race. The largest recorded clutch (1973). *Photo B-U. Meyburg.*

some days the first down is replaced by a thicker, more woolly plumage, and the chicks are now more lively. They move around in the nest on their tarsi and at the end of the downy period learn to stand on their feet and carefully back to the edge of the nest to squirt excrement away.

The downy stage lasts for about one third of the nest period. It is characteristic that during the whole of this period one of the adults is either on the nest or in the immediate vicinity, tearing the prey brought back and dividing it up in small bits to the chicks.

Plumage development

Normally the wing and tail feathers are the first to erupt, which marks the transition to the second phase of development. In this period the chicks become fully fledged, but typically with down still appearing here and there, particularly on the head. Roughly speaking this stage accounts for approximately one-quarter of the period in the nest. At the end of this second phase the beak and legs are fully developed and this is also the time when the chicks are able to feed themselves on the prey brought to the nest.

Last phase in development

The third and last phase in development is dedicated to the completion of the wing feathers. Both parents now hunt and the young begin to exercise their wings as a completion to the period in the nest. This may take only about 23 days in the Merlin, but 130 in the Griffon Vulture.

Independence

Learning to fly is evidently not the end of the breeding period. The young birds have to learn to hunt before they are truly independent. The Red-footed Falcon manages this in 10–14 days, although catching insects is really a very simple process. There are cases in which the young of the Golden Eagle have remained in the territory for about six months after being able to fly.

Vultures are known to feed their young for some months after they can fly, the Californian Condor for seven months. There are cases from the tropics where the parents feed their young for about a year.

The length of the breeding period therefore varies between that of the small species and that of some of the larger species. Small falcons mostly take a total of 90 days, with 30 days for incubation, 30 days in the nest and 30 days to become independent. At the other end of the scale the Californian Condor takes 55, 220 and 210 days respectively, a total of 485 before the young are really independent. This naturally means that they cannot breed every year.

The 'Cain syndrome'

There is good reason for the long period young raptors are dependent upon their parents. Among other things, the young are inexperienced in hunting and they often die of hunger. All the statistics show clearly that mortality is very high during the first months of their independent existence.

However, before a young bird reaches this stage it has already been subjected to a selection process. In many eagles a strange principle takes over. Irrespective of whether there is sufficient food available a larger chick aggressively attacks a smaller one, prevents it from feeding by bullying it to lie still, chases it to the edge of the nest or brutally pecks it. For this reason some species such as the Lesser Spotted Eagle only produce a single fledgling, while Golden Eagles may manage to produce just two.

Most species, however, are not involved in the murder of siblings, but the youngest chicks die owing to lack of food. Such deaths occur particularly during the first two phases of development, the downy phase and when the feathers appear. In the last phase the chicks can feed themselves and also fight for a sufficient share of the food.

Production of young

Considering the losses suffered throughout the breeding period it is clear that the number of young leaving the nest is, on average, considerably lower than the number of eggs laid. A Dutch investigation of 413 Kestrel clutches has shown a loss before the chicks fly of 43.3 per cent. Although the Golden Eagle normally lays two eggs, as a result of the Cain syndrome not more than a third of the clutches produce two young that survive long enough to fly away. An investigation in the Alps showed a production of only 1.13 young per clutch.

Greenlandic White-tailed Eagle young almost ready to fly. *Photo B. Génsbøl/Biofoto.*

In many species, the production of young varies considerably from year to year because of weather conditions and differences in the availability of food. In Germany there have been fluctuations in the production of young Kites of between 0.5 and 2.4 young per clutch. For the Honey Buzzard in central Europe the production of young is normally between 1.3 and 1.5, but in wet summers it may fail completely in certain places. The Rough-legged Buzzard provides an extreme case. Apparently this species only breeds in two years out of the four-year rodent cycle; when food is abundant the production of young is high. In poor rodent years it is possible that the Rough-legged Buzzard may search for areas with better food supplies and breed there.

The examples cited are from populations not particularly threatened by pollution. If this is taken into consideration the figures may be completely different, probably much less.

Non-breeding years

It has long been known that not all the birds in a population breed every year. We now know some of the reasons for this.

The female must be in good condition to start egg-laying, which comes from extra feeding in the short period before the eggs are laid. In the Sparrowhawk, for example, this leads to a weight increase of roughly fifteen per cent. These increased reserves are used partly for egg-laying, partly to survive the incubation and rearing periods in reasonably good shape. If prey is not available there will be no weight increase, and the female will not lay eggs. (There may be other reasons for this too.)

It has also been shown that many raptor species will easily give up breeding sites because of disturbance by man or lack of prey, whereas in good years they will tolerate more disturbance.

These conditions have been investigated in the American species *Buteo regalis*, the Ferruginous Hawk, which is very sensitive to disturbance. In a year when food was scarce, seven out of thirteen nests were deserted because the investigation involved climbing the nesting trees. In another 'good' year this did not happen in any of the thirteen nests subjected to the same amount of disturbance.

For many large species with a long and enervating breeding period, it appears that they cannot attain breeding condition every year; in the large African species investigated, the general picture was that they only bred in two years out of three.

Raptors in the modern world

In recent decades one of the dominant themes has been the extent to which it is possible to maintain a raptor

population, seen in relation to the amount of disturbance to which it is subjected.

Here one of the dominant factors has been pollution, but there have been other forms of disturbance too, such as habitat changes and the hazards for individual birds of high tension cables and barbed wire. Active persecution has also been important. Apart from shooting, both legal and illegal, there has also been raiding of nests for eggs and young.

Pollution

In recent years there have been numerous problems involving substances whose effect was previously unknown to most people. There has been a certain amount of confusion about the individual chemicals themselves, and so they are explained below.

These substances can be divided into a number of main groups, each with a different effect on the environment.

A. Pesticides

These can be divided into sub-groups, based on their chemical composition.

I. Chlorinated hydrocarbons

The best known is the insecticide DDT. This substance has been known for more than a hundred years, but it was first used during the Second World War as an insecticide to combat malaria. At first few, if any, were aware of its powerful side effects, due mainly to the slow rate at which it breaks down. Once an animal has accumulated this substance in one way or another it is very difficult to get rid of it. There has been found to

Peregrine killed by pesticides. *Photo I. Beames/Ardea.*

be a slow build-up of DDT in most prey animals.

Nowdays the use of DDT is forbidden in many countries, which has resulted in an improvement in the environment. Many pests quickly became resistant to DDT (and other substances) but in spite of this it is still used as a pesticide in some parts of the world. The problem continues, and in Africa alone about two million people die every year of malaria.

DDT is lethal to cerebral tissue in a dose of roughly 30 parts per million (= 30 mg per kg of cerebral tissue). It also causes the liver to produce enzymes which disturb the balance of sex hormones.

As it breaks down DDT forms another chemical compound, DDE, and this appears to damage the ability of birds to produce sufficiently thick eggshells. A 15–20 per cent reduction of shell thickness is critical, and an incubating bird may easily perforate the shell with its claws.

Today DDT has been replaced as an insecticide by lindan, which is less injurious to the environment.

Other chlorinated hydrocarbons include dieldrin and aldrin. They work in the same way as DDT but are ten times more poisonous. In Scotland during the 1960s there was a marked decrease in breeding success in the Golden Eagle, from 72 to 29 per cent, and this occurred after dieldrin had been used in sheep rearing. Aldrin has been used, for instance, to treat seed corn.

Finally, there is PCB (polychlorinated biphenyl) which is ten times less poisonous than DDT, but is incredibly stable. It is reckoned that the amount of PCB already present in the natural environment is sufficient to cause irreparable damage. In birds this poison probably affects the production of eggshells. The use of PCB is now forbidden in many countries, or at least without special permission.

II. Organophosphates

These substances are also used as insecticides. They are very poisonous but they break down rapidly, and can cause deaths.

B. Herbicides

These are used to control weeds. They vary considerably both in toxicity and in their ability to decompose. They act on plants as growth hormones causing them to grow fast and exhaust themselves. Any undesirable effects on the environment are not fully understood, but injection of pheasant eggs with a normal dose of one of these substances (2,4 D) produced misshapen individuals in about 50–60 per cent of the chicks.

C. Heavy metals

These substances are used in industry, agriculture and the control of rodents.

For many years mercury has been used industrially, e.g. in paper-making, and for treating seeds. Mercury breaks down slowly; checks on humans who had taken in mercury from a fish diet showed that after 70 days they had lost 50 per cent of the poison, after 150 days 75 per cent, and after a year all of it, provided that they had not in the meantime eaten more food tainted with mercury.

Mercury is lethal in very small amounts and when accumulated in the eggs it kills the chicks. For Sparrowhawks, six parts per million has been shown to be the critical threshold.

In recent years it has been discovered that lead is very injurious. Lead, as a mixture in petrol and more specially as sportsmens' lead shot, infects the general environment; a White-tailed Eagle was affected which had eaten a dead animal with shot in its stomach. Pollution by lead also appears to have an adverse effect on the formation of eggshells.

New investigations suggest that in humans lead may affect intelligence and behaviour. Such observations may in time lead to people taking action to reduce the lead content in air.

Apart from mercury and lead the element thallium may also be injurious. It is used to control rodents.

Observations of injurious effects

In Europe the uncontrolled use of environmental poisons continued for fifteen years before a connection was noticed between their use and long-scale damage to the environment. In Britain a sudden reduction in the number of breeding raptors was observed in the 1950s, but it was not until the 1960s that a connection between this and the poisons appeared to be probable. Scientists in several countries, primarily Britain, Holland and Sweden, set to work investigating what, without exaggeration, could be a serious threat to the lives of both animals and humans.

From numerous places came alarming reports of an uncommonly large decrease in many species. At the start this was most noticeable in the Peregrine Falcon.

The Peregrine in Great Britain

The pesticide crash in population took place during the 1950s. It was first noticed in the south and west and some populations, such as those along the chalk cliffs of Sussex, were completely lost. Sub-lethal effects on breeding success were being reported from many areas and, by 1964, the northern birds were suffering too. However, even at its worst ebb, Britain's Peregrine population was probably still about 50 per cent of the prewar level. In other countries, such as Sweden, thriving breeding populations were all but destroyed – from 350 pairs in 1945 there are scarcely ten left now, and the chicks produced are no longer sufficient to sustain even this meagre foothold.

Poison politics

This unforeseen extermination went on throughout Europe. Where the authorities took action early on, as in Denmark, the damage was not devastating although several species lost much terrain. This happened typically with the Sparrowhawk. In several countries, however, where action was insufficient the losses were very serious. In many European countries almost all the raptor species were reduced catastrophically.

Protection

However, the distressed situation of raptors did lead to some positive action. Particularly in the 1960s, when the seriousness was properly exposed, almost all countries introduced protective measures for raptors. This was, of course, very necessary, yet it is a sad fact that as late as 1967 Norway was still paying premiums for the shooting of eagles.

Restrictions

There was also positive action in the field of the poisons themselves. In many countries the use of some of the most injurious substances was for-bidden, including DDT, aldrin, dieldrin, PCB and mercury.

Re-establishment of the populations

The effects of these restrictions became noticeable little by little, and the re-establishment of raptor populations occurred particularly in places where the restrictions were introduced. The population problem is of course worldwide; there is no sense in providing Denmark's Montagu's Harriers with a relatively clean environment if they are to die of poisoning in their winter quarters. Similarly, other species carrying a load of poison from their winter quarters will either be unable to breed, produce clutches that are too small or lay thin-shelled eggs.

The restrictions introduced have had positive results. In recent years there have, for instance, been local

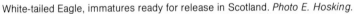

White-tailed Eagle, immatures ready for release in Scotland. *Photo E. Hosking.*

improvements in the populations of Osprey, Kite, Marsh Harrier, Rough-legged Buzzard, Merlin and Kestrel. The reasons for this are not always clear, but in the Sparrowhawk, for instance, it is certainly due to improved living conditions.

The situation of a species can improve in one area but deteriorate in another. Thus, there is a difference between northern and southern Europe, the cleanest environment being in the north.

It is worth pointing out that in the Baltic area the White-tailed Eagles only produce young when fed on poison-free meat, and that the situation of the Peregrine Falcon in Norway and Sweden continues to be a problem. So there is no reason to be over-optimistic, and there may, of course, be other hazards ahead.

Poisoned bait

Locally in Europe the laying-out of poisoned bait has decimated raptor populations, and in some cases has led to extermination. It is mainly strychnine that is used. The poison is poured onto carrion from domestic animals to, for example, shot game, which attracts vultures, eagles, kites and buzzards. This method has been used particularly in the Balkans as a means of exterminating wolves and foxes, and has had a serious effect on raptor populations.

In the Balkans this anti-wolf campaign was mainly responsible for the extermination of the Bearded Vulture (except in Greece), for the disappearance of the Griffon Vulture in Romania and Bulgaria, for its scarcity in Yugoslavia and for the extermination of the Egyptian Vulture in Romania. Furthermore, a threatened population of the White-tailed Eagle cannot tolerate this kind of attack.

However, the problem is not only in the Balkans, for it exists throughout southern Europe, and in Iceland it has threatened the White-tailed Eagle. Today the use of strychnine is forbidden in most parts of Europe.

Habitat changes

Economy today is characterized by commercialism. In the forests, fast-growing conifers are planted at the cost of deciduous trees. An area of swamp, a delta or a shallow sea bay is drained or dammed to yield new land for ploughing, even today when the disappearance of wetlands is a constant subject for discussion. Agriculture continues to employ such modern methods, adversely affecting the range and variety of animals and plants.

All in all, there have been such radical changes in the natural environment as to affect all life around us, including the existence of raptors.

In large areas of Europe the period from the Middle Ages to the beginning of the nineteenth century was characterized by deforestation. In many areas trees became uncommon and new planting took place. The former deciduous woodlands were, however, replaced by conifers which from the biological viewpoint are poorer. Where the former countryside had woodland interspersed with small fields, damp meadows and small lakes, a biologically very productive environment, there were now plantations with much less variety, and this can be seen in the case of raptors and others.

At one time many species bred in a single area, e.g. Kite and Black Kite, White-tailed Eagle, Lesser Spotted Eagle, Buzzard, Honey Buzzard, Hobby, Kestrel, Sparrowhawk and Goshawk; but the plantations that followed the mixed woodland normally held only a few of the commonest species and fewer individuals.

There are two reasons for this. First, the large areas of conifers provided few good nest sites. Larger raptors require old, strong trees for nesting. Secondly, the plantations and their surroundings produce only a fraction of the prey animals.

In addition, raptors are much affected by modern forestry methods, and many clutches have been lost in this way. There was a glaring example of this in West Germany in 1968. Two of the country's last six pairs of White-tailed Eagles deserted their nests as a result of forestry operations in the vicinity. Raptors are particularly sensitive to disturbance near the nest at the start of the breeding season.

When Montagu's Harrier places its nest in a cornfield, the nest and young are often threatened by large agricultural machines. *Photo H. Fr. Hansen.*

Apart from changes in the character of woodlands, considerable losses have been caused by the desiccation of extensive, valuable areas. Swamps and other damp places, shallow lakes and bays are often very productive with good food sources for higher and lower forms of life, including a rich bird fauna; they produce large numbers of frogs, lizards, snakes, rodents, birds, fish and insects. A few raptors (harriers) breed in such areas and many more use them for foraging.

Throughout Europe there is a continuing struggle to increase the amount of agricultural land. At the end of the last century large areas along the Danube included some of Europe's best localities for birds, with large populations of raptors. Control measures preventing the annual floodings have meant that these places have a poorer bird fauna than before. Deltas are dried out everywhere, including large areas of the famous Danube delta, and even today this work continues, for example in Greece. Areas which might sound enticing in the ornithological literature are found to have been transformed into agricultural land and to have become valueless as natural environments. This even happens in northern Europe, as for instance in the newly undertaken attack on the Wadden Sea.

The introduction of agriculture inhibits the development of a rich fauna and flora. Among other things, it means that if no raptors are shot, none disturbed while breeding, none killed by poison or their reproductive success impaired, in other words given 'ideal' conditions, it will still never be possible to attain the population of former times. In the modern world there is simply not enough food for a large number of raptors.

Other problems

There are several other factors, of varying importance, which have an adverse effect on raptors.

The most serious is man's increasing interest in the countryside. In certain areas the birds do not have peace needed for nesting or foraging. Ospreys have lost many clutches because tourists have camped under their nests, and so have White-tailed Eagles, where anglers have been too close to them. The interest of ornithologists in the nests of the rarer raptors has also meant that these have been deserted. In the Soviet Union the decrease in the Black Kite has been associated with mass tourism in the foraging areas near rivers and lakes. In general, disturbance is undoubtedly greatest in the vicinity of lakes, rivers, bays and similar places.

In Scotland it has been shown that it is possible to channel the increasing interest in natural history in a reasonable way. At the end of the 1950s, when the Osprey started to breed there again, a strict watch was kept on the nests, but at the same time the public were allowed to view one of the nests from a suitable distance. The interest proved to be enormous and it had a considerable influence on the story of raptors in the British Isles. This example should be followed in other places.

Raptors often come to grief on barbed wire, here a Montagu's Harrier. *Photo L. E. Nissen/Biofoto.*

found, of which five had flown into high tension or other cables. Large windows also claim victims among birds in general, and especially among Sparrowhawks which often hunt near houses. Barbed wire is also a hazard; many raptors have died when their wings have become caught in the barbs.

Shooting

The factors, hitherto cited, in the reduction of populations have been by-products of other situations, as for instance cases of unintentioned extermination. Mercury, for example, was not used intentionally to kill raptors.

In our time the direct removal of raptors has taken place by shooting. This has usually been done by people who believe that raptors threaten their interests.

From old documents, shooting raptors can be traced back for 200–300 years. From these it appears that the big campaign of extermination started more than 200 years ago, instituted by kings and noblemen who thought their shooting interests were threatened by raptors. Lack of knowledge about the individual species led to the destruction of all of them, even such harmless birds as the Honey Buzzard and Kestrel.

Shooting premiums

In practice the extermination was associated with the payment of premiums on the production of torn-off

A reduction in the amount of shooting has meant that raptors have, in general, become less shy. This can be seen by the presence of Buzzards near roads. In some places they sit and wait for a mouse to appear or for animals that have been run over. Traffic deaths also occur among raptors. In northern Scandinavia Golden Eagles are killed as they sit and eat reindeer that have been run over, and the same happens elsewhere to other heavy eagles.

Collisions with high tension cables also occur. In the period 1952–64, in Switzerland, sixteen Peregrines were

claws or by a kind of tax, every man and family being bound to destroy a certain number of raptors every year.

This happened throughout Europe. In the eighteenth century the numbers involved were still limited compared with what happened later.

As early as 1684–85 a hundred Kites were killed in Kent. A few years later the species was only mentioned a few times in the lists of birds destroyed. The survival of the Kite in Britain, with a present-day small population in Wales, may be because game was not pursued very energetically in Wales.

Old account books going back to the 1700s show the premiums paid in many places. During the period 1705–1800 premiums were paid for 624,087 raptors killed in the Kingdom of Hanover, but it is interesting that there was no drop in numbers during those 95 years. With good conditions, a raptor population can therefore tolerate a high pressure from hunting without being reduced. In the 1700s the habitats, especially the wetlands, were still intact.

In the 1800s the campaign against raptors was stepped up, a situation associated with an increase in pheasant rearing. In the latter half of the century there was a massive increase in shooting. This was rendered more effective by the introduction of breech-loading guns. Very often the state paid the shooting premiums, but it was also common for land-owners to do this. At the end of the century, when a distinction began to arise between 'harmful' and 'less harmful' raptors, the governments tended to not get involved. Premium payments were often taken over by shooting organizations or by pigeon rearers. With such little knowledge available the situation was not very good. Even organizations of bird-lovers paid premiums for 'harmful' species such as Goshawks and Sparrowhawks. So there was no reason for sportsmen, owners of fishponds, pheasant-rearers and farmers to hold back. It is fantastic to learn that in 1877 a German bird protection society in Kassel paid premiums totalling 215 marks for twenty Goshawks and

A hunter's sad booty (from the time of the great anti-raptor campaign). *Photo W. van Wijk.*

thirty Sparrowhawks, among others.

It was prestigious to be able to say that an area's raptors had been exterminated, which is what happened in many of the more densely populated places. Thousands and thousands of raptors were killed throughout the whole of Europe. In the second half of the 1800s a well-known eagle hunter in southern Germany celebrated having killed a hundred Golden Eagles. In Sweden in the 1890s about 325 eagles were killed every year, of which about 70 per cent were White-tailed Eagles. It has been estimated that in Germany around 1860, roughly 400 White-tailed Eagles were shot annually. In Spain there was a campaign against the Imperial Eagle. Nests were destroyed, birds shot and collected. In Romania, over a period of twenty years one man sold at least 400 dead White-tailed Eagles for stuffing.

There was thus enormous pressure on the raptor population, particularly the large species, the eagles, with their late sexual maturity and slow rate of reproduction.

The medium-sized species, such as kites, harriers, Goshawks and buzzards, also suffered and were decimated or locally exterminated.

In the second half of the nineteenth century protection helped to save some of the obviously harmless species or those threatened with extinction. This usually meant protection during the breeding season, but this scarcely helped as sportsmen and pheasant-rearers were still inimical to raptors.

Protection for raptors

In Europe as a whole the First World War was marked by an upsurge of raptors. People had other things to think about than rearing and shooting game. This also happened during the Second World War. It was in the 1950s and 1960s that raptors as a whole ceased to be persecuted in Europe, and since then they have received effective protection. Today they are totally protected in about half the countries of Europe, and partially protected in the rest. The species still hunted in certain parts of Europe include the Goshawk, Sparrowhawk, Buzzard, Rough-legged Buzzard and Marsh Harrier. The large species, eagles and vultures, need widespread protection.

Raptors are still shot in southern Europe in spite of protection laws, but the situation is better in northern Europe, where in recent years shooting has markedly decreased. However, extermination continued right up to this time. Statistics for Norway show that about half a million raptors were killed in the period 1900–1966. The situation was similar in Denmark where game statistics from the start in 1942 to 1966–67 showed about 300,000 raptors destroyed.

Many countries lack complete statistics, but there are figures available for certain areas. Thus, it is probable that in West Germany in the 1950s and 1960s roughly 70,000 raptors were killed annually. In France, during the same period, the annual toll was 100,000–300,000. So it is not too extreme to suggest that in Europe 0.5–1.0 million raptors were shot, at a time when attempts were being made to combat the effects of pollution.

Other forms of 'direct' persecution

Evidently shooting was mainly responsible for the decrease of raptors, but in some places there were other factors which played a part, and some of these involved people with an interest in such birds as raptors.

Falconers

The sport of falconry is about 4000 years old. It almost died out in Europe, but in certain areas it has had a strong renaissance. In spite of its name the sport may also involve other raptors such as eagles and hawks.

In Europe falconers have had a massive drive to obtain new birds. The Peregrine Falcon continues to be threatened with extermination in many parts of Europe, because of environmental factors. The few clutches which the species manages to produce have to be guarded night and day to prevent them being raided by falconers. Oologists (egg-collectors) are also involved. The last time a Peregrine clutch was hatched in Denmark was in 1969 and the chicks were stolen from the nest. In 1967 a German falconer took 23 young of the rare Lanner Falcon from nests in Italy. In Scandinavia there have also been troubles with the Gyrfalcon, the falconer's most popular quarry.

There are numerous falconers in Germany. In February 1968 a Bavarian count showed that in his province alone there were 800–1000 raptors in captivity. With interest on this scale it is small wonder that nests of, for example, the Peregrine Falcon are raided every year. It is also generally known that German falconers, in particular, move round Europe in search of new 'material'. Greenland has also been visited for the greatest prize of all – the white Gyrfalcon.

To a limited extent falconers have started to breed their own birds, but not on a scale sufficient to satisfy the demand for new young.

Egg-collectors

The early days of ornithology were plagued by collectors, but as a science it has long grown out of this phase. On the whole there are enough skins and eggs for the necessary studies. Nevertheless, there are still people who continue; although egg-collecting is on the wane it still exists and is carried out on the principle of the rarer the better. As a result the eggs of raptors are still prime targets for the remaining collectors of eggs.

The fear of such marauders has meant that the breeding sites of rare species are increasingly kept secret, and many are guarded day and night.

Trophies

At one time it was the fashion to stuff raptors and mount them on a perch in the sitting-room or perhaps in the library. The large species were particularly sought-after. An eagle with its wings spread was regarded as a real trophy. In most countries this activity has now been stopped. Schools formerly used this kind of biological collection but they now use other kinds of educational material. However, as long as there is money to be made raptors will continue to be killed and stuffed, in spite of protective measures.

Artificial rearing

Artificial rearing of raptor chicks has been justified on the grounds that it provides a supplement for the wild, free-living raptors. This argument is dangerous and is only valid in special circumstances, namely when the rearing is carried out under scientific control. To allow private persons to perform such illegal rearing might well compromise the wild raptor stocks. It must be remembered that wild raptors are the best rearers of the future generations.

In special cases, however, it may be necessary for humans to help in this way. Thus, artificial rearing under scientific control may help to preserve the Peregrine population in view of the present environmental conditions. In such a case artificial rearing is acceptable.

Goshawk juvenile on the falconer's hand. *Photo A. Christiansen/Biofoto.*

The situation today

In summary, the present prospects are reasonably good for raptors. Shooting has been much reduced throughout Europe, and in northern Europe the environmental situation has been much improved for most species. The results from these two factors have been increased populations in many places.

The negative position is seen in those species which are particularly sensitive to environmental conditions, as for instance when habitat changes occur. The positive side to the picture is seen when conservation organiza-tions seek to prevent, e.g. egg-collect-ing, and the adverse activities of falconers.

It is both sad and encouraging that efforts are made to feed raptors such as vultures and the White-tailed Eagle, so that they can survive lack of food and the hazards of environ-mental poisons. Sad because it shows how far we have to go towards the management of the natural world, encouraging because at least some people are positively contributing towards the conservation of these birds.

In the United States, Peregrine Falcons have been artificially reared for later release in towns. *Photo C. Davidson/Bruce Coleman.*

Honey Buzzard
Pernis apivorus

Distribution
In addition to the areas shown on the map, the Honey Buzzard breeds in the Soviet Union eastwards to the region between the Ob and Yenisei, and also in Iran south of the Caspian Sea. It is not divided into races.

Population estimate
In general, the population of this species is very difficult to record. The birds arrive after the leaves appear and live a very secluded life.

It is probable that the size of the population is under-estimated in sev-eral countries; this has been the case in Denmark in recent decades. Investigations in 1971–74 put the number of breeding pairs at 200–300. Further very detailed observations in Jutland in 1973–81 suggest that the Danish population is about 800–1000 pairs.

The European population, as shown in the table on p. 58, is 33,000–38,000 pairs. Several countries, particularly the Soviet Union, are not included and so it is not really possible to get a true picture of the total population in the Western Palearctic.

There is, however, another possibility. Most Honey Buzzards pass well-known migration stations on the way to winter quarters in Africa. The

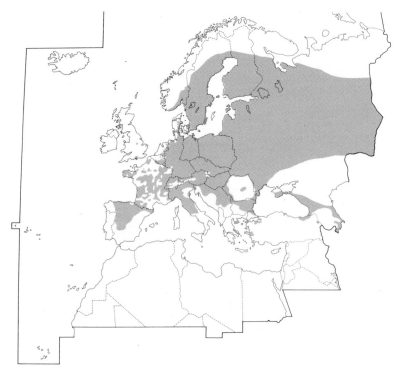

maximum (approximate) numbers are: Gibraltar 126,000; Malta 1000; Bosporus 26,000 and Borcka (N-E Turkey) 138,000. The last figure refers to Soviet birds. Reckoning that half the observed birds are juveniles, it seems that there are roughly 35,000 pairs in the European part of Soviet Russia. For birds from the rest of Europe the other three stations give a total of 153,000 birds or about 40,000 pairs.

Population trends

The Honey Buzzard population appears to have been subject to an enormous decline. It arrives late, departs early and lives a secluded life. In past years it has been much hunted.

Today Honey Buzzards are shot illegally in southern Europe during migration, particularly in Italy, Malta and Lebanon. It is not known whether this affects the size of the population.

The Honey Buzzard has apparently not been affected by environmental poisoning; its food does not accumulate the poisons to any great extent.

In certain countries there is talk of a marked decrease, but in general the population appears to be stable, although there are considerable annual fluctuations related to the weather at the start of the breeding season. Wet and cold springs produce few wasps, its primary food, and so few breeding Honey Buzzards.

In many countries there is a fear that the production of conifers in favour of deciduous trees may tend to reduce the population, but this requires further investigation. In certain areas, including northern Sweden, the Honey Buzzard thrives remarkably well in coniferous forests.

It is perhaps relevant that such

Honey Buzzard adult male. *Photo M. Müller & H. Wohlmuth.*

forests were earlier planted in poor soil, where production of prey was low. However, it seems clear that the species does not thrive in the dark, uniform monocultures of spruce.

Migration

A classic migrant wintering in Africa south of the Sahara, mainly in the wooded parts of the Equatorial regions. Birds from the whole of the European breeding range move out from mid-August to the end of September – the few birds that remain later are youngsters.

Migrating Honey Buzzards are capable of sustained flapping flight, but most soar. They therefore concentrate in large numbers at the well-known sites where the sea-passages are narrowest. Peak autumn numbers, and the years when they were recorded, are as follows: Falsterbo, about 22,000 in 1955; Gibraltar, 126,000 in 1972; Bosporus, about 26,000 in 1971; Caucasus, about 138,000 in 1978. There is certainly a widespread passage of lesser numbers at other sites, with peaks of 1000 in one autumn recorded through Malta. The peak passage at the major sites is generally during the first ten days of September.

Spring return passage is between mid-April and the end of May. There are notable concentrations through Gibraltar and Eilat (200,000 or more a season) in the west and east respectively. An established route lies through Cap Bon (Tunisia), Sicily and up through Italy. 'Tradition' hunting, now illegal, in Sicily poses a threat to this population.

In the breeding grounds to the north of its range, birds generally return mid-May to early June. Birds from the tiny British population are seldom recorded on migration and are unlikely to be concentrated much by the rather narrow eastern end of the Channel.

Habitat

Breeds in wooded areas where its food is plentiful. Most often in deciduous woods, but sometimes in pine forests, and in the most northerly breeding areas in spruce forests. Breeds partly in large forests with clearings or meadows, and partly in small wooded areas where it hunts along the edges.

Voice

Seldom heard. The typical flight call is an attractive, jingling, somewhat sad, high-pitched *'glee-yee'* as the bird loses height. A finer, more musical voice than that of the Buzzard. Also uses it as a one or two syllable call. When relieving at the nest there

Juvenile Honey Buzzard digging up a wasp nest. *Photo I. Trap-Ling/Biofoto.*

Honey Buzzard chick being fed with wasp comb. *Photo D. Skjelle.*

is a sound like a piece of stiff cardboard being hit by a rapidly rotating bicycle wheel.

Breeding

The age at which the birds breed for the first time is not known, but they are believed to pair for life.

The birds appear in late spring (middle to late May); apparently nest-building starts immediately, and egg-laying begins roughly 11 days after arrival.

During the first 2–3 weeks there is often a chance to see the display flight, usually performed by the male. The bird flies upwards in a steep arc, remains stationary in the air, extends the wings almost vertically and beats them 3–4 times very rapidly, clapping them together over the back. It then makes further ascents, not losing height at each performance but rising in a stair-like fashion.

Both sexes take part in building the nest which is placed high up in a tree, often on a side branch. It can be easily distinguished from that of other raptors as it largely consists of leafy twigs. The type of tree varies according to the locality. Red spruce predominates in Finland (89%), beech in Denmark (57%) and oak in the Pfalz in West Germany (58%).

The clutch, which consists of 2 (1–3) eggs, is laid with an interval of two days and is incubated by both sexes from the laying of the first egg. Hatching is after 30–35 days incubation (per egg). The chicks remain in the nest for 33–45 days and are dependent on the parents for about a further 14 days. By then it is late August to September and the autumn migration starts.

The number of pairs which manage to breed varies considerably from year to year, at least in northern

Europe. In cold, wet springs there are few wasps and this evidently reduces the birds' reproductive drive.

The production of young also undergoes considerable fluctuation. In the wet summers of 1965 and 1967 all the young in an area of Switzerland died. On the other hand, in the good wasp years of 1964 and 1968 there were 1.5 young per pair of those that started to breed. Recent investigations of migrating Honey Buzzards in southern Scandinavia also reveal great variety in the production of offspring, almost reaching nil in many years.

Food

A specialist eater, feeding mainly on insects, primarily wasps, and secondarily bumblebees, including larvae and pupae as well as adults. In northern latitudes such food normally occurs in substantial amounts from mid-June until the autumn migration begins.

At the start of the breeding season this food must therefore be supplemented by other food sources, such as various insects, earthworms, spiders, frogs, reptiles, birds (mainly nestlings) and small mammals. In late summer the bird also takes fruits and berries. Wasps play the principal role in the diet of the chicks. In a Danish investigation of 104 identified food sources the percentages were wasp combs 61, bumblebee nests 15, frogs 19, worms 2, birds 2 and lizards one per cent.

In rainy weather Honey Buzzards seem to feed more on frogs and birds.

Foraging methods

Wasp and bumblebee nests are found either when flying at a height of about 15 m or from a perch in a tree. It is thought that Honey Buzzards observe the insects directly when they fly in and out of the nest, but there are also observations which suggest that a bird can find for example a wasp nest, by following wasps over long distances.

The Honey Buzzard takes free-living wasps and those in the ground. The latter are dug out down to depths of 40 cm, using feet and beak. In so doing the bird may be so preoccupied with digging that it is unaware of danger, and becomes vulnerable.

When the nest has been exposed the bird tears the combs apart, eats the larvae and pupae and also any adult wasps. The wasps are probably unable to injure the bird with their sting, thanks to a special adaptation: in the vulnerable area between the eyes and beak there are stiff bristles instead of feathers.

Honey Buzzards can also hunt for food, and in some cases, such as when hunting beetles and grasshoppers, they rise to heights of 500 m before stooping on the prey. Exceptionally they can take flying insects.

Honey Buzzard population in the Western Palearctic

Denmark	800–1000 pairs (1981)[51]	Decline due to change in forest composition with increase in conifers.
Sweden	8000 pairs (1981)[9]	Possibly declining owing to reduction in deciduous

		woodland in favour of conifers, but position uncertain.
Norway	small numbers (1971)[62]	Considerable decline since last century.
Finland	5000 pairs (1985)[10]	Stable.
USSR *Estonia*	? around 100 pairs (1976)[11]	In area in central Russia (270,000 km²) an estimate of over 4000 pairs (1971)[1]. On the whole stable or increasing.
Poland	2500 pairs (1984)[80]	Apparently stable.
East Germany	600 pairs (1983)[87]	Mecklenburg 120 pairs (1979)[52]. Brandenburg 175 pairs (1983)[36].
West Germany	5500 pairs (1982)[22]	
Holland	at least 300 pairs (1979)[53]	
Belgium	200–400 pairs (1979)[1]	
Luxembourg	70–90 pairs (1967)[3]	
England	6 pairs reg. (1986)[18]	Former status uncertain. Apparently never numerous. 1–10 pairs reg. annually.
France	8000–12,000 pairs (1984)[92]	
Switzerland	300–400 pairs (1980)[25]	
Austria	common? (1977)[48]	Commoner than Buzzard in certain alpine valleys.
Czechoslovakia	approx. 600 pairs (1988)[43]	
Hungary	300–350 pairs (1988)[40]	
Yugoslavia	few (1982)[19]	
Romania	approx. 20 pairs (1977)[42]	
Bulgaria	apparently common (1960)[3]	
Greece	approx. 250 pairs (1983)[84]	Decrease.
Italy	100–500 pairs (1982)[19]	Decreasing.
Spain	1000 pairs (1977)[27]	
Portugal	5–10 pairs (1982)[19]	
Turkey	<500 pairs (1982)[19]	
Cyprus	10–100 pairs (1982)[19]	

Black-winged Kite
Elanus caeruleus

Distribution
As shown on the map, this species breeds in the Western Palearctic area only in the Iberian Peninsula and North Africa. In addition, it occurs over large areas of the rest of Africa (the nominate race is also in the Western Palearctic), and in many parts of southern Asia (*E.c. vociferus*). There are four island races: in Sumatra (*E.c. sumatranus*), Java (*E.c. intermedius*), the Philippines, Celebes and Borneo (*E.c. hypoleucus*) and in eastern New Guinea (*E.c. wahgiensis*).

Migration
A non-migratory bird, although some individuals wander. In western Europe seen in, among other places, Holland, Belgium, West Germany, Poland and France.

Habitat
This bird breeds on savannas, steppes, in semi-desert areas and in cultivated

Black-winged Kite with mouse. *Photo B. Génsbøl/Biofoto.*

areas with groups of trees and single trees, as well as along the margins of large clearings. In dry areas it likes to have water in the vicinity.

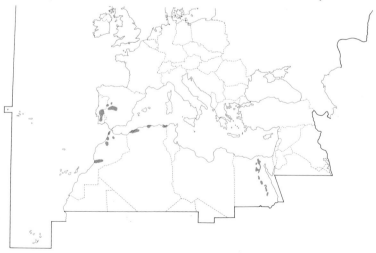

Breeding

There is little detailed knowledge of breeding in the Black-winged Kite.

The occupation of individual territories appears to be very irregular. To show that a territory is occupied the sexes circle together high above the area.

The nest is preferably built in thorny, flat-crowned trees at a height of 3–20 m. Both sexes share in nest-building. Usually the male's role is to fetch material, while the female builds. At this stage in the breeding season the male takes over the care of the female.

In Spain and Portugal the eggs are laid in late February to March. The clutch has 3–4 (2–6) eggs, laid at intervals of 2–3 days. Incubation, mainly by the female, starts with the first egg, so that hatching takes place at intervals. Incubation time is 26 (25–28) days and the chicks remain in the nest 30–35 days. How long the family remains together after that is unknown.

Food

Various small mammals, particularly rodents. In addition they take small birds, almost exclusively species that live on the ground in open country (larks and pipits) and various juveniles. Reptiles, mostly lizards, also play a role; in general, insects are not important, except in some localities.

Foraging methods

A slow flight at a height of 15–20 m when hunting, with frequent calls while hovering. At other times the bird perches in a high position and keeps a lookout. Also in the early morning the bird flies low down like a nightjar.

Small prey is often eaten in the air while larger objects are brought to a branch or rocky outcrop.

Black-winged Kite. *Photo B. Génsbøl/Biofoto.*

Black-winged Kite population in the Western Palearctic

Spain	100 pairs (1977)[1] 60 pairs (1981)[2] >50 pairs (1982)[19]	Estimates fluctuate. Seems to be increasing due to the (otherwise inappropriate) clearing of woods.
Portugal	150–200 pairs (1982)[19]	Increasing.
Morocco	100–500 pairs (1982)[19]	
Algeria	small population (1979)[19]	
Tunisia	<10 pairs (1982)[19]	
Egypt	locally common (1982)[29] 100–1000 pairs (1982)[19]	Decrease in northern part of country. Large population in the south.

Black Kite. *Photo M. Müller & H. Wohlmuth.*

Black Kite
Milvus migrans

Distribution

As shown on the map this species is widely distributed in the Western Palearctic. The breeding area extends eastwards over large parts of Asia. In addition, the Black Kite breeds in Australia, in Africa south of the Sahara and in Arabia.

In the Western Palearctic there are two races: the nominate race in Europe, North Africa and most of the Middle East, and *M.m. aegyptius* in Sinai, the Arabian Peninsula and eastern Africa, a smaller, paler, more rust-brown bird with the tail more deeply cleft. In addition, there are four other races: in Asia (2), the rest of Africa and Australia.

Population estimates

An estimate covering the whole of the Western Palearctic is not possible as there are no figures for many large areas (see table on p. 68). However, most is known about Europe (excluding the Soviet Union). For this area the figures suggest a total population of about 36,000 pairs, of which 25,000 are accounted for in Spain. In fact, Europe only holds a low percentage of the total world population of the Black Kite which is regarded as the world's most numerous raptor.

Population trends

In the Western Palearctic the Black Kite population occupies a rather special position. As in other species, the extensive shooting during the period 1750–1950 naturally resulted in a marked decrease in the population. Nevertheless, from about 1850 the breeding area increased in certain localities. It is remarkable that a species can show an increase under such conditions; the expansion is associated with the fact that the Black Kite thrives in close proximity with man, and it is almost omnivorous.

From 1950 onwards there is a clear change in the trend. There was a marked decrease in shooting in most parts of Europe, but nevertheless there was a distinct drop in population numbers almost everywhere. Although it has not been proved, it is likely that for this species, too, the decrease is due to the unrestricted use of environmental poisons in the 1950s and 1960s.

Subsequently there has been more control over the use of these substances but, as the table shows, this has not led to an improvement in the position. Only a few countries record a stable population.

At a time when we might expect improvement there is still no sign of it. However, the increase in numbers of the Black Kite in southern Scandinavia is possibly a sign of a more positive trend.

The Black Kite has attempted to breed on one occasion (1878) in Denmark.

Habitat

Normally breeds in tall forest in the immediate vicinity of water: lakes, marshes, rivers and wetlands. However, the species is not always dependent upon water and breeding sites at a distance of 8–12 km, even 25 km from water, have been recorded.

Outside the breeding season Black Kites usually live near lakes and rivers.

Migration

The nominate race is mainly migratory, most often with winter quarters in Africa south of the Sahara, secondarily also in the Middle East. A few overwinter in southern Europe. Exceptionally, Black Kites are seen in winter in southern Scandinavia and central Europe. These are probably weak birds unable to fly long distances. The Egyptian subspecies *M.m. aegyptius* is non-migratory.

In Europe, young birds start to disperse in late June or early July. The true autumn migration starts early – late July and August – and by September virtually all Black Kites have left their breeding grounds. Migration is concentrated around the narrow sea passages, with maximum (approximate) numbers for Gibraltar at 40,000 (1972), for the Bosporus 2700 (1971) and for Boreka 5800 (1976). The birds pass Gibraltar in the period August–October with a peak from mid-August to mid-September,

Black Kites consume many fish. *Photo G. Ziesler.*

at the same time as the migration over the Bosporus. Migration over the Mediterranean also takes place by other routes, such as through Italy. With an estimated population for Europe (excluding the Soviet Union) of about 30,000 pairs one could expect an autumn population of roughly 120,000 birds.

In the Mediterranean area the spring migration occurs in February–May with a peak in mid-March to April at Eilat (about 27,000 birds in 1977) and two maxima at Cape Bon and Gibraltar (respectively old and young birds?) in middle to late March and mid-April to early May. Switzerland is reached at the earliest in early March, and the main arrival period here is late March to early April. March observations are rare in East Germany and Poland, where the birds mainly arrive in the first

In southern Europe, Black Kites are often seen at refuse dumps. *Photo C. Frahm/Biofoto.*

half of April.

As might be expected in such a pronounced migrant, the Black Kite is quite often seen north of its breeding range although few make it to Britain, most records being in May or June.

Voice
Similar to that of the Kite and mostly heard during the breeding period. The common, high-pitched call occurs in various forms: drawn out, wailing or whistling.

Breeding
Probably breed at the earliest at three years old. Male and female apparently meet on the territory and resume the connection, so that the same birds often pair year after year. In the mating flight the birds fly close to one another on an undulating course with soft wing beats, rock from side to side and lunge towards one another.

The species generally breeds solitarily but may breed in colonies (as sometimes in Switzerland). The nest is built at the edge of woodland or in a free-standing tree, and outside Europe it often breeds in towns.

Both sexes take part in building the nest, generally at a height of 8–15 m. The nest is often lined with paper, pieces of cloth, plastic and similar materials.

The eggs are usually laid from middle to late April to early May in a clutch of 2–3 (1 to 4 or 5) eggs which are normally incubated by the female alone. Incubation starts when the first egg is laid and lasts for a total of 26–38 days. The chicks remain in the nest for 42–45 (52) days, and are dependent upon the parents for a further 40–50 days.

The production of young is dependent upon the weather. Heavy, persistent rain with cold weather kills many

Black Kite juvenile. *Photo B. Génsbøl/Biofoto.*

chicks, often because water stands centimetres deep in the nest owing to the lining of paper and plastic.

A Swiss investigation in 1958–60 (with a sample of 1477 birds) showed an annual production for each clutch started of 0.71–1.92 young. In years 1952–67 a German investigation based on 134 pairs showed that 64 per cent of the pairs bred successfully, with a resulting 1.23 young per clutch.

Food

Almost omnivorous, with a liking for fish; common species occur most frequently, e.g. various members of the carp family, perch, pike etc.

Birds are also often taken, mostly as fallen game or stolen from other raptors. In addition, Black Kites also catch many birds, mostly juveniles of, for example, larks, members of the crow family, poultry and gulls, waders, ducks and moorhens. In drier areas quite a number of small mammals are taken, mainly field voles, hamsters, sousliks, leverets and rabbits.

Amphibians and reptiles represent a part in certain localities. Insects, earthworms and snails are regularly taken, as well as any kind of carrion and often household waste sometimes eaten from rubbish tips.

Investigations from different parts of Europe show the large range of foods taken: in the Berlin area 102 fish, 16 mammals, 22 birds and one frog; France (Lorraine): 734 fish (mainly various members of the carp family), 651 mammals (mostly moles and field voles), 265 birds (87% young with starlings as the commonest species), 95 amphibians and reptiles and 737 invertebrates (mostly beetles); West Germany (dry area): 247 mammals, 170 birds, 4 fish, 2 amphibians and many insects.

Foraging methods

Flies low over open country at a height of 10–60 m. Also wanders about on the ground in search of beetles etc and can catch insects in flight.

67

Black Kite population in the Western Palearctic

Sweden	approx. 5 pairs (1981)[9]	In Norrbotten. Population trend not known.
Finland	approx. 10 pairs (1985)[10]	Around 20 pairs in 1950s.
West Germany	650–1000 pairs (1982)[22]	
East Germany	800 pairs (1985)[37]	50 per cent decrease 1940–79 in Brandenburg, where 200–220 pairs estimated (1969/70)[36]. Mecklenburg approx. 240 pairs (1974)[52].
Poland	400–450 pairs (1984)[80]	Apparently decreasing. Reason not known.
USSR *Estonia*	? 20–30 pairs (1976)[11]	In a 270,000 km² research area, 6500–9000 pairs (1970)[1]. Probably decreasing steadily on account of mass tourism at breeding sites and foraging places.
France	5800–8000 pairs (1984)[92]	Population has grown in this century. Now stable.
Belgium	at least 2 pairs (1982)[54]	Immigration taking place.
Switzerland	1250 pairs (1969)[25]	The species' best area in Central Europe. Marked increase from about 1850 now replaced by slight decrease.
Austria	a good 20 pairs (1977)[48]	Marked decrease in about the last 100 years.
Czechoslovakia	40 pairs (1988)[43]	Decrease in recent decades.
Hungary	100 pairs (1988)[40]	Considerable reduction in population.
Yugoslavia	approx. 100 pairs (1982)[19]	After decrease, now stable.
Romania	120–150 pairs (1977)[42]	Big decrease. Formerly country's most numerous raptor. At start of this century could be seen in flocks of 50–60.
Bulgaria	few? (1971)[3]	
Greece	approx. 70 pairs (1983)[84]	Apparently decreasing.

Italy	500–1500 pairs (1982)[19]	Population halved since 1945 (shooting, poisoned bait).
Spain	>25,000 pairs (1982)[19]	Stable or possible decrease (shooting, nest raiding).
Portugal	900–1200 pairs (1982)[19]	Probably decreasing.
Turkey	500–1000 pairs (1982)[19]	Big decrease. In 1930 about 500 pairs in Istanbul, now (1977) 10 pairs.
Syria	exterminated? (1979)[1]	Not rare as late as 1968.
Israel	4 pairs (1982)[19]	Decrease due to thallium sulphate.
Egypt	100–500 pairs (1982)[19]	Big decrease.
Tunisia	>200 pairs (1982)[50]	
Algeria	common (1982)[19]	
Morocco	>1000 pairs (1982)[19]	
Cape Verde Islands	50–100 pairs (1988)[45]	Southern Islands: 50–100 pairs hybrids with Red Kite

Kite and Black Kite (*left*) juveniles with carrion laid out. *Photo B. Eichthorn/Dieter Zingel.*

Kite

Milvus milvus

Also known as Red Kite

Distribution

This species has a remarkable small range. It is essentially a European bird, and as the map shows it breeds outside Europe only in small numbers, in North Africa and on islands in the Atlantic.

The population on the Cape Verde Islands constitutes a separate subspecies *M.m. fasciicauda*. It is now threatened by extermination because of hybridization with Black Kites.

Population estimates

The total population in the Western Palearctic is, according to the data on p. 75, roughly 7500–17,000 breeding pairs. The large difference between the minimum and maximum is due to disagreement on the size of the Spanish population. The table shows clearly that from the viewpoint of population the Kite is centred on East and West Germany and probably also in Spain.

Population trends

Over the whole of its range the Kite has suffered a decline during the last 300–400 years, due first to improved hygiene (restricting its food) and secondly to the great campaign of extermination, effected by shooting and nest-robbing in the nineteenth and first part of the twentieth century.

Kite juvenile. *Photo J. Elmelid/N.*

On account of unfavourable living conditions, the species has left several outposts both in the north and the south, namely in Norway, Estonia, large areas of the Balkans, Algeria and the whole of the Middle East.

The Kite is robust enough to withstand pressures of the modern world. This was shown, for instance, during the Second World War when the species regained terrain because its persecutors became distracted from the wildlife. In the northern part of its range this happened later, because shooting raptors was forbidden in large parts of western Europe at the end of the 1960s and the start of the 1970s. The population grew and resumed incursions took place in areas where the species had been exterminated. This upward trend was also encouraged by the restrictions placed on the use of pesticides.

While the trend improved in several countries (see table on p. 75) it nevertheless slipped back in others. This applies to many eastern and southern European countries. In the latter, illegal shooting appears to have been an important factor. In general, countries where the trend has been negative do not have the same control of or restrictions on the use of poisonous substances as in northern and western Europe.

Habitat

The Kite prefers hilly country with woodland, meadows, lakes and rivers. Compared with the Black Kite it is less tied to areas rich in lakes, and thus also breeds in drier, hilly or mountainous areas.

The preferred hunting terrain is cultivated land, lakes rich in fish and rubbish tips and, particularly in winter, main roads where it looks out for wildlife fatalities.

Migration

Red Kites from the northernmost breeding populations may be strongly migratory, some reaching North Africa. However, some stay for the winter in the breeding areas, even as far north as Sweden, and this habit seems to be increasing. It may, in part, be due to a run of mild winters. Some dozens of birds are now involved, and

they are artificially fed during the winter. The birds from the southernmost breeding areas have probably always been sedentary.

Migrant Red Kites are concentrated at narrow sea-crossings but the numbers involved are small. Generally less than 100 are seen in autumn at Falsterbo, and the record at Gibraltar is only 200. Recoveries of Swedish ringed birds indicate wintering in Belgium, France and Spain. German birds have been found in France, Spain and Portugal but also in the Balkans and one in the Ukraine. Autumn passage continues from mid-August through to November. Young birds may not return to their breeding area in their first summer but adults will be back in late March or April. In the areas where the adults do not move out they remain territorial throughout the year.

The isolated breeding population in mid-Wales was thought to be totally sedentary, but ringing has shown that the young birds may move south-east into England for the winter. The July recovery of a bird ringed in Schleswig-Holstein (Germany) within the Welsh breeding range shows that the population is possibly not totally isolated after all.

Voice

Very silent. The voice is heard only near the nest or outside the breeding period in the morning and evening around the assembly places of the species. There are two basic motifs: 1) a buzzard-like mewing and sharp *vee-oo* screech, and 2) whistling or whining rapidly repeated.

Breeding

Kites breed for the first time at an age of 2–3 years. In populations where the pair remains in or near the breeding site the whole year round it seems that the sexes form a more lasting partnership than in migrating populations.

At the start of the breeding season (March–April) the birds can be seen in display flights over the breeding site, often circling at a great height or flying and chasing one another and seizing each other's talons.

Some pairs use the same nest year after year, while others build a new one or renovate old nests of e.g. Buzzard or Rook. Normally the nest is placed at a height of about 10–28 m, and the Kite prefers to build in an oak, beech or fir. The nest cup is typically lined with paper, plastic or scraps of cloth.

Both sexes take part in nest-building; the male's role is primarily to

Kite and Black Kite (*right*) juveniles. *Photo B. Eichthorn/Dieter Zingel.*

bring the nest-building material to the female, who builds the nest.

In Scandinavia, the eggs are normally laid in late April to early May in a clutch of 2–3 (1–4 (5)) at intervals of (2) 3 (4) days. Incubation starts with the first egg, so hatching is asynchronous. The incubation period is 31–32 days per egg, and a typical clutch of three will take 38 days. Normally the female incubates alone, but may be relieved for short periods by the male, who both in the incubation period and in the first fourteen days after hatching feeds both the female and the chicks.

The young are fledged at an age of 48–50 days, in some cases only after 60 (70) days. The length of this period probably depends upon feeding and the degree of disturbance around the nest site. The young appear to become independent of their parents about four weeks after taking to the air.

There have been numerous investigations into chick production. In Sweden (1977–82) on average every fourth breeding attempt failed. Depending upon weather conditions the annual percentages fluctuated considerably. The same investigation showed that, on average, 1.44 chicks survived per breeding attempt. This can be placed in relation to a range from 0.6 (Wales) to 1.68 (West Germany). The very low production in Wales seems to be related to difficulties in obtaining food in a rainy climate.

It is interesting that the population in Wales has been able to treble in 30 years.

Hybridization
Two cases have been recorded of a Black Kite interbreeding with a Kite: East Germany in 1960, and Sweden (1972?–) 1976–81.

Food
Kites have a very varied diet, the composition for each bird depending upon what the locality offers.

Various observations show that bird prey accounts for 22–82 per cent of the total, mammals 13–68 per cent, fish 4–42 per cent. The higher figure for fish seems, however, to be an exception. The Kite does not eat as much fish as the Black Kite.

In a locality where fish was not available, a ten-year investigation of remains in 427 Kite nests yielded 948 mammals and 400 birds, plus insect remains. Over 75 per cent of the mammals were small rodents of various species. There were also 180 hares, mainly young ones. How many of these were actually caught by the Kite is not known.

The dominant birds taken were poultry (109 individuals). Doubtless many of these were taken dead from scrap heaps, but Kites also kill living fowls, particularly chickens. Other birds taken were starlings (46), partridges (36), doves (33), skylarks (31), sparrows (14) and magpies (7). Other investigations record crows, magpies and lapwings as common prey. The insect remains were mainly those of beetles.

In addition, other investigations have recorded amphibians and reptiles as prey.

The remains of domestic animals occur frequently, but these are taken as carrion. It also eats slaughter-house offal.

The Kite is also known to steal prey from other raptors, such as the Peregrine Falcon, Goshawk and White-tailed Eagle.

It is evident that the Kite takes prey which is of interest to man. It can kill in poultry runs and annoy pheasant breeders. It also kills hares. But all in all, it is not a serious menace to man.

In northern Europe, people have come to understand the place of raptors in nature and this attractive species nowadays survives as part of the fauna.

Foraging methods

Hunts while flying low (10–60 m) over open country or water.

Even though the bird does not appear fast in the air, it has been seen to kill both black-headed gulls and rooks which came too near. It can also take insects in flight. More commonly, however, it catches small invertebrates by wandering about on the ground.

Kite with a jay. *Photo G. Ziesler.*

Kite population in the Western Palearctic

Sweden	150 pairs (1987)[50]	Population doubled in 10 years. Increase due to winter feeding, reduced shooting and improved environment, thanks to restrictions in pesticide use.
Denmark	approx. 20 pairs (1986)[67]	Exterminated 1927. Several breeding attempts in following decades. Now seems established again.
West Germany	approx. 2000 pairs (1980–81)[22]	Increasing.
East Germany	approx. 1500 pairs (1983)[87]	Apparently increasing.
Poland	300 pairs (1984)[80]	Increasing.
USSR *Latvia*	rare (1983)[6] few (1983)[34]	
Britain *(Wales)*	57 pairs (1986)[18]	About 15 pairs in 1950s, over 30 pairs at start of 1970s. Increase due to less shooting and better food supply.

Belgium	2–5 pairs (1979)[1]	
Holland	breeds irregularly (1979)[1]	
Luxembourg	approx. 12 pairs (1981)[83]	
France	2300–2900 pairs (1984)[92]	After long period of decline is now increasing.
Switzerland	150 pairs (1979)[25]	Increasing. In 1960 only 90 pairs.
Czechoslovakia	Approx. 30 pairs (1988)[43]	Increasing in some areas.
Hungary	exterminated (1988)[70]	Last breeding record: 1976.
Romania	approx. 10 pairs (1977)[42]	
Yugoslavia	exterminated? (1982)[19]	
Italy	150–300 pairs (1982)[19]	Decreasing. 80–90 pairs Sicily (1982)[19].
Spain	10,000 pairs (1975)[27] 3000 pairs (1979)[1] <1000 pairs (1980)[23] >1000 pairs (1982)[19]	Much disagreement on population size. Apparently decreasing.
Portugal	100–200 pairs (1932)[19]	Decreasing.
Tunisia	only few pairs (1982)[50]	Threatened.
Morocco	10–100 pairs (1982)[19]	
Canary Islands	exterminated	Not seen since 1960's.
Cape Verde Islands	50–100 pairs of hybrids with Black Kites (1988)[45]	Strongly threatened by increase of population of Black Kite.

White-tailed Eagle
Haliaeetus albicilla

Distribution
The map shows the Western Palearctic distribution. Further eastwards the breeding area extends as a broad belt to the Pacific. In general, the northern limit follows the forest tundra, while the southern limit is roughly at the transition between grassland and bushy steppe.

It also breeds in the Nearctic region in Greenland, where the population is reckoned by some to be a separate subspecies *H.a. groenlandicus.*

Population estimates

A total population of approx. 1750 pairs. Within the area described the species has some marked focal points: Norway, about 45 per cent of the total number of pairs. Baltic area roughly 22 per cent and the Volga delta about 13 per cent, making a total of around 80 per cent for these three areas. On the other hand, the large area of south-eastern Europe with Turkey is sparsely occupied with only about 4 per cent of the breeding pairs.

Population trends

As late as the last century the White-tailed Eagle was distributed throughout most of Europe but was exterminated in many places. This was due to shooting, the laying-out of poison and a radical change in conditions at the breeding sites, including an intensification of forestry.

In the middle of this century a new man-made threat appeared, namely the use of environmental poisons. These are the main reasons for the

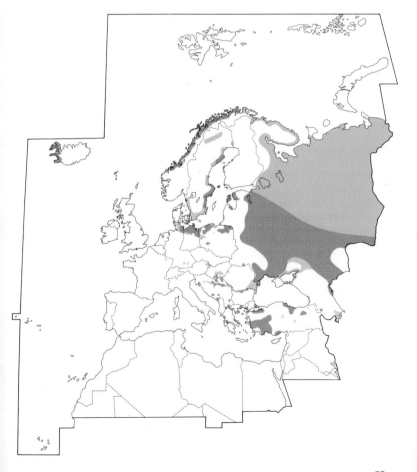

continued threat to the species in Europe. Thus, the population in south-east Europe is faced with extermination. In this area the population has been more than halved in the last two decades. In other places the species has been exterminated, as for example in many Mediterranean countries.

Today, the White-tailed Eagle is largely protected in all its breeding areas but, particularly in eastern Europe, it is still shot illegally and killed by poison laid out as a pesticide. In recent decades considerable attention has been paid both nationally and internationally to the living conditions of the Baltic population. This area's high content of heavy metals and of DDT and PCB has, since the 1950s, produced an especially difficult situation for this species. In their place at the top of the food chain eagles accumulate these environmental poisons with the result that the production of young may fail completely. In 1966 the rather large populations in Finland did not produce a single bird on the wing.

This situation set certain protective measures in motion, in both Sweden and Finland. These included the laying-out of poison-free meat with the aim of detoxicating the birds so that they could again become capable of breeding. To a large extent this has resulted in the survival of many young birds through the hazardous first year of life, and when they become sexually mature they are now far less laden with poison than they would otherwise have been. In Sweden in very recent years there have been records of young birds forming pairs in previously deserted breeding sites. This feeding and other measures such as the outlawing of many poisons has,

in Sweden and Finland, led to a slow increase in the production of young. However, this is still a long way from providing everything for long-term survival.

In both Sweden and Finland attempts are also being made to protect the breeding sites by stopping the felling of nesting trees and by buying up areas around the breeding sites. In Germany captive-hatched young have been placed in the nests, which has made the rearing of more than one young per nest possible. In Great Britain, since 1968, young of Norwegian birds have been introduced in an attempt to re-establish a breeding population, which has now been achieved.

As shown in the table (p. 85), there are only three countries that show an improvement, or a partial one. These are Poland, Norway and Iceland. This is due to the fact that poisons are now much less used, and so conditions have improved. The stable situation or improvement in Poland is due to the breeding sites being inland, where poisoning is much less serious than in the Baltic region. Sweden has a comparable position in Lapland.

In the remaining countries the position is more or less serious, the main threat being a poisoned environment. However, there are also differences from country to country. Finland and Sweden have made great advances and they may well be over the worst. Other countries are also working seriously on the survival of this species. As already mentioned the position is bad in south-east Europe. Here an understanding by the

Adult White-tailed Eagle, taking off from resting place. *Photo B. Génsbøl/ Biofoto.*

human population of conservation problems is generally less effective than in, say, northern Europe. In addition to the poor environmental conditions an additional factor is the long distance between the surviving pairs.

In summary, it can be said that the White-tailed Eagle is not at the moment threatened with extermination, although in the coming years some local stocks will tend to decrease.

Migration

In Europe, White-tailed Eagles capable of breeding are almost exclusively non-migratory. Only those in northern Russia and Lapland leave their breeding sites in winter. The birds may, however, wander about. Old birds are seen from time to time in Denmark and southern Sweden.

Young birds move around more and can almost be regarded as migratory. Young Scandinavian birds may, in some cases, reach as far south as the Balkans, Italy, France and Spain. These movements are, however, related more to the occurrence of waterfowl than to true directional migration.

Over the last decade or more the programme of introductions in Scotland has partly obscured the position of this magnificent bird in Britain. There are some recent records of wild individuals including one which wintered in Buckinghamshire and was admired by many and another, ringed in Germany, that died in May 1985 in Norfolk. Most records of wild birds occur in eastern England from November to March. With the first successful breeding of the birds introduced in Scotland it is possible that

Adult White-tailed Eagle with carrion laid out. *Photo L. Järnemo/N.*

regular wandering, and even wintering, south of the newly established breeding area, may develop in the future.

Habitats

As already mentioned the species is distributed from the northern tundra to more temperate areas, sporadically also in subtropical areas. In its northwestern breeding grounds, namely Iceland, Fennoskandia apart from Lapland, and in the remaining Baltic countries, also in Greenland, this is primarily a coastal bird, while in much of the remainder of its range it occurs near large lakes and rivers.

Pairs which breed on the coast are often close to their favourite foraging areas, but inland pairs may nest 10 km from their food supply.

The birds are very adaptable as regards nest position, building in large trees, in cliffs or even on the ground.

Adult White-tailed Eagle.
Photo B. Génsbøl/Biofoto.

Voice

Often heard during the breeding season, the voice consists of a series of 15–20 loud hoarse screeches as contact calls, often increasing in rapidity and pitch: usually a *klee-klee*. The female's call is definitely deeper than the male's.

Breeding

The plumage of White-tailed Eagles is fully developed at an age of about five years and they are then ready to breed. Young birds can be seen building nests or being partners to older ones but apparently this does not lead to the production of young.

The eagles live in or near their territory throughout the year but in early spring the link between the sexes becomes more noticeable. The

birds are seen in display flights high above the territory. There the two birds fly, often close together, at a maximum height of 200 m and perform various rituals, including stooping towards one another.

Investigations in East Germany show that most of the White-tailed Eagles build a nest at a maximum of 3 km from their principal foraging area. However, about ten per cent nested at a distance of roughly 6–11 km. Typically the nests were built on the edges of woodland (over 80 per cent) and so with direct access to open country or water. As a rule the nest trees were over a hundred years old, with fir as a preference, then beech.

In Norway this species most often breeds on small skerries or larger islands, and in smaller numbers on the mainland coast. In localities un-inhabited by man the nest may be accessible. Where man is in evidence the nest is completely inaccessible, in 50 per cent of the cases on the side of a steep cliff. In southern Sweden eagle nests are typically built on an island about 100 m from the coast in the uppermost third of a large fir tree.

In Scandinavia eggs are laid in March–April. The clutch size varies between one and three eggs. Norwegian investigations (57 clutches) gave 9 per cent with one egg, 70 per cent with two and 21 per cent with three eggs, giving an average of 2.1 eggs per clutch. Earlier on, that is before the arrival of environmental poisons, Sweden averaged 2.3 eggs per clutch and in the 1970s this fell to 1.2.

The individual eggs are laid at intervals of 2–5 days, and as the female starts to incubate with the first egg the chicks do not hatch at the same time. The incubation period varies from 34–42 days (average 38 days). Both sexes incubate, the female does the most, on average 75 per cent of the time.

In the first two weeks of the chicks' life one of the parent birds is always on the nest, almost always the female. When the chicks are four weeks old they can be left by themselves for long

Greenlandic White-tailed Eagle bringing a trout to the nest. The photographer was recording the types and numbers of prey taken. *Photo W. Wille/Leica.*

periods, while both the parents hunt. The young are fledged at an age of about 70 days but the nest is still the centre of their life for 10–20 days. After they are fully fledged it takes a further six months before the young are independent.

As mentioned under population trends the production of young is, in most areas, too small for the population to survive in the long term. One of the populations least burdened with poison, namely the Norwegian, produced 1.2 young per breeding pair in the years 1956–60. For 1982 the production figures for the following countries were: Poland 0.78, Estonia 0.46, Finland 0.49 and Sweden 0.52. It has hitherto been reckoned that 0.70 young per breeding pair must be produced to keep the population stable. In 1982 this figure was achieved by Poland. Perhaps the 0.70 is nowadays too high a figure. The winter artificial feeding already mentioned means that many young birds survive and nowadays there is a lower mortality from shooting. Nevertheless the figures for Sweden, Finland and Estonia are, without doubt, too low.

It is, however, comforting to know that, after the enormous decrease in the 1960s the Finnish and Swedish production figures show an upward trend.

Food

The diet of the White-tailed Eagle covers a wide spectrum. It varies according to the locality and the time of year. Normally, fish make up a large part of the diet. Investigations in southern Greenland during the breeding season, with systematic photographing of prey brought back to the nest, show roughly 91 per cent fish,

mainly sea trout, cod and Greenland cod, three per cent birds, mostly gulls, and in a good year five per cent mammals, exclusively arctic fox.

From Norway there are other figures based on the remains of prey in the breeding season: 36 per cent fish and 56 per cent birds. In all, the Norwegian investigation shows a repertoire of 27 fish species, with cod and lumpsucker as the commonest. New East German investigations of the remains of prey in the breeding season show 56 per cent fish, 37 per cent birds and seven per cent mammals, but the figures for winter were 79 per cent birds, fifteen per cent mammals and only six per cent fish.

There is no doubt that the proportion of fish is set too low in both these investigations. Fish remains are difficult to identify and to use the remains of prey as a basis for food analysis means that fish will be underestimated.

Carrion constitutes a considerable part of the food, mostly, it seems, in winter; this would be the remains of fish, birds and large mammals. Interest in the last food source has, especially some years ago, led to the belief in eagle districts that White-tailed Eagles frequently kill lambs and calves. In fact they are eating carrion. Recent investigations in Greenland suggest that these eagles sometimes kill small lambs. However, this only occurs to a limited extent and has no effect on sheep farming.

The Norwegian research worker J. Fr. Willgohs, who is responsible for many of the foregoing observations, has studied the biology of White-tailed Eagles over a period of several years. He believes that mammals are not normally eaten by these eagles, except as carrion.

White-tailed Eagle juvenile catching a mallard. *Photo J. Elmelid/N.*

Foraging methods

Various investigations show that White-tailed Eagles take about 700 g of prey per day, corresponding to 500 g of pure meat. They use two hunting methods to reach this figure: either perching to watch out for food, or searching for it in flight. They usually fly low or circle at a height of 200–300 m over the foraging area.

The birds catch fish in calm water, where they can see the fish near the surface. Usually the bird approaches, flying low or hovering and then rapidly strikes the talons into the water in an attempt to catch the fish. It may also stoop like an Osprey, but not so often. Finally, this eagle sometimes stands still or wanders about in shallow water in search of fish.

If the fish is too large to lift, the bird may tow it to land by rowing with its wings.

It prefers to take birds and small mammals by surprise. Otherwise hunting for birds on the water may develop into a long-winded affair. Here the eagle uses an exhaustion technique. The prey dives when attacked and the eagle is immediately above it when it re-surfaces. For coots 43–65 attacks have been recorded before the eagle is successful, which may take 35–45 minutes.

Sometimes two eagles may work together. This can involve two mates or two unrelated birds.

The White-tailed Eagle may also steal food from other birds. Sometimes an Osprey surrenders its catch to the Eagle, and the same happens with gulls.

Normally the White-tailed Eagle appears heavy and clumsy in flight but it can catch a flying bird. In this way it has been seen to take a greylag goose, a couple of ducks and a raven. This type of hunting must, however, be regarded as exceptional.

Whie-tailed Eagle population in the Western Palearctic

Iceland	20 pairs (1981)[2]	Population much reduced, but seems now stable, consisting of about 60 young birds in addition to breeding stock.
Norway	800 pairs (1984)[86] 1500 pairs (1988)[70]	Increasing. Production of young in general good, seems not much affected by poisons. Centre of European population.
Sweden	approx. 100 pairs (1987)[75]	Population in 2 parts. (1) Baltic coast approx. 70 pairs, suffering from poisons. Only about 30 per cent of pairs produce viable young. Slowly decreasing. (2) Lapland 30 pairs, apparently doing better, with about 70 per cent now producing viable young.
Denmark	0–1 pair (1982)[8]	In 1979 and 1980 a pair nested on Lolland, without producing viable young. Adults and young seen in summer in recent years.
Finland	approx. 60 pairs (1985)[10]	In spite of low chick production has, in recent decades, managed to survive at 40 pairs. Production now slightly increasing and with a decrease in DDT in the Baltic the population may well survive.
West Germany	6 pairs (1988)[70]	The small, much threatened population is being helped by setting up artificial nests and by introducing captive-bred young.
East Germany	115 pairs (1985)[87]	Production now slightly increasing.
Poland	min 185 pairs probably 210–240 pairs (1988)[45]	Apparently stable or increasing. Reproduction good.

USSR
of which:
   Estonia
   Latvia
   Lithuania
   Moldavia
   Volga delta
	approx. 500 pairs (1982)[6]
	
	20–25 pairs (1988)[45]
	5 pairs (1988)[45]
	1 pair (1988)[45]
	5 pairs (1982)[6]
	200–250 pairs (1982)[6]
		On the whole decreasing Lower Volga population probably the world's densest and seems very stable.

Britain	10 pairs (1987)[45]	Over 82 young Norwegian birds released in Scotland between 1968–1985. First release not successful, but oldest birds from second release have now started to breed.

White-tailed Eagle

Czechoslovakia	5 pairs (1988)[43]	New population based on released birds.
Hungary	25 pairs (1988)[40]	Increasing last years.
Romania	10–12 pairs (1981)[2]	Decreasing.
Greece	2–5 pairs (1988)[70]	Extinction threatened.
Yugoslavia	30 pairs (1982)[19]	Threatened by environmental poisons.
Bulgaria	2–3 pairs (1979)[1]	Information uncertain.
Albania	?	
Turkey	15–25 pairs (1982)[50]	
Algeria	1–2 pairs (1982)[50]	

Pallas's Sea Eagle
Haliaeetus leucoryphus

Distribution
This species has disappeared as a breeding bird in the Western Palearctic, where it was formerly found in the region north of the Caspian Sea (last breeding record in 1947). Widely distributed in central and southern Asia. Probably no longer breeds in the USSR (1983)[6].

Migration
Apparently migratory or mainly so in the northern part of the distribution range, which it leaves in October. The birds usually return to the breeding sites in February.

A rare visitor in Europe outside the USSR. Encountered June–July in Finland (1926), Poland (1943) and Norway (1949), in each case young birds.

Habitat
Breeds near lakes, rivers and wetlands with plenty of food.

Breeding
Where possible the nests are built in trees, but also breeds in areas without trees, where the nest may be placed in a reed-bed, on a sand bank or on a cliff.

In the most northerly part of the range the 2–3 (4) eggs are laid in March (October–February in India).

Food
Mainly fish and birds, secondarily frogs, snakes and water tortoises.

Pallas's Sea Eagle – adult. *Photo K. Halberg/Biofoto.*

Pallas's Sea Eagle – adult. *Photo B. Gensbøl/Biofoto.*

Foraging methods
Often perches on a branch or similar place with a good view. Also flies in search of food, either at a great height or quite low.

Egyptian Vulture – adult. *Photo B. Génsbøl/Biofoto.*

Egyptian Vulture

Neophron percnopterus

Distribution
In addition to its Western Palearctic range (*see* map), the Egyptian Vulture (nominate race) breeds in large areas of Africa north of the equator, in the Arabian Peninsula, in south-western Asia, also in India (*N.p. ginginianus*).

Population estimates
The total population in the Western Palearctic cannot be estimated as there are too many countries without reliable figures. The total European population (*see* table on p. 91) is about 1500 pairs with most living in Spain (1000 pairs).

Population trends
Like the other three European vul-

tures the Egyptian Vulture has been much reduced, a trend which still continues (*see* table on p. 91). In addition, its living conditions have, for hundreds of years, been much reduced by improved hygienic conditions. This negative trend has also been reinforced by shooting and by death due to poisoning.

Nowadays the species is protected in most European countries. However, this evidently does not prevent it being continuously persecuted. On the positive side the reduced food supply had, to some extent, been counterbalanced by feeding projects, including those in northern Spain.

Migration

The Egyptian Vultures of Europe are almost totally migratory, wintering south of the Sahara in the Niger inundation zone, to the west, and the Sudan, in the east. In both areas there are resident populations which lead to some confusion.

It is also clear that many of the European birds do not return northwards in the first or second summer of their lives.

Although capable of considerable water crossings using sustained flapping flight, the majority of Egyptian Vultures use the traditional soaring migrant routes. The Gibraltar route is most important with counts exceeding 6000 in some years, whereas the Bosporus can only muster just over 500. A similar number has been recorded moving from Sicily to Cap Bon. Autumn passage of adults starts in July and juveniles in September, when the peak occurs. Spring return happens from February to mid-April.

A few adults remain on the European breeding grounds during the winter – these are probably older birds remaining on their territories. When the young birds do return – a few years old but substantially in adult plumage – they may wander some distance to the north of the breeding area. There have been records in Britain, Norway, Sweden, Denmark and northern Germany (Schleswig-Holstein) during the summer months.

Habitat

The species is not particularly specialized in its habitat requirements. A fairly ordinary countryside with rocky areas but no great heights will suffice, with bare slopes and valleys that can be seen at a glance. Such conditions provide a good chance for food to be seen and recognized.

Egyptian Vultures like to nest close to rivers, but their flexibility as regards habitat is seen, for instance, when they settle in desert-like areas.

They like to forage in open country such as steppes, savannas and river banks, and also in towns.

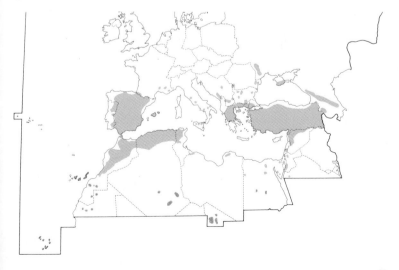

Egyptian Vulture – adult searching the area for food. *Photo B. Génsbøl/Biofoto.*

Voice

The species is normally silent.

Breeding

The Egyptian Vulture usually breeds for the first time at an age of 4–5 years. The birds apparently pair for life. May breed in colonies, but in Europe they generally breed solitarily.

Immediately after arriving the birds start an energetic mating flight, in which they perform impressive stoops or dives which are astonishing for such a large bird.

The nest is often placed on a cliff or in a cleft in the ground, sometimes but not often in a tree. Both birds take part in nest-building. In Europe the 2 (1–3) eggs are generally laid in late March to early April. Both sexes take a share in incubation which lasts 42 days and the young remain in the nest for 70–90 days.

Food

A varied diet, largely depending upon what is available. Typically the birds feed on carrion of small animals, such as rats, squirrels, tortoises, toads and snakes, and also on offal, faeces both of animals and man, and on some insects. The latter are evidently the only food taken alive. Larger carrion only plays a subordinate role, a fact related to the bird's weak bill. Its own strength only allows it to take the eyes, tongue and similar parts and it must otherwise be content with scraps left by larger vultures.

Foraging methods

The bird normally searches its hunting territory very persistently, often only at a height of 10–30 m, but may also fly 30–40 km to areas with plentiful food.

The bird's sight is fantastic. It has been shown that from a height of 1000 m it can discern a food source as small as 4–8 cm.

Egyptian Vulture population in the Western Palearctic

Portugal	40–80 pairs (1987)[45]	Distributed locally. Stable.
Spain	950–1100 pairs (1987)[45]	Of which about 5 pairs in the Balearics. Decreasing.
France	60 pairs (1986)[45]	25 pairs in Provence and Languedoc. 35 pairs in Pyrenees. Stable after decreasing.
Italy	25–35 pairs (1982)[19]	Almost exterminated on mainland, about 20 pairs in Sicily (1981)[2].
Yugoslavia	approx. 50 pairs (1982)[19]	Decreasing.
Albania	?	No recent data.
Romania	4 pairs (1981)[2]	Apparently exterminated around 1966[3]. After this, new colonisation?
Bulgaria	>50 pairs (1960s)[3]	Stable or slightly increasing (1974)[1].
Greece	approx. 250 pairs (1983)[84]	Decreasing.
Cyprus	5 pairs (1982)[19]	

Egyptian Vulture – adult foraging. *Photo J. Robert/Jacana.*

Egyptian Vulture

USSR:		
Moldavia	5–6 pairs	
Crimea	2–3 pairs	
Caucasus	>30 pairs (1979)[1]	
Turkey	500–2000 pairs (1982)[19]	The commonest vulture.
Syria	?	Decreasing, particularly in the large towns (1979)[1].
Lebanon	?	
Israel	86 pairs (1982)[19]	Decreasing.
Jordan	?	
Egypt	10–100 pairs (1982)[19]	Formerly numerous. Steadily decreasing.
Libya	?	Marked decrease.
Tunisia	>200 pairs	
Algeria	Common (1982)[19]	
Morocco	500–1000 pairs (1982)[19].	
Mauretania	?	
Canary Islands	25–35 pairs (1987)[79]	Marked decrease, apparently due to lack of food (1979)[1].
Cape Verde Islands	common (1984)[35]	

Griffon Vulture distribution.

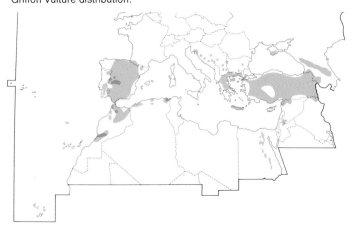

Griffon Vulture
Gyps fulvus

Griffon vulture juvenile searching the area for food. *Photo F. Sahier/Ardea.*

Distribution
In addition to the distribution shown on the map the nominate race of the Griffon Vulture breeds in north-east Africa, the Arabian Peninsula and eastwards through Asia to Kashmir and the Altai region. Here it is replaced by *G.f. fulvescens*, found from northern and central India to Assam.

Population estimates
The Western Palearctic area has a total population of 5000–6000 pairs. Note (table on p. 96) that here again Spain occupies a very special position.

Population trends
The species formerly had a considerably larger population than today. In the thirteenth and fourteenth centuries it bred in southern Germany and it was still in south-eastern Poland in 1914.

However, as for the European vultures in general, its living requirements became much curtailed and this led to a considerable reduction in population, a development which continues today (*see* table on p. 96).

Modern agricultural methods and improved hygiene reduced the food supply (except carrion), shooting oc-

93

curred extensively and still continues, and apparently many die from eating poisoned carrion mostly intended for wolves and foxes.

On the positive side there are reintroduction programmes in Austria and France, and feeding with poison-free meat takes place in the Pyrenees, Sardinia and northern Yugoslavia. In addition, reserves have been established in the Pyrenees, southern Spain and northern Greece, while the species is completely protected in Italy, Spain, France and Greece.

Migration

Old birds are apparently non-migratory, while young ones wander about or are partial migrants. The winter quarters are not known, evidently because they are confused with local populations. Migratory movements have been confirmed at Gibraltar in late July to mid-November (more than 600 at the start of the 1970s) and at the Bosporus (maximum 163 in 1969) in September–October. Gibraltar is passed again in February to early June with a maximum in April–May. So it is clear that the migratory birds must be young individuals. At this time the old birds are breeding.

Mainly young birds can be seen far to the north of the breeding area, most often in April–October as far north as Finland, Sweden and Denmark.

Habitat

For the breeding area there are three main requirements: there must be cliffs to provide nesting sites, plenty of food and a countryside where wind thermals facilitate hovering. The latter develop particularly well in countryside scored by rifts or in more open

plains with hills. Dry areas are preferred.

In Europe the nests are normally placed at altitudes from 0–1000 m, however in the Caucasus they may be found up to 2750 m.

Voice

Frequently used when the birds occur in flocks around carrion: hissing, shrieking and hiccuping.

Breeding

Nests in colonies of 2–100 pairs, but most commonly 15–20. Solitary nesters also occur especially in areas with numerous possible nesting sites. In rare cases they may also nest in trees.

Breeding first takes place at 4–5 years old. The pair probably remains together year after year.

In the breeding season there are display flights, generally performed close to the nesting or sleeping places. The sexes then fly with synchronized movements along a cliff face, one above the other. This phase is succeeded by circling flight, the pair flying upwards side by side in a close spiral.

Griffon Vultures breed early in the year. In southern Europe the single egg is normally laid from mid-February to early March. The sexes help one another in nest-building, in incubation and in feeding the young. Incubation takes 52 (48–54) days. The young spend 110–115 days in the nest, and are still dependent upon the parents for some weeks.

Flight of adult Griffon Vultures. *Photo Jacana.*

Food

Griffon Vultures live exclusively on carrion, mainly of medium-sized and large mammals, but in certain cases on larger birds and fish.

From time to time they also take sheep afterbirths. This has led to the unconfirmed claim that they kill new-born lambs.

Foraging methods

Typically the mode of procedure is as follows: the flock takes off, flies in the same direction and spreads out over the area. At the same time as they are searching for food, each individual bird keeps an eye open for those flying close by. They observe not only the behaviour of members of their own species, but also that of other carrion-feeders, such as magpies, crows, ravens and other vultures.

When carrion is sighted the bird drops down and its fellow vultures soon realize the presence of food and move in.

Griffon Vultures' sight is quite fantastic. It has been shown that they can discern an item of food about 30 cm across from a height of 3690 m.

Griffon Vulture population in the Western Palearctic

Portugal	158 pairs (1987)[45]	Only in the eastern parts. Apparently decreasing.
Spain	4000 pairs (1982)[19]	Steadily decreasing.
France	110 pairs (1982)[19]	Stable. From 1982 breeding in the Cevennes, as a result of an attempt to re-establish a population in the area. In 1987 12 young hen.
Italy	22–23 pairs (1982)[19]	Only breeds in Sardinia. Extermination on the mainland and Sicily.
Austria	1 pair (1980)[33]	Free-flying pair from Salzburg Zoo bred in nearby mountains. 20–30 non-breeders every summer in the Alps.
Yugoslavia	<200 pairs (1982)[19]	Decreasing?
Albania	?	No recent data.
Romania	extinct	Last breeding record around 1960 (1974)[3].
Bulgaria	extinct	Few pairs possibly breed (1977)[1].

Greece	approx. 450 pairs (1983)[84]	Decrease in the lowlands, about 250 pairs in Crete (1932)[19].
Turkey	500–1000 pairs (1982)[50]	Decreasing.
Cyprus	10–100 pairs (1982)[19]	
USSR *Crimea* *Caucasus*	approx. 10 pairs approx. 50 pairs (1979)[1]	
Syria	?	Decreasing (1968)[1].
Israel	74 pairs (1982)[19]	Decreasing due to use of poisons to control rodents and wild pigs.
Tunisia	extinct (1979)[1]	
Algeria	few (1982)[50]	
Morocco	100 pairs (1982)[19]	Decreasing. Threatened.

Griffon Vultures and Black Vulture (*centre*) with carrion. *Photo P. Petit.*

Lappet-faced Vultures at one of their very few breeding sites in Israel. *Photo R. Staav.*

Lappet-faced Vulture
Torgos tracheliotus

Distribution
Breeds in the Western Palearctic only in Israel, Egypt and Morocco, but is widespread over large parts of Africa south of 20°N. Divided by some authorities into two or three races on the basis of differences in the colour of the head and the size of the lappets. Others maintain that these differences are not geographical but characteristic of the individual.

Population trends
There has been a marked decrease in the Middle East and in North Africa. There is little information available, but apparently the species is close to extinction in the Western Palearctic.

Migration
Non-migratory, but young birds wander about. A single bird recorded from Europe (France) in the 1800s.

Habitat
Breeds in bushy steppe country, in desert areas and mountains, especially in places where domesticated animals and game are present.

Breeding
The species breeds when 4–5 years old The pair remains together throughout the year and, it seems, for life. In contrast to many other vultures the Lappet-faced Vulture breeds solitarily in an extensive territory.

The nest is built at the top of a tree or, if there are no trees, on the side of a cliff. In Israel the egg is laid in January, in North Africa in November–March. It is incubated for about 55 days and the young remain in the nest for approximately 125 days. The period during which the young are dependent upon the parents is probably some months.

Food
Mainly carrion from domesticated animals and larger game. The bird can kill smaller helpless mammals and birds.

A large vulture which itself opens the carrion. It often eats the tough muscles, and is normally the dominant bird in a flock of vultures feeding on carrion.

Foraging methods
Flies over the territory at moderate heights.

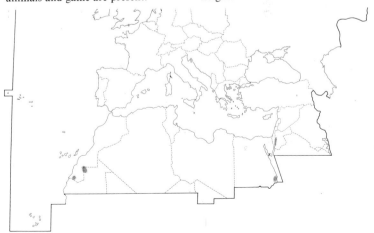

Lappet-faced Vulture population in the Western Palearctic

Israel	1 pair (1986)[96]	In 1945, 30–40 pairs (Negev Desert). Reasons for the decline are not clear, but may be lack of food, shooting and thallium poisoning.
Egypt	few pairs (1983)[82]	Near frontier to Sudan.
Tunisia	extinct (1982)[50]	Bred last century in southern part of the country.
Algeria	extinct? (1962)[1]	Once locally common.
Morocco	extinct (1982)[19]	Perhaps breed in areas indicated on the map, irregularly.
Mauretania	?	Formerly bred in the northern part of the country. No recent information (1962)[1].

European Black Vulture
Aegypius monachus

Distribution
Apart from the range shown on the map, the species is distributed in a broad belt eastwards to China.

Population estimates
Nearly all the population figures in the table on p. 103 are from 1983[31]. Thus, the total population in the Western Palearctic is 740–1250 pairs. Of these Asia Minor and the Caucasus account for 350–450, so southern Europe has only approx. 380 pairs remaining.

Population trends
In historic times the species has a considerably larger population than today, with breeding sites as far north as France, Czechoslovakia and northern Romania.

Right up to very recent years the population has steadily decreased and there was doubt whether it would survive in the Iberian Peninsula and the Balkans. It seems that the position has now become stable, thanks to feeding with poison-free meat and the establishment of reserves, including attempts to prevent the felling of nesting trees.

The European Black Vulture must, however, be regarded as one of Europe's most threatened raptors. Its requirements have been much reduced by the improved hygiene of modern agriculture and by a reduction in the stock of sheep, which both result in less carrion. In addition, there is some direct persecution by shooting and to a certain extent deaths due to strychnine poisoning.

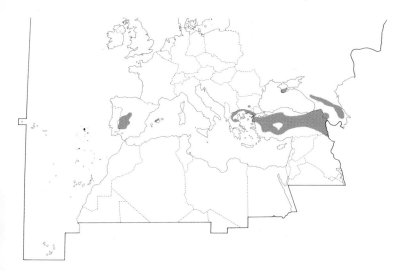

Migration

Non-migratory but wanders about. The old birds remain in or near the breeding sites throughout the year. The young wander more, but only a few go outside the breeding area. When the population was larger this happened more frequently. Thus, there are five old records from Schleswig-Holstein (several small flocks) and one or two from Denmark. Nowadays sightings in such northerly latitudes are apparently (perhaps exclusively) escaped captive birds.

Black Vulture sunning itself and at the same time shading the chicks. *Photo B-U. Meyburg.*

Adult Black Vulture. *Photo B-U. Meyburg.*

Habitat

Lives in lowland areas, plateau land and mountains, where there is sufficient food in the form of large game or cattle stocks. Prefers nesting in trees growing on slopes with good upward air currents which provide good conditions for flights in and out and also for display flights.

The species usually breeds alone, but there are also several records of loosely structured colonies.

Voice

Normally silent.

Breeding

The species normally breeds for the first time at an age of 5–6 years, at the same time as the adult plumage is complete. Pairs remain together throughout life.

In the first part of the breeding season display flights are seen in the vicinity of the nest. One bird flies directly over the other. The uppermost bird touches the other's back with its talons, then the lower one turns on its back and the two engage their talons and fall towards the ground.

The birds show an interest in the nest as early as October. They normally build in trees (5–20 m high), but may exceptionally build on a cliff side (e.g. in Majorca). Both sexes build, and the female usually lays her egg from late February to early March. The egg is incubated by the male and female and it hatches after 50–55 days. The young remain in the nest for 100–120 days but it is not known how much longer it is dependent upon the parents.

Food

Lives almost exclusively on carrion, but may also catch slow or sick animals if dead ones are not available. There is information from Asia that the European Black Vulture has caught tortoises, squirrels and marmots, and has occasionally taken newborn lambs. Fish remains have also been found in the nest.

The species prefers carrion from small game animals. Larger game may remain untouched for several days.

Foraging methods

The preferred mode of hunting is to fly low, searching over familiar terrain. Less commonly they may perch somewhere in the territory watching out for food.

A comparative study of a Griffon Vulture imm. and a Black Vulture ad. (*right*). *Photo P. Petit.*

Black Vulture population in the Western Palearctic

Spain *Mainland* *Majorca*	365 (1987)[45] 2 pairs[89]	Heavily decreased this century. Now increasing on mainland where the population has doubled in 10 years, but steadily decreasing in Majorca.
Portugal	probably exterminated (1982)[19]	
Italy	no longer breeds (1983)[31]	1–2 birds in Sardinia.
Yugoslavia	extinct? (1983)[31]	Possibly a few pairs near Albanian frontier.
Albania	?	No recent information.
Romania	extinct (1983)[31]	Last breeding record 1964.
Bulgaria	1–2 pairs? (1983)[31]	Probably a few breeding birds in Rhodope Mountains near Greek frontier.
Greece	approx. 15 pairs (1983)[31]	The sad remains of the Balkan population. Feeding project started 1987.
Turkey	100–500 pairs (1982)[19]	
Cyprus	2 pairs? (1982)[19]	
Israel	extinct	
USSR *Crimea* *Caucasus* *Armenia*	5–8 pairs 200–300 pairs } (1983)[31] approx. 50 pairs	

Bearded Vulture
Gypaetus barbatus

Distribution

As shown on the map the Bearded Vulture breeds in North Africa (nominate race), southern Europe, Asia Minor and the Middle East. The distribution extends eastwards to Mongolia and China (European and Asiatic birds belong to the subspecies *G.b. aureus*). Finally, the somewhat smaller subspecies *G.b. meridionalis* breeds in parts of East and South Africa.

Population estimates

The total European population is roughly 91–102 pairs, and there are 200–300 birds in all (*see* table on p. 106).

Population trends

As late as the last century, and in some areas also at the start of this century, the Bearded Vulture was a very common bird in the mountains of many southern European countries. But the species is vulnerable. Of the four European vultures it is the first to disappear when conditions deteriorate owing to a reduced food supply, massive shooting and the laying out of strychnine-poisoned carrion to control wolves and foxes. Poor living conditions led to its extermination in Austria, Switzerland, Italy, Romania and Bulgaria, and as the table on p. 106 suggests it is almost disappearing in other countries. To-

Adult Bearded Vulture. *Photo G. D. Plage/Bruce Coleman.*

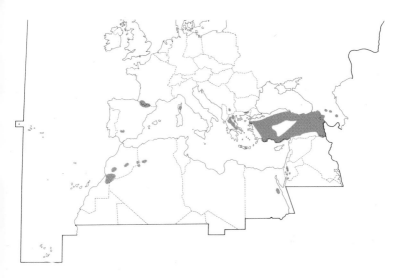

day the Bearded Vulture is by far the rarest of Europe's vultures.

For some years work has gone on to re-establish a population in the Alps, starting in 1974 when birds from Afghanistan were introduced. Now attempts are also being made with captive breeding, with a view to re-leasing young birds.

Migration
Non-migratory, remaining on the breeding sites throughout the year. The young birds wander about, but only exceptionally leave the mountains.

Habitat
This vulture breeds in mountainous regions with valleys and peaks at different heights where there is a good population of ibex, chamois, wild sheep and feral domestic animals. It also seems important that there should be a stock of hunting animals, such as wolves, lynx and Golden Eagles from

which it can take its share of the prey. In Europe the breeding places normally lie at an altitude of 1000–2000 m.

Voice
Normally silent. During display flights one hears some chirping calls, strikingly thin for such a large bird.

Breeding
The species usually starts to breed at an age of five years, at the same time as the adult plumage is acquired. The pair remains together year after year. In southern Europe preparations for breeding start early: even in October–November the birds show interest in the nest sites, and display flights can be seen in December–January. The sexes chase one another, fly higher, seize each other's talons and allow themselves to fall towards the ground.

The nest, which is apparently built by both sexes, is placed inaccessibly on a cliff wall or in a small cave. The 1–2 eggs are laid from late December

or early January (southern Spain) to late January or early February (Pyrenees). Both sexes incubate, the female apparently more than the male. Hatching takes 55–60 days, fledging 100–110 days. Although the two-egg clutch is common, usually only one chick survives.

Food and foraging

In its diet the Bearded Vulture is scarcely a typical vulture. It prefers fresh flesh from a newly dead animal, together with the bones. If thus is not available it can also take carrion and various forms of offal.

Bones are swallowed whole, the bird's stomach juices being capable of dissolving them. Larger bones are dropped from a height of 50–80 m. If they do not splinter, the bird tries again. The same technique is used in dealing with living land tortoises.

Most of the food comes from carcases, but this species can also catch live prey. In many cases it has been seen to kill weak, sick or wounded animals. It attacks them on steep slopes with beats of the wings.

Prey or carrion is found by regularly flying over the territory. Often the male and female hunt together, flying at a height of about 50 m. This searching proceeds very regularly so that day after day the birds can be seen at the same time and the same place.

Bearded Vulture population in the Western Palearctic

Spain		
Andalusia	1 pair (1986)[96]	After declining is now increasing, mainly due to reduction in use of strychnine.
Pyrenees	45–49 pairs (1982)[30]	
France		
Pyrenees	15–20 pairs (1982)[19]	Stable in both areas.
Corsica	9 pairs (1986)[96]	

Greece		Exterminated in many parts of the country. Threatened on the mainland because of poisoned carrion used to control foxes and wolves. Stable in Crete.
Mainland	15–20 pairs (1982)[30]	
Crete	10–12 pairs (1982)[30]	
Yugoslavia	1 pair (1982)[30]	
USSR		
Caucasus	5–10 pairs (1982)[1]	
Turkey	100–150 pairs (1982)[19]	
Israel	4–5 pairs (1982)[19]	
Iraq	perhaps few pairs (1979)[1]	
Egypt	<10 pairs (1982)[19]	
Algeria	<8 pairs (1982)[19]	
Morocco	10–100 pairs (1982)[19]	

Left: Adult Bearded Vulture. *Below*: Bearded Vulture adult, together with Alpine Chough. *Photo R. Ridman/G. D. Plage/Bruce Coleman.*

Short-toed Eagle
Circaetus gallicus

Distribution
In addition to the distribution shown on the map, the Short-toed Eagle breeds in the Soviet Union eastwards to the area around Lake Baikal, in parts of Iran and in India. It is not divided into races. Similar populations in Africa are today regarded as separate species.

Population estimates
It is not really possible to give a total figure for the Western Palearctic as data are lacking for the Soviet Union and elsewhere. Excluding these the total population for Europe can be estimated at around 5000 pairs, again with the majority in Spain.

The maximum number of Short-toed Eagles migrating south over Gibraltar and the Bosporus is roughly 11,000, which agrees well with the total figure for breeding pairs in Europe.

Population trends
During the last hundred years the breeding area has been considerably reduced. In the 1800s the northern limit lay in southern Jutland, where the last breeding record is from 1877.

The fanatical campaign against raptors hit the Short-toed Eagle hard; this happened at the same time as changes in the pattern of land use. The species ceased to breed in Denmark, Germany, Belgium, Switzerland and Austria. In western Europe

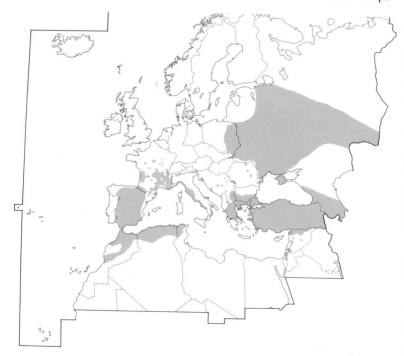

the breeding limit retreated some 1000 km to the south.

Today persecution no longer plays an important role, although it may be a problem locally. The reduced population is due to a poor supply of food. Reptiles do not thrive in areas with intensive agriculture.

It seems that the bird does very well in places where its requirements are adequately fulfilled, and protection measures are respected.

Migration

Essentially a migratory species with winter quarters in Africa south of the equator. There are a few records of winter sightings in southern Europe.

In autumn Short-toed Eagles almost exclusively follow the routes over the Caucasus, Bosporus and Gibraltar with approximate maximum numbers of 250, 2350 and 9050 respectively. These movements take place from mid-August to mid-October with a peak between mid-September and early October; however, the Gibraltar passage starts in early August.

The spring migration passes the Middle East, Caucasus (?), Bosporus and Gibraltar and (secondarily) Cape Bon in Tunisia in the period March–May, with a peak in the second half of March.

Although there have been many sightings of Short-toed Eagles north of the breeding range on the Continent, and around the North Sea from Belgium to Denmark, there are none from Britain. The 31 Swedish records (to end of 1982) are taken mainly in the autumn but the fewer Danish records are divided equally between spring and autumn.

Habitat

As a reptile specialist the bird favours

Short-toed Eagle. *Photo B. Génsbøl/Biofoto.*

regions offering good conditions for its prey; in general, areas with a warm and dry climate. In the northern part of the range the Short-toed Eagle likes to breed where damp low-lying country alternates with heath, grassland and forests, in the southern part in dry, stony or sandy terrain with maquis vegetation or open country with scattered woodland. The species has a preference for undulating hilly country where there are good thermal conditions. It does not thrive in areas with intensive cultivation, where its prey disappears.

Voice

Heard very often. Various complex harmonious, whistling sounds, of which one is rather like the call of a golden oriole and the other resembles the screech of a herring gull.

Breeding

Probably breeds for the first time at an age of 3–4 years. The same birds often mate year after year, meeting on the common territory in the spring.

The display flight, seen at the start of the breeding season, is of the type with a descent of about 15 m followed by an ascent and a new descent.

Both sexes take part in building the nest which is normally placed in a tree at a height of 6–10 m. The female lays a single egg in late March (south-west Europe) or late May (Russia). Incubation lasts 45–47 days, and is mainly by the female. The fledging period is 70–75 days. It is not known how long the chicks are still dependent, but they are usually seen migrating south with their parents.

Food

Feeds overwhelmingly on reptiles, with a preference for snakes (up to 1.80 m long). The bird searches mainly for non-venomous species, such as the European whip-snake, Montpellier snake, Aesculapian snake, grass snake, viperine snake and smooth snake, but also catches adders. Of 34 identified snakes brought to a nest only one was an adder. The bird also catches lizards.

Less important elements in the catch are slowworms, toads, frogs, various small mammals and birds, earthworms and beetles.

Investigations show that in rainy summers when reptile catching fails, the Short-toed Eagle can replace this prey with mice and fledglings of small birds, so that its own young do not die of starvation.

Short-toed Eagle killing an adder. *Photo Jacana.*

Short-toed Eagle feeding young on snake. *Photo Y. Eshbol/Bruce Coleman.*

Foraging methods

Searches while hovering at a height of 20–30 m, from which it drops on to the prey like a parachute, often in several separate descents. The bird can also stoop from a great height (up to 400 m).

Short-toed Eagles sometimes perch on a pylon, tree or post looking out for prey, and they also walk along the ground in search of something edible.

They catch snakes by seizing them at the nape. Small specimens are immediately lifted up into the air, the 'neck' broken, and often decapitated. Larger snakes are killed on the ground before the bird flies off with them.

Short-toed Eagles are not immune to snake venom but they are protected to a certain extent by their scaly feet and dense plumage.

Short-toed Eagle population in the Western Palearctic

Spain	approx. 3000 pairs (1982)[19]	Perhaps decreasing.
Portugal	80–100 pairs (1982)[19]	Stable.
France	>1000 pairs (1984)[92]	Reduction by 60–75 per cent since 1940s. Now stable.
Italy	100–200 pairs (1982)[19]	Decreasing.

USSR	rare (1979)[1]	Decreasing. Thought to be threatened in European Soviet (1983)[6].
Latvia	5 pairs (1983)[34]	
Poland	15–30 pairs (1983)[80]	Apparently stable.
Czechoslovakia	7 pairs (1988)[43]	Stable.
Hungary	45–50 pairs (1988)[40]	Stable.
Yugoslavia	approx. 200 pairs (1982)[19]	Apparently stable.
Albania	?	Seem to be breeding birds (1968)[1].
Romania	approx. 30 pairs (1977)[42]	Decreasing.
Bulgaria	very common? (1971)[3]	
Greece	approx. 300 pairs (1983)[84]	Stable.
Cyprus	3 pairs? (1982)[50]	
Turkey	100–1000 pairs (1982)[19]	
Israel	100–200 pairs	
Tunisia	>200 pairs (1982)[50]	
Algeria	few (1982)[50]	
Morocco	>1000 pairs (1982)[19]	

Marsh Harrier – adult female above breeding site. *Photo B. Génsbøl/Biofoto.*

Marsh Harrier
Circus aeruginosus

Distribution
As shown on the map the Marsh Harrier is widely distributed in the Western Palearctic. It also extends eastwards in a broad belt to the Pacific Ocean.

Most of the Western Palearctic has the nominate race which is replaced in North Africa by *C.a. harterti*, in which the male has a paler underside and darker upperparts, the female almost white on the head, back and breast. The race *C.a. spilonotus* occurs from Lake Baikal to northern Mongolia and eastwards. In this form the male is easily distinguishable from the nominate race by the white head, neck, underside and the foremost part of the back.

In addition there are five races in Madagascar, New Guinea, Australia, New Zealand and islands in the Pacific Ocean.

Population estimates
It is not possible to estimate the population in the Western Palearctic as a whole because there are no data for such a large area as the Soviet Union. For Europe, excluding the Soviet Union, however, the information is fairly good (*see* table on p. 118) and on the basis of this the total population of this area is of the order of 10,000 pairs, with Poland and East Germany as the focal points.

113

Marsh Harrier – adult male. *Photo H. Fr. Hansen.*

Population trends

The Marsh Harrier was so affected by the great anti-raptor campaign that it was completely exterminated at the beginning of this century in the British Isles and in more recent decades also in Syria (?) and Israel. In many other countries the populations were so much reduced that the species was threatened with extinction.

The factors involved were persecution by shooting, draining of the breeding habitats and possibly also the use of poisons.

Even in the 1950s and 1960s when the species was protected in many countries, the trend continued to be negative.

However, in the middle of the 1970s something suddenly happened in northern Europe. The populations started to grow at an astonishing speed. This positive development was particularly marked in Denmark. In 1970 the population was reckoned at 80 pairs. Counts throughout the country showed 310 pairs in 1979, 336 pairs in 1980, 412 pairs in 1981, 445 pairs in 1982, giving an annual growth of 8–23 per cent.

Positive trends also appeared in Sweden, East Germany, West Germany, Holland and Britain. On the other hand, there was a steady decrease in populations in southern Europe and almost all the countries of eastern Europe. This is due to habitat destruction and shooting (legal in several countries), as well as reed harvesting and various disturbances at the breeding sites.

The reason for the sudden upsurge in the populations in northern Europe is not known. There has been a clear improvement in living conditions: the environment has become cleaner and shooting has been reduced. This perhaps means that the more confident birds are no longer shot, and they can settle in more restricted habitats in the vicinity of man.

Migration

Northern and eastern populations are migratory with winter quarters in the Mediterranean area and in Africa, mainly south of the Sahara. Southern populations migrate partially or disperse. The North African population *C.a. harterti* is apparently non-migratory.

Northern birds migrate south-west and south-south-west. Thus, those from Scandinavia move south-west via France and Spain, Finnish birds mainly through Italy to Africa.

As is typical for harriers this species is a broad front migrant. The concentrations at the big migration stations are therefore relatively low: Galsterbo maximum 142 (1982), Stignaes maximum 143 (1981), Gibraltar 359 (1972), Bosporus maximum 10 (1971–80) and Borcka-Arhavi 385 (1976).

Ringing recoveries show that some British birds certainly move into Africa, but birds are regularly recorded in eastern England during the winter and some of these are undoubtedly of British origin. European migrants move south by October and return by April. Apart from the British birds, and those in countries bordering the Mediterranean, regular wintering in Europe is only reported

Marsh Harrier – adult female with nest material. *Photo H. Fr. Hansen.*

Marsh Harrier – adult male with a bream for the young. *Photo A. Christiansen/Biofoto.*

from Holland and from Lake Neusiedler (Austria).

Habitat

The nests are mostly placed in large dense reed-beds with good possibilities for foraging and relative quiet, either by lakes, marshes, lagoons or fjords. Narrow reed belts along rivers may also be regularly used for nesting.

Exceptionally, in the absence of the preferred habitat, the nests may be placed in cornfields, among heather, in thickets or in overgrown plantations.

The species mostly hunts over reed-beds, but neighbouring usually uncultivated areas are also searched.

Voice

Almost only used during the breeding season. During the mating flight there is an attractive, sonorous, pee-wit-like call, and when attacking an intruder a hoarse *kyekyekye*. When prey is brought the female has a high-pitched, piping call.

Breeding

Normally breeds for the first time at an age of two or three years, but may breed at one year. The sexes form pairs on the territory. They *may* nest year after year, but this seems to be uncommon. Polygamy occurs.

The mating flight is seen immediately after arrival at the breeding site. The male flies up and performs various forms of aerial acrobatics, diving down onto the female, who wards him off with her talons.

The nest, normally placed in the

densest part of the reed-bed, is built mainly by the female. The male often makes a simple platform for his own use, for resting and feeding.

The 3–8 (–10(–12)) eggs are laid in southern Europe in late March, in Denmark in late April to early May and in Finland at the most northerly breeding sites in late May to early June. Incubation, by the female alone, takes 31–38 days per egg. It starts with the first, second or third, so they generally hatch at different times. In large clutches the youngest often die, probably due to lack of food.

The male brings food to the female during incubation and also hunts alone when the chicks are very young. The prey is delivered in the characteristic harrier mode, the male throwing it to the female who catches it in the air.

The chicks spend 30–40 days in the nest and are dependent upon the parents for a further 15–25 days.

Many clutches are lost: around 19–34 per cent in all. In two investigations in East Germany and one in Finland the production of young per clutch was 1.75, 2.30 and 2.29 respectively.

Food

In general, quite varied. However, during the breeding season there may be a high degree of specialization.

A collection of 2146 prey animals from various investigations shows the range of food taken: 954 small rodents the size of voles (44 per cent), 302 small birds up to the size of a hawfinch (14 per cent), 194 larger birds, such as poultry, ducks and larger waders (9 per cent), 189 larger rodents and insectivores such as water voles, rats, hamsters and moles (9 per cent), 124 larger small birds and smaller waders (6 per cent) and 121 frogs (6

Marsh Harrier – adult female on the nest. *Photo B. Génsbøl/Biofoto.*

per cent). The remaining 12 per cent consists of leverets and young rabbits, insects, fish, birds' eggs, shrews, snakes and lizards in that order.

However, a statement of the numbers of prey animals does not give a complete picture. For example, nine per cent of larger rodents would, from the viewpoint of weight, give a larger share than nine per cent and therefore a much greater nutritional value.

The bird prey consists primarily of chicks. The Marsh Harrier can also catch coots and moorhens, taking them by surprise.

During the rearing period the main food sources vary from country to country and from area to area according to the frequency of the individual prey animals. In an investigation in Austria this was shown to be sousliks, in Holland (two areas) rabbits and frogs, in East Prussia and southern Finland small birds and gull and wader chicks, in England poultry, in Germany field voles, in Denmark coot chicks.

Foraging methods

Flying low, the bird tries to surprise the prey by suddenly appearing.

In terrain that is difficult to take in at a glance, an unsuccessful hunt is quickly abandoned, but over open water the Marsh Harrier can exhaust birds by forcing them to dive continuously.

Marsh Harrier population in the Western Palearctic

Denmark	445 pairs (1982)[56]	After being almost exterminated around 1914 because of shooting, it slowly increased in subsequent decades, particularly from mid-1970s.
Sweden	approx. 520 pairs (1979)[9]	Few at start of this century. Marked increase from mid-1970s.
Norway	irregular breeder	First breeding record 1975.
Finland	230 pairs (1985)[10]	Arrived around 1890. Increasing.
USSR *Estonia* *Latvia*	? approx. 100 pairs (1976)[11] approx. 100 pairs (1983)[34]	A 270,000 km² area in central Russia estimated to have 200–1000 pairs (1970)[3].
Poland	1500–2000 pairs (1984)[80]	Increasing.
East Germany	approx. 1500 pairs (1985)[87]	Stable. Brandenburg 650–700 pairs (1971)[36]. Mecklenburg 900–1000 pairs (1975)[52].
West Germany	725–850 pairs (1982)[22]	Decrease of 60–80 per cent from 1940s to mid-1970s, then an increase.

Holland	725–800 pairs (1979)[53]	Considerable increase following more suitable habitats (damming) (1970, 60–90 pairs).
Belgium	15–20 pairs (1979)[1]	Not common recently.
Britain & Ireland	33 pairs (1986)[18]	Exterminated at start of this century. New immigration in 1920s. Now increasing very slowly.
France	740–900 pairs (1984)[92]	Stable or possibly decreasing.
Spain	150–200 pairs (1982)[19]	Marked decrease due to draining.
Portugal	30–40 pairs (1982)[19]	
Italy	40–50 pairs (1982)[19]	12–18 in Sardinia. Extermination threatened by draining and shooting.
Czechoslovakia	approx. 600 pairs (1988)[43]	Increasing.
Hungary	min 1000 pairs (1988)[40]	Increasing.
Austria	50 pairs (1977)[48]	Marked decrease. (Environmental poisons?)
Yugoslavia	common (1982)[19]	
Albania	?	Common in 1930s. No more recent information.
Romania	several hundred pairs (1979)[1]	Marked decrease.
Bulgaria	approx. 100 (1976)[1]	Marked decrease.
Greece	approx. 130 pairs (1983)[84]	Marked decrease, due especially to cultivation of river deltas.
Cyprus	1–10 pairs (1982)[19]	
Turkey	100–250 pairs (1982)[50]	
Syria	extinct? (1979)[1]	
Lebanon	possibly still breeding birds (1979)[1]	
Iraq	?	
Tunisia	50 pairs (1982)[50]	
Algeria	?	
Morocco	100–500 pairs (1982)[19]	Decreasing.

Hen Harrier
Circus cyaneus

Distribution

In addition to the distribution shown on the map, the nominate race of the Hen Harrier breeds in a broad belt eastwards through the Soviet Union to the Pacific Ocean. On the other side of the sea, in the Nearctic region, it is replaced by the race *C.c. hudsonius*. There are also two races in South America. As with *C.c. hudsonius* some ornithologists regard these as separate species.

Population estimates

It is not possible to give a total figure for the Western Palearctic because of the lack of data for the huge Soviet breeding range. For the remainder of Europe, without the Soviet Union, the table on p. 124 suggests a total of the order of 3000–10,000 pairs.

These figures should be taken with some reservations. The Hen Harrier is one of the species that is difficult to record. Furthermore, the number of breeding pairs varies considerably from year to year, depending upon fluctuations in rodent populations.

Population trends

In this century the Hen Harrier has, generally speaking, suffered a marked decrease in the densely populated, industrialized and intensively cultivated areas. This is due to a reduction in the number of suitable breeding habitats, to various forms of disturbance, and particularly, in earlier decades, to shooting. Several minor breeding

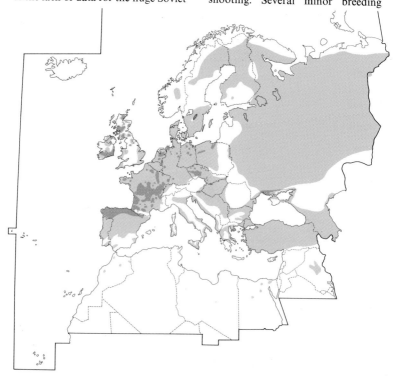

Hen Harrier – adult male. *Photo P. Petit.*

areas have been abandoned, such as Belgium, Luxembourg, Austria, Hungary and Italy.

The situation in the British Isles shows clearly how extensive shooting was responsible for a decline. Here the population was, generally speaking, exterminated by shooting and only survived in the Hebrides and Orkney Islands. However, after protection from the end of the 1930s, a positive development ensued, and it is remarkable that the Hen Harrier in the British Isles was able to expand even during the 1950s and 1960s when threatened by chemicals.

The table on p. 124 shows clearly that the populations in Sweden and Finland are developing favourably, which is due to a considerable reduction in persecution and surely also to a cleaner environment. In addition, the original habitats here are, generally speaking, still intact.

From the viewpoint of population the species has certain encouraging areas, namely Sweden–Finland, the British Isles, and France–Spain. In all, these three areas have roughly 95 per cent of the breeding pairs in the Western Palearctic, excluding the USSR.

Migration

Hen Harrier movements are complicated by the current increases developing in some areas (e.g. Scotland) from whence it seems surplus birds are colonizing new areas – as evidenced by the ringing recoveries from Orkney. The species is also influenced by the small mammal populations available – particularly in the northern parts of its range where it is, in any case, almost completely migratory.

As with the other harriers the birds move on a broad front with relatively little concentration at the short sea-crossing stations. The peak autumn figure for Falsterbo was 221 in 1977; since few leave Europe, the Gibraltar peak is about the same, and only a handful are seen at the Bosporus. The small African wintering population remains in the Mahgreb and does not cross the Sahara. The autumn movement is generally rather late, its peak being toward the end of September or in early October. The spring return of the breeding birds is during March or April. Young birds may carry on moving around into the summer, and can sometimes be found well away from the usual breeding areas.

The winter records south of the breeding range on the east coast of England are generally of 'ring-tails' rather than full-plumage males. The ringing recoveries show that these may be from the British population or from the Dutch Polder birds. There has also been a British recovery of a Finnish bird, and others have been found south to Italy and France.

Habitat

This species prefers open low-lying country such as heathland, uncultivated grasslands, marshes and other wet areas, but may also breed in mountainous regions as, for instance, in Norway and Sweden. The species has also adapted itself to cultivated terrain and breeds in cornfields and other cultivated areas.

It hunts mostly over agricultural land, meadows and wetlands. In winter it is often seen close to inhabited areas.

Voice

Often heard during the breeding season. During the display flight the male has a high-pitched, plaintive *pee-you*, with the tone reducing. Any disturbance at the nest is marked by a rapidly repeated *kee-kee* call, and when prey is being handed over the female has a piping *psee-oo*.

Breeding

The species normally first breeds at an age of 2–3 years, although one-year-old birds occasionally breed, particularly in years when plenty of food is available.

Pair formation takes place in the territory. Most of the birds are monogamous, especially where an individual pair is very isolated. Polygamy is very common in populations resembling colonies where the nests may be placed only 50 m apart. In

Hen Harrier: the youngest chicks, dead from starvation, are torn up and fed to the remaining young. Note the size difference of the young. *Photo P. Petit.*

such conditions a single male may have 2–3 females, and up to six have been recorded.

The display flight is very distinctive. The male performs a tern-like flight at great height, then falls in an impressive dive before immediately rising and diving again and so on, 20 or 30 times or more. The repertoire includes flying backwards, somersaults, rolls and spins. The female's role is normally restricted. She *may* take an active part but is more often a target for the male's dives. She wards them off by turning on her back and showing her talons.

The nest is placed on the ground, whether dry or damp, and normally in very tall vegetation. The female does most of the nest-building.

In central Europe and Scotland the 3–6 (2–8 (12)) eggs are laid from late April to mid-June, most often in the second half of May, and in Scandinavia from early May to mid-June. The size of the clutch varies according to the amount of food (rodents).

Incubation, which starts with the second, third or fourth egg, is by the female and varies from 29–39 days per clutch (29–31 days per egg). The fledging period is 32–42 days.

During the incubation period and when the chicks are small, the male looks after the female and delivers prey in a fascinating way. He announces his arrival with a call. She takes off and flies towards him, begging loudly. Just before the two meet the male drops the prey. The female turns elegantly on to her back and seizes it with her talons, lands close by and either eats it or flies to the nest to feed the young.

When the chicks are fledged the male departs from the breeding site, leaving the female to find food for 2–3 weeks until the young are independent.

Like the clutches themselves the production of young varies according to the food supply. The best investigated is the population on the Orkney Islands, where the number of young per year has fluctuated between 0.7–2.2 (mean 1.3) per clutch started. The population here is very dense with many cases of polygamy. Experience has shown that this means a low production of young.

Food

The most marked specialist among the harriers. Generally speaking the Hen Harrier only eats small mammals and birds. Locally, insects may also be eaten, as well as amphibians, reptiles and fish.

Among the small mammals the main prey consists of field voles. A French investigation showed that in good vole years these accounted for about 90 per cent of the catch, in bad years 21 per cent.

Of the birds it particularly likes ground-nesting species, such as pipits, larks and buntings, also thrushes and young waders, ducks and poultry.

The distribution of prey can be illustrated by citing four investigations: two German, one Dutch and one Norwegian, with a total of 624 prey animals: small rodents 346 (55 per cent), small birds 150 (24 per cent), young rabbits and leverets 55 (9 per cent), larger small birds and small waders 39 (6 per cent), ducklings and poultry 19 (3 per cent). The remaining 3 per cent consisted of larger rodents, shrews, insects and lizards. Thus, small rodents and small birds accounted for approximately 80 per cent of the total prey.

Foraging methods

Low flight over open land. Occasionally the species also hunts from an elevated perch.

Hen Harrier population in the Western Palearctic

Denmark	only very few pairs (1988)	No regular breeding.
Sweden	1000–2000 pairs (1981)[9]	Migration figures at Falsterbo show increase since 1940s and 1950s.
Norway	>10 pairs (1971)[62]	As regular breeder only known from Dovre and Finmark.
Finland	3000 pairs (1985)[10]	Migration figures show an increasing population.
USSR Estonia Latvia	approx. 100 pairs (1976)[11] few pairs (1983)[34]	500–1000 pairs (1970)[3] in a 270,000 sq. km area in central Russia.
Poland	50 pairs (1984)[80]	Considerable decrease due to habitat destruction.
East Germany	30 pairs (1985)[87]	Brandenburg 45–50 pairs (1983)[36]. Mecklenburg about 20 pairs (1979)[52]. After big decrease at turn of the century, now apparently stable.
West Germany	15–20 pairs (1982)[5] near extermination (1987)[79]	Considerable decline due to habitat destruction, persecution and disturbance at breeding sites. Now stable. Under protection.
Britain & Ireland	750–800 pairs (1977)[1]	Threatened with extinction at start of this century. Big increase following protection. Recent decrease in Ireland.
Holland	100–130 pairs (1979)[53]	Increase since 1960s due to new suitable habitats following damming.
Belgium	5 pairs (1986)[79]	No breeding 1969–85.
France	2500–3600 pairs (1984)[92]	Decrease of over 50 per cent since 1930s. Steady negative situation?
Spain	500 pairs (1982)[19]	Probably decreasing (habitat destruction? environment poisoned?).
Portugal	5 pairs (1982)[19]	

Czechoslovakia	max. 10 pairs (1988)[43]	Irregular.
Yugoslavia	irregular? (1982)[19]	Said only to breed in northern part of country. In 1978 the author saw several males in a suitable breeding habitat near Greek border.
Cyprus	1–10 pairs (1982)[19]	

Hen Harrier – adult male. *Photo P. Helo/Bruce Coleman.*

Montagu's Harrier

Circus pygargus

Distribution

As the map shows, Montagu's Harrier is distributed in the most central part of the Western Palearctic. From there the range extends eastwards through the Soviet Union to the region around the Yenisei. The species is not divided into races.

Population estimates

Lacking figures for the Soviet breeding range, it is not possible to give a total for the Western Palearctic.

For Europe, excluding the Soviet Union, there are population figures for almost all the countries (*see* table on p. 130). The estimate for the region is 7800–9300 pairs.

The species has population centres in France/Spain/Portugal with 7000–8300 pairs, and in the Soviet Union (Poland ?). Thus, there are only 600 pairs in the rest of Europe.

Population trends

The position has been atypical. At the beginning of this century when shooting weighed heavily on raptor populations, Montagu's Harrier managed to expand northwards. For instance, the species bred for the first time in Denmark around 1900, and three years later there were approximately 200 pairs there. From the 1940s onwards it decreased rapidly, not only in Denmark but in Europe in general, and this was in a period when shooting was decreasing.

There were, however, other nega-

tive factors. Environmental poisons were much used at this time, draining and cultivation of good habitats flourished, shooting during migration was still a problem in southern Europe and many clutches were killed by harvesting machines.

On the negative side the birds are still apparently poisoned in their winter quarters, where they commonly spend the night in paddy fields sprayed with dieldrin.

All these factors have resulted in a considerable decrease in the population, particularly in intensively cultivated areas, and this is still going on. As shown in the table on p. 130, populations are still decreasing, except in the Soviet Union, Czechoslovakia, Sweden and Denmark.

The surprisingly positive trend in Sweden may perhaps be due to the relatively good conditions in the eastern part of the country.

Locally in the different countries the position is somewhat varied. In France, for example, the general picture shows a decrease, but in Alsace there has been an almost explosive increase during recent years. It is probable that access to suitable breeding habitats is responsible for this development.

Migration

This species is a long distance migrant with the European population wintering in Africa south of the Sahara. Western birds do not reach the Guinea coast but many eastern ones cross the Equator and some reach South Africa. There are a few winter records in Europe.

Migrant birds travel over a broad front but there are good concentrations at Gibraltar in particular, with a record total of 1700 during autumn 1972. The first birds start to move at

Montagu's Harrier – adult female. *Photo B. Génsbøl/Biofoto.*

the beginning of August and most are out of Europe by mid-October. Spring return peaks in April, although there is some evidence that immature birds stay in the winter quarters during their first summer. Whilst the British population was declining during the 1950s, ringing recoveries implicated hunting pressure on passage birds in France.

Habitat

This is intermediate between the habitat of the Marsh Harrier and the Hen Harrier. The species prefers to breed in broad river valleys, uncultivated plains, moorland and the margins of lakes and marshes. It has also become adapted to certain cultivated areas, especially in grasslands and cereal crops.

Montagu's Harrier hunts in open country over wetlands, fields with low vegetation, meadows, heathland, and particularly in the autumn in vineyards.

Voice

Only heard a little, and almost exclusively in the vicinity of the nest. During the display flight the male has a hoarse, staccato, very high-pitched *kyek-kyek-kyek*. The female has a piping *psee* when prey is handed over and when the nest is threatened.

Breeding

Montagu's Harriers normally breed for the first time when two or three years old. Occasionally one-year-old females are seen on a nest.

Pair formation takes place on the territory. The birds are tied to former breeding sites, so it is probable that two old adults will often mate again. The display flight, like that of the Marsh Harrier and Hen Harrier, is seen immediately after their arrival.

The species breeds solitarily or, with good conditions, in loose colonies, often with nests placed 10–100 m apart. As with the Hen Harrier, polygamy is common.

The nest, built mainly by the female, is placed on the ground among tall vegetation. In Scandinavia and central Europe the 4–5 (2–20) eggs are normally laid in mid- to late May, and are incubated by the female for 27–40 days per clutch (27–30 days per egg). The eggs do not all hatch at the same time.

The male feeds the female both during incubation and while the chicks are still very young, bringing prey in the mode characteristic of harriers (*see* Hen Harrier).

The young are fledged at an age of 28–42 days and are independent 10–14 days later.

In many areas investigated the production of young appears to be very low. On Lüneberg Heath in West Germany twenty per cent of the clutches were lost. In Schleswig-Holstein, Bavaria and Brandenburg the production of young per clutch begun was respectively 1.30, 1.40 and 1.09. Apparently this is too low for the species to maintain its population under the existing living conditions.

In years when the birds breed late there is a serious problem, for the fields may be harvested before the young are fledged. In an instinctive attempt to protect themselves they lie on their backs when the machines approach, so that sometimes their feet are chopped off.

Food

This consists mainly of small prey. In various investigations (mainly French) this proved to be: 41 per cent small rodents, 37 per cent insects, 11 per cent small birds, 4 per cent eggs of small birds and 4 per cent lizards. The remaining 3 per cent consisted of snails, frogs, snakes, larger birds and larger rodents.

Among the small rodents the main prey consisted primarily of field voles, secondarily of water voles and hamsters. Larger rodents, such as sousliks, rabbits and hares are only taken when young, but in very limited numbers.

Most of the insects taken were dragonflies and large beetles. Birds were the small ones from open country, such as larks, pipits and buntings.

Montagu's Harriers may catch many more lizards than the four per

Montagu's Harrier – adult male. *Photo H. Fr. Hansen.*

cent mentioned above. In regions where they are numerous, lizards may account for 56 per cent of the prey (Kazakstan).

Foraging methods

The species hunts in the typical harrier fashion, in low flight over the countryside. It is capable of stopping very rapidly and of changing direction when prey is sighted. Like the other harriers, it can also catch small birds in flight.

Montagu's Harrier population in the Western Palearctic

Denmark	approx. 50 pairs (1982)[56]	Immigrated around 1900, about 200 pairs 1930s. Decrease 1940–60, and breeding area restricted to South Jutland. Then stability or slight increase. Many nests destroyed every year during hay harvest.
Sweden	55 pairs (1982)[57]	Only a few pairs from immigration in 1920s and 1930s till about 1950. Then a marked increase which still continues. Spreads from its base on Øland.
Finland	0–3 pairs (1985)[10]	Immigrating?

Melanistic Montagu's Harrier – adult female. *Photo P. Petit.*

Montagu's Harrier – adult male, with a small bird in its talons. *Photo B. Génsbøl/Biofoto.*

West Germany	50 pairs (1985)[79]	Considerable decrease, mostly due to habitat destruction, shooting, disturbance and poison. Population centre in Schleswig-Holstein.
East Germany	approx. 35 pairs (1985)[87]	Brandenburg 46–54 pairs (1970)[36], Mecklenburg 25–35 pairs (1975)[52]. Seems to be decreasing.
Poland	200–300 pairs (1984)[80]	Decrease due to habitat destruction.
USSR *Estonia* *Latvia*	 50 pairs (1976)[11] few pairs (1983)[34]	500–1500 pairs (1981)[2] in a 270,000 sq. km area in central Russia. Increasing.
Britain	approx. 10 pairs (1986)[18]	Apparently always in small numbers. Reached a maximum of 40–50 (70–80?) pairs in 1950s. Thereafter decreased, and now threatened with extinction. 2–10 pairs last 10 years.
Holland	25–35 pairs (1981)[2]	Decreasing. 30–50 pairs in 1977.
Belgium	approx. 5 pairs (1981)[2]	Decreasing. 15–25 pairs in 1967.
France	3000–4000 pairs (1984)[92]	Decreasing, due to habitat destruction?
Spain	3000 pairs (1982)[19]	Decreasing due to habitat destruction and nest destruction.
Portugal	1000–1300 pairs (1982)[19]	Decreasing.
Italy	200 pairs (1982)[50]	Decreasing due to habitat destruction and shooting.

Montagu's Harrier/Pallid Harrier

Italy	200 pairs (1982)[50]	Decreasing due to habitat destruction and shooting.
Switzerland	very few pairs (1980)[25]	Breeds irregularly.
Austria	5–10 pairs (1976)[2]	Decreasing.
Czechoslovakia	5 – 20 pairs (1988)[43]	Always been in small numbers. Irregular.
Hungary	approx. 100 pairs (1988)[43]	Decreasing.
Yugoslavia	rare (1982)[19]	Probably decreasing.
Bulgaria	1–2 pairs (1981)[2]	Apparently does not breed regularly.
Albania	?	No recent data. Population apparently small.
Greece	10–20 pairs (1982)[19]	
Turkey	50–100 pairs (1982)[50]	
Tunisia	<10 pairs (1982)[50]	
Algeria	?	
Morocco	100–500 pairs (1982)[19]	Decreasing.
Cyprus	10 pairs? (1982)[50]	

Pallid Harrier – adult male on elephant dung. *Photo A. Christiansen/Biofoto.*

Pallid Harrier
Circus macrourus

Distribution
This map shows that this species only breeds in the eastern part of the Western Palearctic. From there the range extends eastwards through the Soviet Union to the region around the River Yenisei. The species is not divided into races.

Population estimates
The table on p. 135 shows that it is not really possible to give an estimate.

Population trends
Cultivation in the USSR of the southern steppes and felling of forests in the north have perhaps changed the distribution and pushed the limits of the breeding area northwards.

There are several breeding records far to the west of the real distribution range: eastern Finland 1933; Sweden, 5–6 pairs in 1952 (Øland and Gotland); East Germany 1879 and 1952 (2 pairs); West Germany 1850s, 1901, 1933 and 1952. In addition there are occasional poorly documented records of breeding in Austria, Czechoslovakia and Hungary. Note the invasion-like records in 1952 and to a lesser extent in 1933.

These are evidently chance records of breeding rather than a 'purposeful' expansion.

Migration

A typical migratory bird with winter quarters in India, and in Africa mostly south of the Sahara and usually east of Lake Chad. The bird may exceptionally overwinter on the edge of the breeding range. In winter it is regularly seen in central and southern Europe and in the Middle East.

The migration is on a broad front and thus without marked concentrations at the narrower sea passages. Nevertheless 133 Pallid Harriers were recorded in north-east Turkey (Borcka) in late August to early October, with a peak in late September.

Generally speaking the migration in the eastern Mediterranean and Middle East reaches a peak in mid-September to early October.

The spring migration has a more westerly direction. Thus, more than 30 Pallid Harriers were recorded at Cape Bon in Tunisia in early spring (first in the 1970s). In the Mediterranean region the spring migration is mainly seen from mid-April to mid-May.

This species is regularly recorded well to the west of its normal breeding range. There have been over 120 records in Sweden and more than 30 in Denmark, with less frequent vagrants found in Britain, the Benelux and even Spain. Such records are often in autumn but may occur at any time from March to October. The species is undoubtedly often overlooked, particularly immatures and females, and many of the records logged are of adults.

Habitat

The basic breeding habitat is open, dry steppe country, but the species is also seen in habitats typical for Montagu's Harrier, and also in cornfields.

Voice

Seldom used outside the breeding area. Very similar to that of the Hen and Montagu's Harrier.

Breeding

The species probably breeds for the first time at an age of 2–3 years. Exceptionally a one-year-old bird is seen on a nest.

Arrives in April, apparently already mated. The territory is marked by a

Pallid Harrier – adult male. *Photo E. Engqvist.*

display flight very similar to that of the Hen Harrier. Like the Hen and Montagu's Harrier, the present species may make nests close to others (100 m apart) in loose colonies.

The nest is made on the ground, protected by tall grasses and preferably close to water. The 4–5 (3–6) eggs are laid in late April (most southerly) or mid-May (most northerly) and incubated by the female for 29–30 days per egg. The chicks are fledged at 33–45 days and are independent of the parents after a further 15–20 days.

Food
Primarily small rodents, particularly lemmings, but also wood mice, field voles, harvest mice, sousliks and hamsters. In years with few rodents this species catches many birds, mainly nestlings of larks, pipits and the young of poultry. Occasionally it also takes reptiles (lizards) and insects.

The Pallid Harrier is so dependent upon small rodents that the number of breeding pairs fluctuates with these.

Foraging methods
Low flight, as is typical for the harriers.

Pallid Harrier – adult female. *Photo B. Génsbøl/Biofoto.*

Pallid Harrier population in the Western Palearctic

USSR	?	Common in suitable habitats. The limit of the breeding area appears to have retreated northwards, with fewer breeding pairs to the south. Occasionally breeds in the Baltic (1951)[1].
Romania	few pairs (1979)[1]	Recolonising? Formerly thought to have disappeared (1974)[3].
Bulgaria	few pairs (1971)[3]	Observed on various occasions in the north-east.

135

Dark Chanting Goshawk on a lookout perch. *Photo J. Robert/Jacana.*

Dark Chanting Goshawk

Melierax metabates

Distribution

As the map shows this bird only breeds, in the Western Palearctic, in Morocco (10–30 pairs – 1982[19]), isolated from the remainder of the range and only in small numbers. The true distribution covers large areas of Africa south of 20°N as well as coastal parts in south-western Arabia. There are several races.

Population trends

Appears to be threatened with extinction in the Western Palearctic.

Migration

Said to be non-migratory, although to some extent it wanders about after the breeding season. Recorded in Spain in July 1963.

Habitat

Mainly tropical and subtropical savannas but also seen in more dense vegetation such as plantations and on the outskirts of deserts.

The species needs trees for nest-building.

Breeding

Full details are not known. In Morocco, egg-laying takes place in Feb-

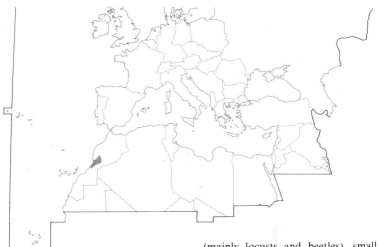

ruary–March. The nest is built in a tree with dense foliage at a height of (3) 6–7 m. Normally the female lays only one egg, exceptionally two.

Food

Principally reptiles: lizards, chameleons and snakes, but also insects (mainly locusts and beetles), small rodents and birds.

Foraging methods

From a perch on a branch, termitarium or similar, from which it pounces rapidly on prey. It also wanders about on the ground searching for prey.

Dark Chanting Goshawk with a weaver-bird. *Photo A. Christiansen/Biofoto.*

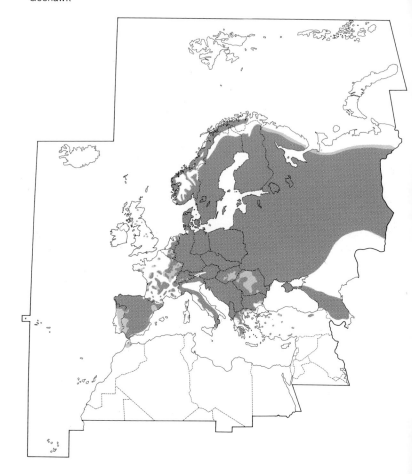

Goshawk

Accipiter gentilis

Distribution

The Goshawk breeds in most parts of the Western Palearctic. To the east the range extends to the Pacific Ocean and continues on the other side in North America.

The species is divided into nine races, the present, nominate race covering most of the Western Palearctic. Corsica and Sardinia have *A.g. arrigonii* (small, very dark with pronounced stripes). The race *A.g. buteoides* from northern Sweden and Finland extends eastwards to the Lena area; it is pale, greyer and a little larger, the young birds having white spots on the upperparts.

Population estimates

The data in the table on p. 144 are not sufficient for a total estimate for the

Western Palearctic. For Europe, excluding the Soviet Union, the population is 40,000–45,000 pairs.

However, this may well be an underestimate, especially for larger areas where it is difficult to get an overall picture. The Goshawk is not easy to record at the breeding sites unless one frequently visits an area.

Population trends

This is one of the most persecuted raptors in Europe. It thrives, for example, in Fenno-Scandia's large forests in thinly populated regions, but does not do so well in densely populated areas where it is relatively easy to find the nests.

Statistics for Goshawks killed in Norway, Sweden and Finland at the end of the nineteenth and beginning of the twentieth century show a fluctuating, but on the whole stable, population.

During the same period the situation was different in densely populated Denmark. The extensive persecution by pheasant rearers, dove and poultry breeders and by hunters in general led to a marked decrease in the population.

Around 1950 the pressure from shooting abated in northern Europe and in many places there was a positive trend, helped no doubt by the establishment of very suitable habitats (increased number of small woods) and by improved access to food, primarily wood pigeons and tame doves.

The progress stopped suddenly in the middle of the 1950s, and there was a considerable population decrease up to around 1970. Holland, for instance, had 180–200 pairs in 1955, but dropped to 20 pairs in 1963, because of the unrestricted use of poisons.

Around 1970 a number of the worst environmental poisons were outlawed and the population re-established itself rapidly. Thanks to much reduced

Goshawk – adult male on a lookout perch. *Photo B. Lundberg/N.*

persecution the Goshawk population is now, in many countries, above its level for the last hundred years.

In southern Europe the situation is otherwise. Here shooting is still at a high level and the environment considerably burdened by poison.

Today the Goshawk is the species most often excepted from protection measures. Under certain conditions the bird may (1982) be killed in Denmark, Sweden, Finland, East Germany, Czechoslovakia, Hungary, Austria, Romania and Greece. In addition the species is, in many countries, subject to intensive illegal shooting.

The present-day positive population trend is largely due to living, in many places, with little contact with man.

Migration

The characteristic movements of this species are best described as 'oriented dispersal'. Northern populations are much more likely to move than southern ones, but a handful of birds move over the Straits of Gibraltar and across the Bosporus. In the Fenno-Scandian populations birds breeding in the north move, on average, 210 km, but those from the south only 50 km. Concentrations of more than 100 birds during the autumn are recorded from several Finnish stations, but numbers at Swedish observatories are much lower.

Wandering birds start to move in August, but oriented southwards migration is mainly in October and November. Northern populations move most in years when prey species are at a low ebb, and a 3–4 year cycle has been demonstrated. Return passage takes place from March to early May. In mid-European populations most movements are only over a short distance with, for instance, only 4.5 per cent of the German recoveries showing movements of more than 50 km.

Those that do move are almost always young birds. It seems likely

Goshawk – adult male with grouse. *Photo P. J. Tömmeraas.*

that this will prove to be the case with the population of Goshawks building up in Britain, for they should have little problem in finding food in the winter.

Habitat

Prefers countryside where woodland alternates with open areas, and for breeding a wood with an area over 100 ha. A smaller wood sometimes suffices and the species has been found nesting in tree groups in Jutland. The nest is normally placed in a tall tree, generally a conifer, sometimes a beech.

Mainly hunt in the vicinity of the nest (up to 6 km away). In winter, when hunting is less productive in woodland, Goshawks can be seen over open country.

Voice

Mostly used early in the breeding season. Two types: (a) usually a rapid, rhythmical, sonorous call with coarse *gyak-gyak-gyak*. This is used when there is disturbance near the nest and as a contact between the sexes. The series often starts slowly, rising in both pitch and speed. (b) A drawn out, rather buzzard-like *yu-heeyy*, used by the female to keep in touch with the male.

Breeding

Usually breeds for the first time at an age of 2–3 years, but one-year-old birds also take part to a certain extent in breeding, especially when older birds are not available, for example after a harsh winter. Apparently mating is for life, at least for non-migratory birds.

In Denmark the territory is already occupied in January. In central Europe and Denmark nest-building takes place most often in February; in

Goshawk – adult. *Photo J. B. Bruun/Biofoto.*

Norway and Finland in March. During this period there are two types of display flight. Either a circling flight over the nest site, with slow wing beats, the tail spread out and the under tail-coverts raised as a white fan, the wings raised high as in a pigeon, or in the form of a powerful dive as in the display flight of a Buzzard.

The nest is built by both sexes, normally at a height of 10–20 m in a fir or spruce, sometimes in a beech.

In spite of the climatic differences, egg-laying takes place at the same time in central Europe and Fennoscandia, namely late March to late April or early May. The clutch of 2–5 (1–6) eggs is mainly incubated by the female for 35–38 days per egg. Incubation starts with the first or second eggs.

The chicks are fledged at 35–42

days and they are independent after about another 35 days.

Many clutches are lost, roughly nineteen per cent, according to an extensive Danish investigation during recent years. This is due largely to raiding by martens. In the same investigation the average production of chicks (in around 1000 clutches) was 2.1 per breeding pair.

Food

All types of food, with special emphasis on birds, but there are many local variations.

In Sweden, Norway and Finland the principal birds taken are jays (25–50 per cent) and other corvids (15–23 per cent), in West Germany often domesticated doves (13–37 per cent), and magpies in some places. In a locality in East Germany 35 per cent were waterfowl, mostly coot and mallard; in one area in France the main prey consisted of corvids, thrushes and starlings, and in Denmark woodpigeons and mallard (37 per cent).

A German investigation of 9022 prey animals showed the remains of 8309 birds from 123 species and 713 mammals from 16 species. Apart from the birds mentioned, Goshawks also took poultry and several small birds, as well as owls and smaller raptors. Mammals taken were mainly rabbits, hares, squirrels, field voles, shrews and, locally, marmots.

Although the number of mammals was not particularly marked, their weight was quite considerable (25 per cent has been confirmed). In addition, a much higher production of young has been recorded in good rodent years, and this suggests that Goshawks can alter their diet when the occasion demands.

An investigation in Schleswig-Holstein (1950–55) of one pair's food (3874 prey animals) gives an idea of variations throughout the year: starlings in June 20 per cent, in October 1 per cent; woodpigeons in June 7 per cent, in October 40 per cent; crows in June 16 per cent, in October 2 per cent. Partridges were mostly preyed upon in April with 15 per cent, least in October with 3 per cent. In general, domesticated doves accounted for 20 per cent, but in August only 11 per cent. Hares and rabbits were, in general, 23 per cent, but only 11 per cent in September.

In earlier times, when there was ignorance about the place of Goshawks in the natural economy, it is not surprising that this raptor, with its widely based diet, was much hated in shooting circles, by pigeon breeders and in certain cases by people rearing poultry.

In recent years, it has been clearly shown that in the case of wild game and doves, the Goshawk mainly catches sick or severely weakened individuals. An investigation in southern Sweden showed that in one year Goshawks took a good 25 per cent of the pheasants which died in winter. The explanation was that the pheasants had tuberculosis and were therefore an easy prey. A year later, with a healthy pheasant stock and still with several Goshawks in the area, their share was only 8 per cent.

Other Swedish investigations show that Goshawks can seriously affect a population of pheasants, especially when large numbers have been released, which attracts many of these birds.

A British investigation of winter mortality in woodpigeons revealed that 25 per cent of those caught were in such poor condition that, even without persecution, they could not have survived the next month.

In northern Europe, at any rate, there has fortunately been a change in attitude towards raptors in general and this, of course, also applies to Goshawks. Many of this species' former persecutors have come to realize that there is no sense in hunting a country's original animal life in order to protect, for instance, an introduced Asiatic game bird.

So anyone who wishes to keep pheasants, tame doves or poultry should give them some form of protection or pay the price to predators.

Foraging methods

The Goshawk usually uses a surprise attack, flying low over the ground. The bird can accelerate very rapidly, but can usually only maintain high

Goshawk juvenile with squirrel. *Photo A. Limbrunner.*

speeds for 500 m at the most. It only follows flushed birds for a short distance.

When hunting mammals Goshawks fly low, almost hovering over the ground.

Goshawk population in the Western Palearctic

Denmark	650–700 pairs (1986)[67]	Formerly hard-pressed by hunting, in the 1950s and 1960s also certainly by environmental poisons. Partially protected in 1967, followed by substantial increase.
Sweden	approx. 5000 pairs (1985)[95]	Development of the population not known at the moment.
Norway	approx. 2000 pairs (1976)[88]	Apparently decreased in the 1960s, possibly due to environmental poisons (1974)[3].
Finland	6000 pairs (1985)[10]	Seems to be decreasing – probably due to shortage of food.
USSR	?	Around 1600 pairs and stable in a 270,000 sq. km area in central Russia (1979)[1].
Poland	7000 pairs (1984)[80]	Increasing.
East Germany	1500 pairs (1983)[87]	Brandenburg around 140 pairs (1983)[36]. Mecklenburg around 400 pairs (1979)[52]. After big decrease now stable or increasing.
West Germany	2700–3200 pairs (1982)[22]	Schleswig-Holstein about 400 pairs (1980)[59]. In 1950s and 1960s a decrease of 60–80 per cent due to shooting.
Holland	400 pairs (1980)[38]	Marked increase in recent years after being close to extinction (about 20 pairs in 1963).
Belgium	150–250 pairs (1979)[1]	Increasing.
Luxembourg	approx. 20 pairs (1970)[3]	
Britain	max. 112 pairs (1986)[16]	Almost extinct around 1900. Present population seems based on escaped falconry birds. Increasing.
France	3000–4400 pairs (1984)[92]	Apparent decrease of 60 per cent since 1930s. Situation now stable.
Switzerland	approx. 600 pairs (1980)[25]	After big decrease in 1950s and 1960s (environmental poisons) now stable or slightly increasing.

Austria	60–80 pairs (1977)[48]	Stable after considerable decline.
Italy	200–400 pairs (1982)[19]	Big decrease due to hunting (legal and illegal). Sardinia 20–40 (50) pairs (1977)[41].
Spain	approx. 3000 pairs (1982)[19]	Marked decrease, mainly due to reduced rabbit population (myxomatosis).
Portugal	min. 100 pairs (1982)[19]	Probably decreasing.
Czechoslovakia	approx. 2000 pairs (1988)[43]	Trend unknown.
Hungary	1500 pairs (1988)[40]	After considerable decrease, now increasing.
Yugoslavia	common (1982)[19]	
Romania	100–120 pairs (1977)[42]	Was common in many areas in the 1950s.
Bulgaria	few pairs (1971)[3]	Decreasing (1979)[1].
Albania	?	No data.
Greece	approx. 500 pairs (1982)[19]	
Cyprus	6–8 pairs (1985)[5]	
Turkey	100–250 pairs (1982)[19]	
Morocco	10–100 pairs (1982)[19]	
Tunisia	1–10 pairs (1982)[19]	

Goshawk – adult and White-tailed Eagle at laid-out carrion. *Photo B. E. Swahn/N.*

Sparrowhawk
Accipiter nisus

Sparrowhawk juvenile. *Photo J. Østeng Hov/NN.*

Distribution

A widely distributed bird in the Western Palearctic with a range which extends eastwards in a broad belt to the Pacific Ocean, with a separate enclave in the Himalayas.

Most of the Western Palearctic is covered by the nominate race. To the east there is the somewhat larger race *A.n. nisosimilis*, and in the Himalayan area the similarly large and somewhat dark *A.n. melachistos*; in Corsica and Sardinia the small, very dark race *A.n. wolterstorffi*, in the Canaries and Madeira the small, dark *A.n. granti* and finally in North Africa the large, pale *A.n. punicus*.

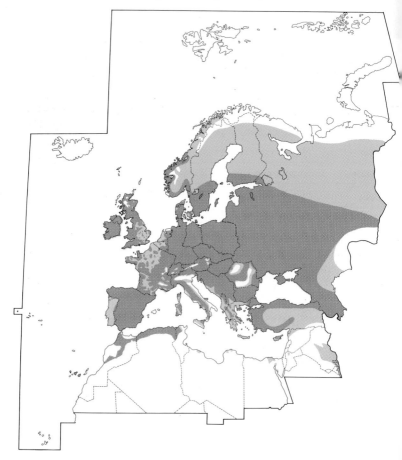

Population estimates

The Sparrowhawk is a difficult species to record in the breeding season. It lives quietly and hides its nest surprisingly well. Generally speaking the populations are therefore underestimated. A great deal of basic research would be needed to obtain a true picture of a country's total number of breeding pairs.

From the available information (*see* table on p. 152) it is not really possible to provide an estimate for the Western Palearctic as a whole, partly because there are no figures for the Soviet Union.

For Europe, excluding the Soviet Union, the information is reasonably good and it is possible to give a total population of 90,000 – 125,000 breeding pairs.

Population trends

Apart from the decrease in population resulting from the general persecution of raptors in the last two centuries, the Sparrowhawk is one of the species which suffered greatly in the 1950s and 1960s as a result of extensive environmental poisoning. It has been suggested that populations fell by 60–90 per cent, depending upon the amount of chemical used.

Until then the Sparrowhawk had been Denmark's commonest raptor, due to its position as a hunter of small birds and its easy access to such prey. The species could no longer maintain this position.

Today with the much reduced use of DDT, PCB and dieldrin the situation has greatly improved. In northern Europe the Sparrowhawk has regained lost terrain, although not to its former extent.

On the other hand, in southern Europe, as the table shows, there is no ground for optimism. Here one has, in many places, to combat the outdated attitude that raptors are a menace to game, which is particularly absurd in so far as the Sparrowhawk is concerned. Thus, illegal shooting and raiding of nests are still real problems in both southern and eastern Europe.

Here it is relevant to mention that in several countries it is quite legal, with certain reservations, to kill Sparrowhawks: in Denmark, Finland, East Germany, Austria, Czechoslovakia, Channel Islands, Bulgaria,

Sparrowhawk. *Photo K. Bjerre.*

Romania and Greece. The situation outside Europe is not known.

Migration

In the north of its range the Sparrowhawk is a true migrant with the whole population moving southwards; however, the southern birds are probably wholly sedentary. For such a common species, only a few birds cross the Mediterranean; up to 1000 a year at Gibraltar and about half this number over the Bosporus. A few cross the Sahara and even reach south of the Equator, to eastern parts of Africa.

Since they concentrate at the short sea crossings, the most spectacular movements are at the major Fenno-Scandian stations. At Falsterbo the maximum recorded was 17,000 during 1984 with the passage generally extending from mid-August to mid-November. Such migrations involve not only Swedish but also Finnish and Russian birds. The spring migration through the same areas extends through April and into May.

The analysis of ringing recoveries of Continental birds shows that youngsters migrate further than old birds and that the males move further than the females. Since females are so much larger than the males they are probably better able to cope with cold conditions. Both young birds and males tend to migrate earlier than old birds and females respectively. The distances moved may be very substantial with recoveries in Spain coming from Sweden, Finland, Russia and Czechoslovakia.

The birds breeding in Britain disperse short distances in random directions with less than 7 per cent of recoveries showing movements of 50 km or more. However winter migrants to Britain have proved to be from Germany, Denmark, Norway, Sweden and even Finland, and others were ringed as passage migrants in North Sea coastal countries. It is not known how many such migrants reach Britain each year but it is probably rather few, and certainly no

British sites have been found where passage birds concentrate in any quantity.

Habitat

For breeding this species prefers an area where open country alternates with deciduous and coniferous woodland. The nests are placed in 20–50-year-old woods where they can be hidden and where conditions are good for flying.

The inner parts of large, dense forests are usually avoided. On the other hand, Sparrowhawks may well nest in small woods down to an area of 10 ha, and they are beginning to move into towns.

Woods are often forsaken in winter and the birds then hunt to a consider-

Sparrowhawk – adult male. *Photo R. J. C. Blewitt/Ardea.*

Sparrowhawk – adult with blackbird.
Photo K. Weile.

able extent in towns, including the vicinity of food shops.

Voice

Most often used close to the nest during the breeding season. A series of rhythmical *kew-kew-kew* sounds, performed at various speeds, depending upon whether the call is used in a display flight, as a warning, when returning to the nest with prey, or as a morning duet and so on.

Breeding

Normally breeds for the first time at an age of 1–2 years. Pair formation often extends over a single breeding season, but in areas where the birds remain on or near the territory throughout the year it is also common for a pair to remain together year after year. A few cases of poly-gamy and polyandry are known.

At the start of the breeding season some pairs, but apparently not all, perform a display flight over the nest.

In Denmark, the nest is usually placed in a spruce forest and is rebuilt every year. Typically it is constructed at the boundary between the live and dead branches of the spruce, at a height of 5–8 m.

Both sexes build, but mostly the female. The 4–6 (1–7) eggs are usually laid in early May at intervals of two days and are incubated by the female for 33–35 days per egg (normally 39–42 days for a clutch). The chicks remain in the nest for 24–30 days and are dependent on the parents for a further 20–30 days.

In the 1950s and 1960s the production of young was very low. The species appears to be particularly sensitive to environmental poisons, and the percentage of clutches lost rose markedly. In England the number of eggs broken due to thin shells increased from 4 to 30 per cent.

Since then conditions have improved. Recent Danish investigations show that, in the years 1974–76, 2.3 young were produced per breeding pair – enough to allow the species to expand. However, many breeding attempts fail: 33–50 per cent annually, often when one of the old birds dies. Also, nests are sometimes raided, usually by Goshawks or martens.

Food

Intensive investigations (Holland and Germany) on roughly 62,000 prey animals collected in the breeding season show that small birds account for 98 per cent of the total food, the actual species taken depending upon which were the most numerous.

The investigation gave the following distribution of those occurring most frequently: thrushes 13 per cent, house sparrows 11 per cent, *Sylvia* species 9 per cent, tits 8 per cent, chaffinches 7 per cent, larks 7 per cent, buntings 6 per cent, swallows 5 per cent, warblers 5 per cent, tree sparrows 4 per cent, starlings 4 per cent and pipits 3 per cent, in total 82 per cent. In all 150 species were identified.

Game birds or similar accounted for small amounts: doves 0.7 per cent, gallinaceous birds 0.2 per cent, including a few pheasant chicks.

A winter investigation showed the same (with roughly 5000 prey animals). The distribution by species was slightly different, because several had migrated. House sparrows were the most important at 20 per cent. Secondary food sources included smaller mammals, mainly various mouse and vole species. In years with large numbers of rodents these would account for up to 16 per cent in the breeding season in Finland.

The Sparrowhawk is harmless in relation to game. Newly fledged Sparrowhawks may perhaps take pheasant chicks now and again, but these soon become too large for the raptor.

Foraging methods

Low flight while foraging, as the bird tries to surprise its prey, which it has perhaps seen from a perch in a tree or when flying at a certain height. When hunting, this hawk flies low over the ground, making use of cover such as hedges, bushes and buildings, so as to attack suddenly, perhaps a flock of sparrows or finches feeding in the open.

Usually the small birds are hidden, so the hawk tries to chase them out by striking at protecting branches, or by wandering over them if in a hedge. Normally they remain where they are and the Sparrowhawk disappears. It seems to be successful in less than five per cent of its attempts.

Sparrowhawk covering prey. *Photo E. Hansen/Biofoto.*

Sparrowhawk population in the Western Palearctic

Denmark	3500–5000 pairs (1981)[51]	After a big decline (at least 65 per cent in the 1950s and 1960s (poisons)) the population grew markedly and now seems stable.
Sweden	30,000 pairs (1977)[58] 14,000 pairs (1981)[9]	Disagreement on the population size. After decline in the 1950s and 1960s the population has increased again.
Norway	very common (1971)[62]	
Finland	10.000 pairs (1985)[10]	In the 1950s and 1960s decrease due to poisons of about 80 per cent. Then re-establishment.
USSR *Estonia*	? approx. 800 pairs (1976)[11]	4000 pairs (1977)[1] in a 270,000 sq. km area in central Russia. Increasing. The figures seem very small.
Poland	2000–4000 pairs (1984)[80]	Probably decreasing. Reasons unknown.
East Germany	800 pairs (1985)[87]	Mecklenburg: <100 pairs (1979)[52]. Brandenburg: 40–50 pairs (1983)[36]. Now increasing after considerable decline.
West Germany	1200–6600 pairs (1982)[22]	Reduction of up to 80 per cent, due to shooting, poisons, falconry and other nest-raiding.
Holland	approx. 1200 pairs (1978)[53]	Now increasing after a decline.
Belgium	200–300 pairs (1979)[1]	Now apparently stable after a decline.
Luxembourg	approx. 50 pairs (1971)[3]	Big decrease.
Britain & Ireland	15,000–20,000 pairs (1976)[47]	Now re-establishing after typical decline in 1950s and 1960s (poisons and persecution).
France	10,000–20,000 pairs (1984)[92]	Recovered after big decrease in the 1950s and 1960s.
Switzerland	?	After considerable decline now apparently re-establishing (1980)[25].

Sparrowhawk – adult male. *Photo B. Génsbøl/Biofoto.*

Austria	?	Breeds in all parts, except perhaps Vienna (1977)[48].
Italy	>1000 pairs (1982)[19]	Sardinia 100–200 pairs (1977)[41]. Population halved since 1945 (hunting, poisons, falconers).
Spain	approx. 9000 pairs (1982)[19]	Decrease due to environment poisoning.
Portugal	>300 pairs (1982)[19]	Decreasing.
Czechoslovakia	approx. 2500 pairs (1988)[43]	Stable or increasing.
Hungary	6–700 pairs (1988)[40]	
Romania	100–120 pairs (1977)[42]	The figures do not differentiate between Sparrowhawk and Levant Sparrowhawk.
Bulgaria	few (1971)[3]	
Yugoslavia	few (1982)[19]	
Albania	?	No recent data. Probably breeds.
Greece	>3000 pairs (1982)[19]	
Turkey	1000 pairs (1982)[19]	
Cyprus	20 pairs (1982)[19]	Probably no breeding birds.[85]
Tunisia	25–50 pairs (1982)[19]	
Algeria	common (1982)[19]	
Morocco	500–1000 pairs (1982)[19]	
Madeira	?	Probably in decline (1965)[1].
Canary Islands	locally numerous (1970)[1]	Probably decreasing.

Levant Sparrowhawk
Accipiter brevipes

Distribution
Apart from the breeding range for the Western Palearctic shown on the map, the Levant Sparrowhawk breeds only in northern and western Iran.

Population estimates
The available information from different countries (table on p. 156) is insufficient to provide an estimate of the size of the population.

On the other hand, the migration figures provide a clue. In 1978 the maximum for the Bosporus between middle and late September was 7150 migrating Levant Sparrowhawks (personal observations). Excluding young birds this figure suggests around 2000 breeding pairs. These birds come from the Balkans and from most of the Soviet breeding range, thus representing a large part of the whole population.

With the number of breeding pairs of this order it is likely that this species is more numerous than the figures in the table suggest.

Population trends
The few data available do not give a clear picture but suggest that the species was formerly more common.

Migration
A typical migrant. The winter quarters are not known, but are probably in the highlands of Ethiopia.

In autumn the migration is concentrated at the Bosporus between mid-August and early October, with a peak in the second and third week of September. The route through the Caucasus is apparently only of secondary importance (290 at Borcka in 1976). Thus, it seems that most of the Soviet population uses the Bosporus route, but this requires further investigation.

In spring the migration is seen in Israel mainly in mid-April, and at the Bosporus in late April.

In contrast to the Sparrowhawk, it is characteristic that this bird's migration is very concentrated. The greater part of the whole population often passes in just a few days.

Habitat
This is a typical bird of deciduous woodland. It prefers hilly country, with enough trees, or at least patches of taller scrub. It often breeds close to water.

Levant Sparrowhawk – adult female. *Photo A. Limbrunner.*

Breeding

Not very well known. It may breed at an age of one year but it is not known whether this is common.

The nest is built in a (deciduous) tree, normally at a height of 5–10 m. The 3–5 eggs are usually laid in middle to late May and are incubated by the female for 30–35 days (per egg). The chicks are apparently fledged at 40–45 days and are dependent upon the parents for around a further 15 days.

Food

More varied than that of the Sparrowhawk: small mammals in the form of various mice and squirrels and several bird species, including tits, warblers, finches, buntings and sparrows.

The species also takes bats, reptiles (grass snakes) and larger insects.

Foraging methods

Birds are hunted in the same way as the Sparrowhawk. The species often hunts ground prey from a perch.

Levant Sparrowhawk – adult male.
Photo M. Müller & H. Wohlmuth.

Levant Sparrowhawk population in the Western Palearctic

USSR	?	Status not clear. Probably decreasing (1979)[1].
Hungary	max. 5–10 pairs (1988)[40]	Breeding irregularly?
Yugoslavia	50 pairs (1982)[19]	Numerous in parts of the country at the start of this century (1974)[3].
Albania	?	Breeding bird. Status unknown.
Romania	rare (1977)[42]	Together with Sparrowhawk population estimated at 100–200 pairs.
Bulgaria	few (1979)[1]	
Greece	>400 pairs (1982)[19]	
Turkey	10–100 pairs (1982)[19]	

Shikra
Accipiter badius

Breeds only irregularly in the Western Palearctic. The only nest recorded was in Azerbaijan in 1933. The actual range includes Africa and southern Asia. Divided into several races.

Migration
The northern population is said to be migratory[1], and to fly in September–October to winter quarters, from Iran to north-western India and back again to the breeding sites in April–May. This species is, however, seen in the area south of the Caspian Sea in the winter, so perhaps the old birds are non-migratory.

Habitat
During the breeding season prefers steppes, savannas, the edges of deserts and oases, but is also frequently found in cultivated land, among trees near houses, in churchyards and in woodland bordering rivers.

Food
Mainly lizards, larger insects and birds, including poultry chicks and moorhens, bee-eaters and sparrows. It also takes small rodents, amphibians and bats.

Shikra immature. *Photo B. Génsbøl/Biofoto.*

Buzzard

Buteo buteo

Distribution

The Buzzard breeds in almost the whole of the European part of the Western Palearctic. The distribution extends eastwards through the forest belt to the Pacific.

There are numerous races. The nominate race covers most of the Western Palearctic. Others are *Buteo buteo arrigonii* in Corsica and Sardinia (paler and smaller); *B.b. rothschildi* in the Azores; *B.b. insularum* in the Canaries; *B.b. bannermanni* in the Cape Verde Islands; *B.b. vulpinus*, the Steppe Buzzard, in northern Scandinavia, Finland, much of the Soviet Union and eastern Poland; and *B.b. menestriesi* in the Crimea, Caucasus and Turkey (very like the Steppe Buzzard).

Population estimate

An estimate is not possible for the

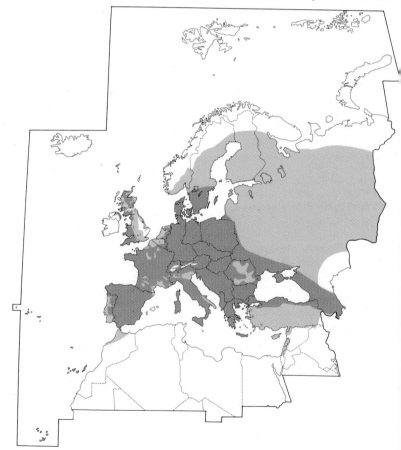

whole of the Western Palearctic as there are no figures for the USSR. For Europe, excluding the USSR, there are probably around 230,000–300,000. This makes the Buzzard the second commonest raptor in the area.

Population trends

The Buzzard is one of the most robust raptor species in the Western Palearctic. Among other things this is shown by the speed with which it has reacted to improved living conditions, more widespread protection and a cleaner environment, during the last 10–15 years.

The table on pp. 164–65 shows a population decrease in some areas. This applies to Italy and the Balkans where illegal shooting is a continuing problem, perhaps also environmental poisoning. But in many other areas there has been a population increase. In certain localities the birds have re-occupied old breeding sites from which, on account of game interests, they had formerly been shot out of.

Nevertheless, in some places (e.g. southern Zealand) ideal Buzzard habitats remain empty. The only explanation for this is shooting.

It will be interesting to follow the trend in the coming years. With the reduced pressure from shooting the Buzzard has, in general, become less shy and the species does well in the vicinity of man. The least shy probably have access to many food sources, e.g. game killed by traffic, and have therefore a greater chance of survival in winter than others which are more shy. A few years ago it would have been absurd to think that the Buzzard could, for instance, nest quite close to or in a town. Nowadays it sometimes does, when not persecuted.

Buzzard juvenile. *Photo B. Génsbøl/Biofoto.*

Migration

One race, the Steppe Buzzard *B.b. vulpinus*, is wholly migratory, moving from its breeding grounds in eastern Europe and Siberia down into Africa as far south as the Cape Province. A few winter in southern Europe and northern Africa and some in the Arabian peninsula, but most go to East Africa. Nominate *B. buteo* from western Europe are sedentary in the south, but quite strongly migratory in the north. Southern and island races are wholly resident.

Since they are soaring birds their migration is highly concentrated to avoid direct flights over water. The Steppe Buzzard moves quite late, with the movement through the Bosporus concentrated from mid-September to mid-October. Peak autumn counts there were in 1969 with 32,900, but these are dwarfed by the Caucasus stream. In north-east Turkey at Borcka-Arhavi over 200,000 were counted in 1976, with an incredible 135,000 on one day (28th September). They reach the southern wintering grounds from mid-October and start to return during February and March. In spring the migration over Eilat (Israel) may involve more than 300,000 birds mostly at the end of March and beginning of April. The scale of movement is best illustrated by the 13,000 km travelled by a South African ringed bird, found in Siberia.

At the central and western Mediterranean crossings many of the birds resemble *B.b. vulpinus* or are intermediate between this and the nominate race. Autumn counts at Gibraltar have almost reached 3000, and the Tunisia/Sicily route in spring may be used by more than 1000 birds. Further north the passage out of Sweden through Falsterbo was 36,600 in 1950 but has been fewer recently (17,200 in 1974); it extends from late August to November. The return passage through Denmark over Skagen (northern Jutland) extends from late March to mid-May, and peaked at 5500 birds in 1974.

Ringing studies in western Europe have shown that many northern Swedish birds winter in France (often in the Paris area), southern Swedish birds mostly stop in Denmark and the majority of Danish birds had moved

Buzzard and Pheasant in peaceful co-existence. *Photo B. Génsbøl/Biofoto.*

less than 100 km. The Danish birds that do move out are found in north-west Germany, Holland, Belgium and northern France. Only 26 per cent of British ringed birds had moved more than 50 km, and 100 km movements are exceptional. One from Hampshire went to northern France but no foreign ringed birds have been recorded in Britain.

Habitat
Prefers a countryside where small areas of woodland alternate with open, undulating terrain and meadows, marshland and heath.

Mainly lives in the margins of woodland. Only a few pairs will be found in dense forests without clearings. Buzzards forage primarily in open country.

During winter the species occurs in completely treeless areas.

Voice
Used almost exclusively in the territory and most often in the breeding season. Characterized by a mewing hiss, heard for instance when the nest is disturbed and during courtship.

Breeding
Normally breeds for the first time when 2–3 years old but may breed when only one year old. It seems that non-migratory birds may pair for life. Occupation of a territory is marked by soaring and screeching.

At the start of the breeding period the display flight is often seen. The birds stoop from a height of 30–40 m, and then rise almost vertically before stooping again. Now and then the higher flying bird rushes against the other which turns and parries with its talons. Shortly afterwards the talons may interlock.

Buzzard with mouse. *Photo A. Christiansen/Biofoto.*

Buzzards usually build a new nest every year but may also renovate one from the previous year. Both sexes help with building the nest which is placed in a tree, normally at a height of 6–27 m.

Egg-laying starts in the middle of March in central Europe, and late March in Denmark, but ends in mid- to late April in northern Scandinavia. The 2–4 (5–6) eggs are laid at intervals of 2–3 days and are incubated by both parents for 33–38 days per egg. The chicks remain in the nest for 50–55 days and are independent after a further 40–55 days.

The production of young varies considerably according to the food supply. A German investigation in the period 1960–71 showed that the number of young varied from 0.42 to 2.13 per breeding pair.

In northern Europe the number of young produced is somewhat lower.

Buzzard – adult with a rabbit in its talons. *Photo A. Brook/Ardea.*

Food

Consists primarily of small rodents and other small mammals, but also birds, reptiles, amphibians, large insects and earthworms.

Four central European investigations show the variation in food sources. Small mammals fluctuated between 70–98 per cent, birds between 3–24 per cent, reptiles 1–15 per cent, amphibians 3–11 per cent. Insects and worms could scarcely be recorded.

Buzzards prefer to hunt over open country. Among the small rodents taken there are, therefore, field voles, bank voles and water voles, and locally rabbits where they are numerous. Other animals taken regularly include moles, leverets, shrews, wood mice, squirrels and rats.

Buzzards are not fast hunters, so their bird prey consists largely of young and newly fledged individuals, particularly starlings, various thrushes, members of the crow family, tits, finches, buntings, larks and woodpeckers, and to a lesser extent the chicks of pheasants, partridge and domestic fowls.

The reptiles taken are mainly lizards and slowworms, and to a lesser extent snakes (various species of colubrids and vipers). Amphibians taken include both frogs and toads, insects include a large number of forms such as beetles, bees and butterflies, but normally not as a significant part of the diet. On the other hand, earthworms may play a significant role.

In the period October–February carrion can be quite important as a part of the diet. This is usually dead game but also offal from slaughter-houses.

On the basis of a long series of stomach analyses it has been reckoned that, by weight, the diet consists of: various mice and voles, 46 per cent; moles 14 per cent; other mammals 16 per cent; reptiles, amphibians and fishes 10 per cent; birds 9 per cent and carrion 5 per cent. The weights of in-sects and worms can scarcely be estimated.

Buzzards are strong enough to take prey weighing up to 500 g. Anything in excess of this is taken as carrion or is killed when it is in a much weakened condition.

Foraging methods
Mainly from a perch, usually from a branch or similar, often waiting pati-ently. When prey is seen, the Buzzard glides down to the ground and seizes it with its talons.

The bird also flies low over the area, sometimes hovering, and often wanders about on the ground.

Buzzard at laid-out slaughterhouse offal. *Photo B. Génsbøl/Biofoto.*

Buzzard population in the Western Palearctic

Denmark	4500–5500 pairs (1981)[51]	After much persecution the population has grown markedly since 1970, by about a third. Suitable habitats remain unoccupied due to shooting.
Sweden	18,000 pairs (1981)[9]	Probably decreasing due to habitat changes (including afforestation of former agricultural areas).
Norway	few (1971)[62]	After marked decline this century, now apparently increasing.
Finland	8000 pairs (1985)[10]	Reduction by 50 per cent since 1930s. Now stable.
USSR *Estonia* *Latvia*	? >1000 pairs (1976)[11] common (1983)[34]	16,000–18,000 pairs in an area of 270,000 sq. km in central Russia. Slowly increasing after protection (1979)[1].
Poland	32,000 pairs (1984)[80]	Increasing since 1940s due to protection.
East Germany	15,000–25,000 pairs (1985)[87]	Mecklenburg: 5280 pairs (1979)[52]. The country's commonest raptor.
West Germany	50,000–90,000 pairs (1982)[22]	Schleswig-Holstein: fluctuates between 1700 and 3600 pairs (1981)[59], depending upon food supply.
Holland	1650 pairs (1980)[53]	Marked increase since 1970.
Belgium	1200–2000 pairs (1979)[1]	Marked increase since early 1970s.
Luxembourg	1000–4000 pairs (1970)[3]	
Britain	8000–10,000 pairs (1970)[1]	Reached maximum in 1950s. Breakdown of rabbit population (myxomatosis) led to decrease. Now stable?
Ireland	13 pairs (1986)[35]	Exterminated in 1880s. Attempts at re-colonisation since 1950s.
France	45,000–50,000 pairs (1984)[92]	After marked decline, now increasing (1977)[1].
Spain	15,000 pairs (1977)[27] >5000 pairs (1982)[19]	Disagreement on population size.
Portugal	2000–3000 pairs (1982)[19]	Stable. The country's commonest raptor.
Italy	>1000 pairs (1982)[19]	Population halved since 1945, due to shooting, poisoned baits and environment poisons (?). Sardinia 250–350 pairs (1977)[41]. Sicily 1000–1500 pairs (1982)[19]. Total figure set too low.

Switzerland	common (1980)[25]	Together with Kestrel the commonest raptor. Stable since about 1960.
Austria	common (1977)[48]	Stable since mid-1960s. Together with Kestrel the commonest raptor.
Czechoslovakia	approx. 8500 pairs (1982)[19]	Trend unknown.
Hungary	2000 pairs (1988)[19]	Now increasing after the worst environmental poisons were forbidden.
Yugoslavia	common (1982)[19]	Marked decline this century.
Albania	?	No information.
Romania	240–300 pairs (1977)[42]	Marked decline.
Bulgaria	few (1974)[2]	
Greece	5000 pairs (1982)[19]	Apparently decreasing this century.
Turkey	1000–5000 pairs (1982)[50]	
Cyprus	10–100 pairs (1982)[19]	
Azores	max. 400 pairs[44]	Uninhabited on the islands of Flores and Corvo.
Canary Islands	?	After a decrease, now increasing on some of the islands (1979)[1].
Cape Verde Islands	few (1984)[35]	100 birds (1963–68)[13], not on all islands, sometimes moving temporarily to West Africa.[94]
Madeira	not uncommon[86]	

Buzzard on carrion. *Photo H. G. Arndt.*

Rough-legged Buzzard

Buteo lagopus

Rough-legged Buzzard juvenile. *Photo K. Bjerre.*

Distribution

As the map shows, this buzzard is distributed in the northern part of the Western Palearctic. The distribution extends eastwards, mainly through the tundra zone, to the Pacific Ocean, where it follows the coastal region southwards to Sakhalin and continues on the other side of the Pacific in the northern region of North America. The distribution is therefore almost circumpolar.

The nominate race covers the Western Palearctic. In the Yenisei area this is replaced by the somewhat larger and paler *B.l. menzbieri*, which is a winter visitor in parts of southern and south-eastern Europe. There are two other races.

Population estimates

For Fenno-Scandia the total population is around 16,000 pairs (*see* table on p. 170). However, this figure is on the low side because the information for Norway is from a period when the populations were apparently lower than today.

It is possible that there has, to a certain extent, been an interchange between populations in different countries.

Population trends

Counts in the breeding area have not been undertaken to any great extent, but the number of migrating birds in Finland and Sweden (Falsterbo) has shown a positive trend. These figures suggest that the population was markedly increasing up to the 1950s and 1960s, when the species was subject to a considerable decrease in numbers (based on migration figures). This was apparently due to environmental poisoning.

The reason for the subsequent population increase is not known, but it is possibly due to a reduction in shooting, a cleaner environment and the considerable stocks of rodents in 1973–74 and 1977–78, on a scale not seen since the 1930s.

Migration

This is a migratory species whose movements are much complicated by the effects of fluctuating rodent populations in the bird's breeding range. Young birds settling to breed, and even adults after a rodent population crash, may be 1000 km or more from where they were the previous summer. For instance a four-year-old bird from Norway was found 2700 km away in Yamal (USSR).

In years with good rodent populations the movement south may not start until October, but in bad years movement may start in August. The normal breeding range is wholly vacated, although some birds may remain in the southern Baltic. Some wintering birds continue to wander southwards until December, then return from February onwards.

Many of the birds move south or south-south-east but, in good years,

Rough-legged Buzzard approaching its nest. *Photo A. Christiansen/Biofoto.*

stragglers get as far south and west as Spain and even North Africa. On average the winter recoveries are some 2000–2500 km from the breeding area.

The fluctuations in numbers moving are best illustrated by the Falsterbo autumn figure for 1978 (best year recently) with 1619, and the following year's total of 141. The Danish return movement after the 'best' year included 2336 passing through Skagen in northern Jutland. Wintering is regular in Denmark and the Low Countries but the numbers reaching Britain in poor years (that is with good numbers of rodents) may be very much reduced with only a handful along the east coast. However, in good years there may be more than 100 records of birds not only along the east coast but inland, particularly in southern England. The only evidence for the origin of these birds is two ringing recoveries of Swedish-ringed nestlings, but rather few are ringed in the eastern part of the bird's range.

Habitat

Prefers to nest on tundra or in the transition areas between this and forest. In Scandinavia up near the tree limit and just above it.

In good rodent years the species also breeds in woodland with large open areas, and in such years may nest far south of its true breeding range.

Outside the breeding season this is a typical bird of open country which hunts both cultivated and uncultivated areas.

Voice

Heard almost only when the bird is disturbed at the nest. It is very similar to the screech of a Buzzard, but is usually longer (twice as long) and at a higher pitch.

Breeding

Probably breeds for the first time at an age of 2–3 years. Apparently pair formation only lasts for a single season and this probably takes place in the winter quarters, for the birds often arrive already paired at the breeding sites.

The breeding population fluctuates markedly in relation to a 4-year rodent cycle. In an area of 32 sq km in Lule Lapmark in Sweden the numbers of breeding pairs in the years 1970–78 were: 9, 0, 0, 8–10, 11, 7, 0, 6 and 11. So there are years when the Rough-legged Buzzard does not breed at all.

Russian investigations show that the species wanders far and wide, and that in years with few rodents it may move to other areas with better food prospects, where it then breeds.

Shortly after the territory is occupied the species performs a form of courtship display like that of the Buzzard, but unlike it in that the voice is not used.

In mountains the nest is usually placed on a cliff, in forests in a tree and on tundra directly on the ground. The 3–4 (3–7) eggs are laid – mostly in years with plenty of food – in late

Young Rough-legged Buzzards almost ready to fly. *Photo P. Lindberg/N.*

Rough-legged Buzzard

Rough-legged Buzzard juvenile on a lookout post. *Photo J. Elmelid/N.*

May to mid-June and are incubated mainly by the female for 31 days (per egg). The fledging period is 34–43 days, and this is followed by a few weeks during which the young are becoming independent.

Rough-legged Buzzard juvenile. *Photo A. Christiansen/Biofoto.*

Food

Mainly small rodents, accounting typically for 80–95 per cent of the food, where they occur in large numbers. They include field voles, lemmings and bank voles, secondarily also leverets and stoats. The rest of the prey consists largely of birds, such as young grouse, ducks, waders and various small birds.

When the rodent stock is low birds become the most important part of the diet (up to 94 per cent has been recorded), and these come from a wide variety of species.

A very minor component of the food may consist of amphibians, fishes and insects, including mosquitoes.

Outside the breeding season the composition of the food shows the same pattern but with birds less commonly caught. In an investigation in northern Germany there were only 19 birds out of 1425 vertebrates.

In winter they often feed on carrion.

Foraging methods

This usually consists of hovering at a height of 10–15 m. Typically a single area is searched for 4–20 seconds before the bird flies off to a new one.

When prey is discovered the bird stoops, often in stages, at a moderate speed, and tries to seize with the talons extended. The species also hunts from a fixed perch.

Rough-legged Buzzard population in the Western Palearctic

Norway	>6000 pairs (1961)[61]	Figure calculated as an average of good and bad years. Commonest raptor.
Sweden	7000 pairs (1981)[9]	Fluctuates considerably. The figure shows the population in a good year.
Finland	2500 pairs (1985)[10]	Much fluctuation.
USSR	?	

Long-legged Buzzard
Buteo rufinus

Distribution

In addition to the distribution shown on the map this species also breeds eastwards through the Soviet Union to Mongolia, in parts of Iran and in scattered places in the Arabian Peninsula.

In North Africa the birds belong to a separate race *B.r. cirtensis* which is smaller with a paler head and tail.

Population estimates

It is not really possible to give a total for the Western Palearctic (*see* table on p. 174). The population in the Balkans appears to be less than 100 pairs (1975)[1].

Population trends

The picture is unclear. In the last century the Long-legged Buzzard was only known in Europe from the Soviet Union and southern and central Greece. The distribution recorded today suggests a slow expansion towards the north-west.

On the other hand, information from the USSR records a reduction in the breeding area in recent times.

Migration

Non-migratory or partial migration, but northern populations are migratory with winter quarters mainly in Africa south of around 10°N. Birds also overwinter in Greece and Turkey.

Only small numbers have been recorded at the Bosporus (maximum eleven in 1973) and at Borcka (five in 1976 and 1977). This may be because observations at both places had stopped before the real migration started.

At Suez in 1981, 1816 migrating Long-legged Buzzards were seen.

The spring migration has been recorded in Israel from mid-February to late April. Breeding sites are occupied in Turkey in mid-March, in Bulgaria in late March and in the southern Soviet Union in mid-April.

In this century the species occurs more frequently north of the breeding area than formerly (? expansion), but

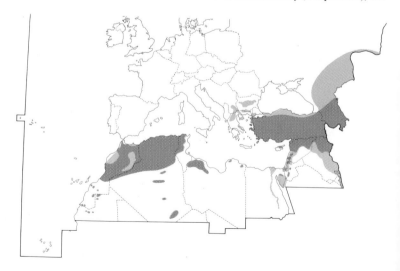

A very pale Long-legged Buzzard. *Photo G. K. Brown/Ardea.*

it is only an accidental visitor north of the Balkans. However, even Scandinavia has been visited – Denmark: 4 records (1987), Sweden: 2 records (1987), Norway: 1 record (1986).

Habitat
Dry steppes and semi-deserts, also true desert areas with sufficient food and water in the vicinity.

In the Balkans the species is also found in wooded, hilly areas and low mountains with cliffs suitable for nests and open areas for hunting.

Voice
Seldom heard. Similar to that of the Buzzard, but shorter and more high-pitched.

Breeding
Probably first breeds at an age of 2–3 years, like the Buzzard.

The mating flight resembles that of the Buzzard. The nest, most often placed on a cliff face, is built by both sexes. In the Balkans eggs are laid in late March to mid-April, the clutch having 3–4 (2–5) eggs which are incubated for about 28 days.

Many details of the breeding cycle are unknown.

Food
Mainly small and middle-sized mammals, such as voles, lemmings, desert rats, ground squirrels, and secondarily hedgehogs, leverets, moles and weasels.

They also take reptiles (lizards and snakes, including adders), amphibians (frogs and toads), insects, including locusts and birds from lark-size up to pheasant. A Russian investigation (1961–62) of 279 pellets yielded the remains of 222 mammals, 105 reptiles, 82 larger insects, 32 amphibians and 30 birds.

In winter the species also feeds on carrion.

Foraging methods

Often circles at a height of 30 m or hovers. Also hunts from a perch and wanders along the ground.

Long-legged Buzzard population in the Western Palearctic

USSR	?	Breeding area seems to be moving eastwards (1979)[1].
Bulgaria	few (1984)[89]	Only scant data, but apparently breeds in many parts of the country. May be increasing.
Yugoslavia	approx. 20 pairs (1982)[19]	Apparently only occurs in the southernmost parts of the country. No sign of expansion northwards.
Albania	?	Probably breeds in small numbers (1972)[1].
Greece	approx. 60 pairs (1983)[84]	
Turkey	1000–1500 pairs (1982)[19]	Scattered breeding (1979)[1].
Cyprus	10 pairs (1982)[19]	
Syria	?	
Lebanon	?	Very few breeding records (1979)[1].
Israel	common (1982)[19]	Decreasing (environmental poisons).
Jordan	?	
Egypt	1–10 pairs (1982)[19]	
Libya	?	Apparently breeds in the areas shown in the map, but possibly also further south (1979)[1].
Tunisia	400 pairs (1982)[19]	
Algeria	numerous (1982)[19]	
Morocco	>1000 pairs (1982)[19]	Apparently decreasing locally.
Mauretania	?	

Long-legged Buzzard with a lizard for the young. *Photo A. Limbrunner.*

Golden Eagle

Aquila chrysaetos

Distribution

In addition to the range shown on the map, the Golden Eagle breeds in large areas of Asia eastwards to the Pacific Ocean, and also in North America (race *A.c. canadensis*). Most of the Western Palearctic is covered by the nominate race which is distributed through Asia to the regions around the Altai. The smaller and somewhat darker race *A.c. homeyeri* breeds in the Iberian Peninsula, North Africa, Crete, the Middle East, Caucasus and Iran. In addition, the Asiatic race *A.c. daphanea* extends from Turkestan to Manchuria and south-eastern China, *A.c. kamtschatica* eastwards from Altai, and finally *A.c. japonica* in Korea and Japan.

Population estimates

An estimate of the total population (*see* table on p. 182) is not possible as

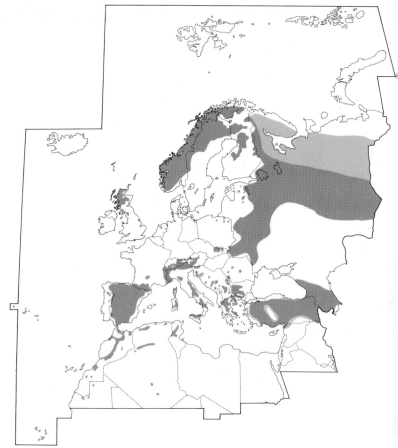

A pair of Golden Eagles on the nest. *Photo C. Pissavini/Jacana.*

there are no data from most of the Soviet Union. The populations are known in almost all the countries in the rest of Europe. The total for Europe (excluding the USSR) is 3,300–3,700 pairs, or a good half of the Danish Buzzard population, so not particularly imposing for such a large area.

In this figure it is likely that the population in the Alps has been underestimated (total: 500 pairs in 1979[81]).

Population trends

During the great campaign of extermination in the last century these eagles had the rather enviable role of being the most hated and the most persecuted, both as prey and for trophies. For large parts of the human population such a position naturally had consequences, partly for the distribution, partly for the population's density. Generally speaking, the species was exterminated in the easily accessible lowland areas and survived in the more thinly populated mountainous areas, which were more difficult for the persecutors to reach. Thus, the species became extinct in Ireland in about 1910. In Germany it was exterminated in the lowlands and lower hills and only survived in the Bavarian Alps. Here and in the inaccessible parts of the Alps the species was fighting for existence. Thus, around 1900 there were only 2–3 pairs in the Austrian Alps. In Sweden the species originally bred in most parts of the country, but on account of shooting it only survived in the upland areas of the north.

During the 1950s and 1960s raptors were much troubled by poisons in the environment and at this time there was a complete change of heart. The Golden Eagle and most of the other raptors were completely protected in most parts of Europe and, most

Golden Eagle juvenile. *Photo A. Niklasson.*

important, in many countries with the support of the local population, particularly in northern Europe.

The result of this change in circumstances can be seen in the table on p. 182. Throughout the whole of northern and central Europe populations have been stable or have been increasing. It has not been so good in southern Europe where, in many countries, the stocks have been decreasing. Here there have been problems with shooting, nest-raiding, poisoning and the collection of skins, phenomena which are still known in the rest of Europe but not to an extent that might threaten the population.

Evidently the Golden Eagle has no great problems in improving its position in the modern world. It also appears to have adapted well to conditions in cultivated areas. It will be interesting to observe the extent to which the species can regain its lost terrain. This depends perhaps on how we can prevent shooting of the more trusting individuals.

In Sweden the species has re-taken Gotland (10 pairs in 1983) and in 1971 a pair attempted to breed in Scania.

Migration

In the western and central part of its European range, adult Golden Eagles are largely resident, although young birds may move southwards from the most northern areas. Few Swedish birds leave the country, and the southern records are almost exclusively youngsters. Severe winters, when prey is in short supply, may trigger more movement and then even adults may be forced southwards. There are regular records (5–10 annually) in Denmark but few in the Low Countries. Young Finnish birds regularly move southwards, with ringing recoveries in White Russia (3), Ukraine and Hungary, the furthest distance being 2100 km.

Daily movements may of course be extensive, and the pair which bred on Rathlin Island (N. Ireland) regularly crossed 22 km to Kintyre to feed. From Scottish ringing the furthest recorded movement is 120 km, and it is certain that the British birds do not move south of the breeding range even during severe winters.

Habitat

Nowadays Golden Eagles breed in the mountains of most of the Western Palearctic. Where the human population is not too dense, and thus there is little disturbance, they are also seen in low-lying country, e.g. in Russia, Sweden and Finland.

The species must have access to several alternative nesting-places, either on cliff faces with an overhang or in large old trees. In Sweden the latter may have a confirmed average age of 320 years.

Likes to hunt over the forest edges with alternating open country and rocky areas, covering large territories, such as 225–625 sq km in the Alps, 40–75 sq km in Scotland.

Voice

Seldom used, even in the breeding season. There are two types of call: yelping screeches during the mating flight, and mewing as a warning and

Golden Eagle juvenile (raven in the background). *Photo B. Lundberg/N.*

during the mating flight. However, when several birds overwinter together they may be quite talkative.

Breeding

In general, Golden Eagles breed for the first time when the adult plumage is acquired, at about five years old. Individuals in juvenile plumage are exceptionally seen at a nest, and have also been recorded as breeding successfully. Golden Eagles pair for life.

The territory is frequently occupied throughout the year. Display flights are most often seen in the true breeding season, usually February–May. There are two types: diving towards a lower flying mate which turns on its back and wards off the other with the talons, and flying with short descents followed by ascents.

Golden Eagles generally have two or three alternative nesting-places, but up to fourteen have been recorded. The nest is placed in a large, very old tree or on an inaccessible cliff ledge.

The 2 (1–3) eggs are usually laid from early March to early April at intervals of 3–4 days and are normally incubated by the female alone for 43–45 days per egg. The fledging period is 65–70 (80) days. The young remain a long time in the territory, in Scandinavia and Scotland often until October, in the Alps sometimes until January or, if the parents do not breed again, even right up to the next summer.

In Sweden considerable variations have been recorded in the number of pairs that breed; this is probably dependent upon the food supply in

Golden Eagle – adult landing on the nest with a fox cub in its talons. *Photo U. Berggren/Ardea.*

early spring. Thus successful breeding may, in any one year, vary between 21 and 85 per cent of the population. On average the production of young was 0.64 per breeding pair.

This may be seen in relation to the Scottish figure of 0.66 for a territory with good food supply and 0.52 for one with a poor supply, and 0.48 in the Pyrenees. For a population without noticeable human persecution this figure for the production of young should be sufficient for the maintenance of the population.

Food

Very variable, depending upon what is available. According to the locality, species may dominate: marmots, sousliks, hares, rabbits, tortoises, various gallinules, the young of chamois, roe deer, red deer and reindeer, and various domestic animals usually taken when weak or as carrion.

Among mammals the birds also take the young of foxes, badgers, lynx and, on a smaller scale, squirrels, weasels, martens, lemmings, hedgehogs, cats, rats, field voles and moles. Among the birds taken are various ducks, waders, gulls, doves, herons, cranes, cormorants and passerines. In southern Europe reptiles may also play a role.

Four investigations show the share of birds taken: in the Alps 19 per cent, in Norway 44 per cent, in Finland, south and north 64 and 74 per cent, with gallinaceous birds the principal items, followed by ducks, cranes and crows. The remaining percentages were covered almost completely by mammals: in the Alps marmots (over 50 per cent), mountain hares (10 per cent), and the kids of chamois and roe, sometimes as carrion.

During the winter Golden Eagles frequently appear at feeding places

Golden Eagle juvenile. *Photo J. Østeng Hov/NN.*

where poison-free meat is put out for raptors.

With a list of prey as given already it is surely not surprising that Golden Eagles have been energetically persecuted. Fortunately, it is now the general opinion that, as is typical for raptors, the Golden Eagle mostly kills weakened animals, leaving room for others.

Foraging methods

Golden Eagles often hunt by keeping watch from a branch, cliff or other

181

Golden Eagle – adult. *Photo I. Stenberg.*

outlook. They may also search the territory for hours at a time, flying low at tree-top height, suddenly appearing in a surprise attack.

Birds are normally taken either on the ground or when flying up; larger mammals are usually chased when the bird is flying low over the ground.

Evidently this eagle is by no means successful every time. Thus, a falconer's eagle only catches a hare at every twentieth attempt, but it becomes more skilful with the years and may surprise hares in their form.

Domesticated eagles quickly take to catching wandering cats which are easy prey, but also quickly lose interest in pheasants and partridges which are more difficult to catch.

A Golden Eagle can lift up to 4–5 kg. Occasionally two individuals have been seen to hunt together.

Golden Eagle population in the Western Palearctic

Britain	425 pairs and 87 individual birds (1982/83)[93]	After considerable decline, re-establishing after 1945, then fresh decrease due to use of dieldrin in sheep-farming in the 1960s. New increase. Two pairs in England, rest in Scotland.
Norway	250–500 pairs (1977)[49]	First protected in 1971. Previous big decrease. Now apparently stable.
Sweden	300–400 pairs (1983)[28]	Formerly distributed throughout the country. Now only breeds in more remote areas. Stable.

Finland	200 pairs (1985)[10]	Formerly much persecuted by e.g. reindeer breeders. Now increasing.
USSR	?	Some thousands of pairs estimated for the
Estonia	20 pairs (1983)[95]	whole country, including the Asiatic parts
Latvia	5 pairs (1982)[34]	(1983)[6]. Apparently decreasing to the south
Lithuania	exterminated (1964)[1]	(European area), possibly expanding northwards.
Poland	10 pairs (1984)[80]	Apparently stable.
Czechoslovakia	c. 50 pairs (1988)[43]	Stable or increasing.
Hungary	2 pairs (1988)[40]	New breeding bird in the country.
Austria	39–51 pairs (1977)[48]	Now increasing after near extermination.
Switzerland	100–120 (150) pairs (1980)[25]	Rare around 1900. Increasing after protection in 1952.
West Germany	12–25 pairs (1982)[22]	Now stable, after decreasing and restriction of breeding area.
France	190–236 pairs (1982)[93]	Now stable, after a decline. Pyrenees 36–39 pairs (1981)[39], Corsica about 16 pairs (1977)[14].
Italy	250 pairs (1983)[93]	Apparently still decreasing, due to shooting, nest-raiding and poisoning. 10–12 pairs in Sicily.
Spain	340–970 (1987)[45]	Considerable decrease due to habitat changes, persecution, myxomatosis in the rabbit population and poisoning.
Portugal	23-30 pairs (1987)[45]	Decreasing.
Yugoslavia	c. 100 pairs (1982)[19]	Decreasing
Romania	30 pairs (1977)[42]	
Bulgaria	200 pairs? (1975)[1]	Apparently increasing after persecution was reduced.
Albania	?	No recent information, but probably breeds.
Greece	c. 250 pairs (1983)[84]	Decreasing in 1974[3].
Turkey	100–1000 pairs (1982)[19]	
Cyprus	2 pairs (1982)[19]	
Israel	10–17 pairs (1982)[19]	Increasing. First nesting record confirmed in 1972.
Egypt	1–2 pairs (1982)[19]	In Sinai.
Tunisia	40–50 pairs (1982)[19]	
Algeria	frequent (1982)[19]	
Morocco	100–1000 pairs (1982)[19]	

Black Eagle
Aquila verreauxii

Distribution
The real breeding range lies outside the Western Palearctic in eastern and southern Africa. The species has evidently attempted to breed (1–2 pairs) in Israel and it is perhaps a regular breeding bird in Sinai (1986)[96].

Migration
Apparently non-migratory, but young disperse widely.

Habitat
Rocky country far from human habitation.

Breeding
No data from the Western Palearctic.

The nest is built on a cliff face, sometimes in a tall tree. In Sudan the eggs are laid in December–March. The 2 (1–3) eggs are incubated by both parents for 43–46 days, and fledging takes 84–99 days. The young may be dependent upon the parents for a further six months. Only one chick reaches fledging age; the youngest dies from being persecuted by its elder sibling.

Food
Mainly medium-sized mammals, particularly hyraxes (up to 98 per cent), and secondarily birds and reptiles (lizards).

Foraging methods
All the prey is taken on the ground. The bird often searches by flying low over the terrain, but it also hunts from a perch.

Black Eagle – adult. *Photo A. S. Weaving/Ardea.*

Imperial Eagle

Aquila heliaca

Distribution

In addition to the distribution shown on the map the Imperial Eagle breeds in a belt to the east, through the steppe zone to the areas around Lake Baikal. The birds in the Iberian Peninsula are in a separate race, *A.h. adalberti.*

Population estimates

Data are lacking for most of the Soviet breeding places in Europe (*see* table on p. 189) so an estimate for the total population is not possible. For the rest of Europe (excluding USSR) the estimate is approx. 275 pairs.

Population trends

A sad story. At one time several thousand pairs bred in Bulgaria, with one pair for every 3 km along the Danube in Romania (1925). In Greece in the 1940s there were 25–40 pairs, but only in the region of Salonika.

Evidently the important factor in the drop in numbers has been persecution, which still happens in certain places. However, the extent to which changes in habitat have played a role is not known. The species prefers flat, uncultivated country, which has become increasingly cultivated over the years. Nor do we know the extent to which poisoning has affected the situation. Generally speaking there have been few restrictions in the use of poison in the countries where the bird breeds.

Imperial Eagle juvenile on the nest. *Photo B-U. Meyburg.*

As shown in the table on p. 189, there has been a steady reduction in almost all these countries. If the European population is to be saved, the birds must be effectively protected against persecution, with laws to enforce this.

Today the Imperial Eagle appears to be the most threatened eagle species in Europe, and it is particularly serious that the Iberian population consists of only approx. 100 breeding pairs.

Migration

In the Iberian race the old birds are non-migratory, the young ones wander to a certain extent. In the nominate race the species is migratory or partially so. Some birds overwinter at the edge of the breeding range, but in general the winter quarters are in North Africa, Arabia, the Middle East and Iran. Young birds migrate furthest. In severe winters the whole population evidently leaves Europe. The old birds do not usually migrate far.

Young birds start to wander as early as August. True migration takes place from mid-September to late October. This is evidently concentrated at the Bosporus and at Borcka (N-E Turkey), but the numbers are small, the maxima respectively being 18 (1966–75) and 29 (1976–77).

In spring the old birds pass through the Middle East from mid-February to mid-March, the young birds usually from late March to early April.

From observations by the author at Bharatpur, India, of Siberian birds in winter quarters it seems that, in suitable localities, families of a pair with young may overwinter together.

The wanderings of the young may lead them far from the breeding grounds. Thus, there are eight records from Sweden (1987) and twelve from Denmark (1987), all in the period late May to late October.

Habitat

For breeding the species prefers low-lying country of a park-like character, usually where groves of e.g. birch and aspen and wooded valleys alternate with wet areas, uncultivated grasslands and even cultivated land.

In winter the birds seek similar habitats, but with more emphasis on the wet areas.

Voice
Mostly used in the breeding period, but also heard in the winter quarters, often when other raptors intrude on their foraging territories. The call is a hoarse, rhythmical raven-like *grrr-grrr-grrr*.

Breeding
The full plumage is acquired at an age of 4–5 years and this is when the birds probably breed for the first time. Younger birds are exceptionally seen in pairs. With migrant birds it seems to be normal for the pairs to remain together throughout the year, and for life.

Remarkable display flights are seen at the start of the breeding season, in

Imperial Eagle (race *adalberti*): a pair on the nest, female on *right. Photo B-U. Meyburg.*

Imperial Eagle juvenile. *Photo B. Génsbøl/Biofoto.*

times. They are fledged at 65–77 days and are dependent upon the parents for a further, unknown period although the family may apparently remain together in the winter quarters.

The parents may quite regularly get 2–3 young on the wing. A Czech investigation of seventeen successful pairs gave an average as high as 1.94 young per clutch (5 with three young, 6 with two and 6 with one).

Food

This is generally medium-sized mammals and birds, carrion and, exceptionally, reptiles. For the nominate race the main prey consists of sousliks and leverets, for the Iberian race rabbits. Other important food sources are hamsters, field voles, young marmots and the young of pheasants, moorhens, ducks, geese, spoonbills, flamingos, bustards, magpies and crows, as well as passerines. Exceptionally poultry, frogs and insects are also taken.

A Spanish investigation from a habitat close to water gave around 42 per cent mammals, 55 per cent birds, 3 per cent reptiles and 0.2 per cent fish.

Carrion is taken throughout the year, but is most important in winter.

Foraging methods

Most prey is taken on the ground. The bird is too large and heavy to hunt birds more actively but often takes them at the moment they fly up. It uses a perch on a tree, haystack or similar, from which to strike prey after a short chase. It may also stoop while circling above, usually using natural camouflage to surprise its victim. It sometimes wanders about for frogs, reptiles and insects.

Two birds often work together when hunting. One startles the prey, the other does the actual catching.

Spain in January, in south-east Europe in March. For hours at a time the birds may circle over the territory screeching loudly, then performing impressive dives, gripping one another's talons and dropping together towards the ground.

The nest is normally 10–25 m up in tall trees and is built by both sexes. The clutch of 2–3 (1–4) eggs is laid in Spain in mid-February to late March, in eastern Europe late March to late April. They are incubated by both sexes and hatch in 43 days (per egg). Incubation starts with the first egg so the chicks hatch at different

Imperial Eagle population in the Western Palearctic

Spain	104 pairs (1986)[97]	Formerly considerable decrease. Now increasing in spite of habitat changes.
Portugal	5 pairs (1982)[19]	No breeding records in a number of years.
Czechoslovakia	25 pairs (1988)[43]	Increasing.
Hungary	21 pairs (1988)[40]	Increasing.
Yugoslavia	20 pairs (1982)[19]	Threatened with extinction.
Romania	100–110 pairs (1981)[2]	Formerly much reduced. Now stable?
Bulgaria	approx. 10 pairs (1979)[1]	Decreasing – 2000 birds in last century.
Greece	2–6 pairs (1982)[19]	Decreasing.
USSR *Moldavia*	? approx. 10 pairs (1979)[1]	In the whole Soviet Union, including the Asiatic areas, some hundreds of pairs (1983)[6]. Decrease in European breeding sites, stability in the Asiatic.
Turkey	50–150 pairs (1982)[19]	
Cyprus	10 pairs (1982)[19]	Decreasing.

Imperial Eagle juvenile. *Photo B. Génsbøl/Biofoto.*

Steppe Eagle
Aquila nipalensis

Some workers regard this bird as a species on its own, others consider it a race of the Tawny Eagle, *Aquila rapax*.

Distribution
As shown on the map, and extending in the steppe zone through Asia to Manchuria. The European and western Asiatic birds belong to the race *A.n. orientalis*. From around Lake Baikal this is replaced by the nominate form.

The most westerly breeding sites are in the Ukraine, with only a few pairs. The true distribution today is as far east as the region north of the Caspian Sea. Here there is a dense breeding population of around 5000 pairs (1983)[6], and in certain areas a density of 3–5 pairs per 100 km².

Population trends
In the last 50 years intensive cultivation of the steppe has considerably reduced the distribution range. In the first half of the present century the Steppe Eagle still bred in Moldavia but this area has now been completely forsaken (last breeding record 1958), and so has most of the Ukraine.

In the western part of the distribution range there has been a steady decrease as a result of cultivation. In addition, many Steppe Eagles are said to die in electric cables as a result of short circuits.

Habitat
In the breeding season this species lives typically in the open, flat steppes, but is also found in open hilly country, to a certain extent in mountains and in semi-deserts. The eastern race is more a mountain bird. The winter is also spent in open terrain, which is mostly savanna-like.

Migration
The western race is a long-distance migrant with winter quarters mainly in Africa. The birds overwinter in northern Africa and Arabia, and in small numbers in the Middle East. The young birds are mainly found in East Africa, and south to Zambia, Malawi and Zimbabwe.

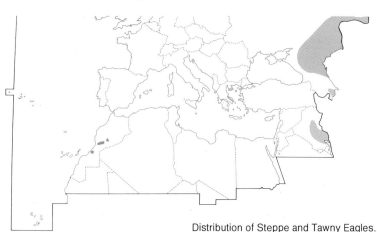

Distribution of Steppe and Tawny Eagles.

Steppe Eagle – adult. *Photo B. Génsbøl/Biofoto.*

In late August to early October the breeding places are left in a broad front migration through Turkey, Armenia, Azerbaijan, the Middle East, northern Iran and Afghanistan, which continues into early November.

The spring migration is more concentrated in the Middle East in the period mid-February to late April, with a maximum for old birds in late February to early March and for the young in late March to early April. The numbers at Eilat in Israel have reached the imposing maximum of around 29,000 (1977).

Young birds wander far from the breeding places, and are seen in many European countries. These include Scandinavia where Norway has two records (1986), Sweden fourteen (1987) and Denmark four (1987), in the period early March to late October. Some of these are probably birds escaped from captivity, but it is not easy to know how many. In the wild the species is often surprisingly trusting.

Breeding

Not known in detail, nor is the age at which the birds first breed. The adult plumage is fully acquired at an age of six years.

The birds arrive, often in pairs, at the breeding sites from mid-March. The size of the territory varies considerably according to the actual food supply, e.g. numbers of sousliks. In good years nests are found at a distance of as little as 300 m from each other.

In undisturbed areas nests are found on hillocks in the terrain, but with increasing cultivation and persecution often on haystacks or in trees. Both sexes take part in nest-building. The clutch of 2 (1–3) eggs is laid in mid-April to early May and is apparently incubated by the female alone for about 65 days. The chicks are fledged roughly 60 days later.

In good years 2–3 young per pair may be reared successfully. On the other hand, nests placed on the ground suffer big losses due, for instance, to predators. Thus, in one year only 3 pairs out of 21 bred successfully.

Food

A very typical food specialist among the *Aquila* species. In the breeding grounds the birds live largely on sousliks (up to 100 per cent has been recorded). Secondarily they take leverets, various small rodents, young birds (from quail to great bustard), snakes, lizards and insects. Carrion is taken throughout the year.

In its winter quarters the Steppe Eagle mostly takes carrion, various small rodents, snakes, lizards and insects, including many termites. It also steals prey from other raptors.

Foraging methods

Mainly hunts from a low perch, striking prey after a short chase. May also circle and stoop. Occasionally it is seen to hunt on foot.

Steppe Eagle, immature. *Photo B. Génsbøl/Biofoto.*

Steppe Eagle, immature. *Photo M. Müller & H. Wohlmuth.*

Tawny Eagle

Aquila rapax

Often regarded as a race of the Steppe Eagle.

Distribution

As shown on the map on p. 190, this form only occurs in the Western Palearctic as the race *A.r. belisarius* in north-west Africa. In addition to south-west Arabia it breeds over large areas of Africa south to about the equator, where it is replaced by the nominate race. It also occurs in northern India and Burma as the race *A.r. vindhiana*.

Population trends

As indicated in the information from various countries (*see* table on p. 194), the Tawny Eagle has become much reduced in numbers. The reason is not known.

Habitat and migration

Mountains and wooded savanna. Non-migratory.

Breeding

Apparently in most respects as for the Steppe Eagle. However, the adult plumage is acquired at an age of four years, so pair formation probably occurs somewhat earlier. In North Africa the eggs are laid from mid- to late March.

Food

In principle the same as for the Steppe Eagle, but more varied.

193

Tawny Eagle population in the Western Palearctic

Tunisia	exterminated? (1979)[1]	Bred in the last century and may still occur in the southern part of the country.
Algeria	exterminated? (1982)[19]	Common in the last century, but considerable decrease since then. Only a single breeding record in recent times.
Morocco	10–100 pairs (1982)[19]	Probably breeds in the areas shown on the map. Threatened (1982)[19].

Tawny Eagle, pale form. *Photo J. Wightman/Ardea.*

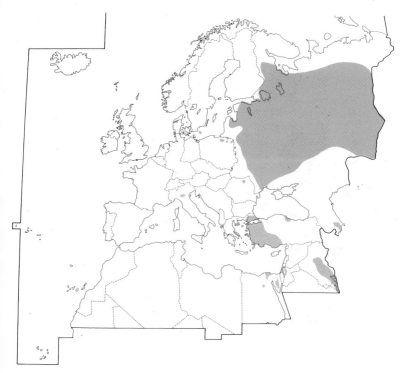

Spotted Eagle
Aquila clanga

Distribution
In addition to its range in the Western Palearctic (*see* map) this species also breeds in a wide belt eastwards through the forest zone to the Pacific Ocean.

Population trends
There is little data available (*see* table on p. 198). In former times the decrease in population was doubtless due to shooting, and today it may be due to a reduction in suitable habitats.

There have been reports on breeding from Norrbotten in Sweden (1973 and 1974), from southern Finland (up to the 1940s), Czechoslovakia (1877, 1945–50?, 1956?), Hungary (1949–51), Yugoslavia (1905 and 1954) and Israel (up to about 1960). It is, however, doubtful whether these represent a former larger distribution. They are more likely to have been the results of chance incursions. Furthermore, it is not always possible to be certain that the identifications have been correct.

Migration
This is a migratory species with few, if any, of the birds wintering within the breeding range. The situation is confused by problems of identification, but it is clear that the autumn movement takes place in September and October and that breeding birds

Spotted Eagle – juv. *Photo B. Génsbøl/Biofoto.*

are back by March or April. No notable concentrations have been reported at the major migration stations (annual maximum for any site less than 30) and so broad front movement is likely. Wintering birds reach East Africa as far south as Kenya but small numbers are also found in the Balkans, the Po Valley (Italy) and even southern France.

Spotted Eagles are regularly recorded in Sweden (232 records up to and including 1982) and are almost annual in Denmark and the Netherlands. The Swedish records are mostly from the autumn and in the south-eastern areas, Danish birds were seen during migration and the Dutch ones were mostly wintering. However the number of records in western areas has decreased this century and the last record for Britain was more than 50 years ago.

Habitat
For breeding the species prefers large forests, especially where these are interspersed with lakes, meadows and heathland. However, it also occurs in small groups of trees and may even breed in free-standing trees. At all times of the year it is much-associated with watery areas.

Voice
Very vociferous especially where several birds are living together. Both flying and sitting birds produce a high-pitched, very melodious screech at intervals of half a second: *dip-dip-dip-dip*.

Breeding
Not known in detail. Probably breeds for the first time when the adult plumage is fully complete, at an age of four years.

Shortly after their arrival, which in Poland and the Baltic takes place between 22 March and 28 April, the birds are seen in a display flight over the territory. This is in the form usual for raptors with impressive stooping and with much use of the voice.

The nest is built in trees, mainly at a height of 8–12 m, with a preference for fir, oak, alder and willow. The clutch of 2 (1–3) eggs is normally laid in early May. Incubation, by the female only, starts with the first egg, so the chicks hatch at slightly different times. The period of incubation is 42–44 days, followed by 60–65 days for fledging and a further 20–30 days of dependence upon the parents.

The smallest chick often dies, but it is not uncommon for two to be reared successfully. In this species it is less common for the larger chick to peck the smaller to death.

A Russian investigation of 43 clutches (1938–51) showed that those begun early produced an average of 0.67 fledged young per clutch. This is in keeping with the production of young in the Lesser Spotted Eagle.

Food

Varied, depending upon what is available locally. In years with numerous small rodents these form the principal prey, in others it may be birds. Supplementary food sources include reptiles, amphibians, fish, insects and carrion.

A Russian investigation of 357 remains of prey showed 58 per cent mammals with field voles (34 per cent), sousliks (8 per cent), moles (5 per cent), bank voles (4 per cent), and water voles (3 per cent). Birds accounted for 35 per cent of prey taken, of which 16 per cent were young rooks, the remainder the young of herons, Black Kites, rollers and turtle doves. In addition, reptiles made up 4 per cent of prey, carrion 3 per cent and amphibians and fish under one per cent.

Other investigations established that water voles may form a basic food and that reptiles, mostly smaller snakes, may account for 24 per cent.

Spotted Eagle, juv. *Photo B. Génsbøl/Biofoto.*

Spotted Eagle

The Spotted Eagle may be a considerable raider of nests in bird colonies; for instance, rooks, herons and the black-headed gull. Thus, around 70 per cent of the bird prey consisted of unfledged individuals.

Smaller amounts were taken of game such as various ducks, grouse, quail, corncrakes and hares, but not to an extent likely to worry sportsmen.

Foraging methods

Like the Lesser Spotted Eagle this species has three forms of hunting: soaring at moderate height (30-50m), sorties from a tree or stake, and wandering on the ground.

It also hunts near open water, and although it does not appear particularly agile is quite capable of catching adult coots on the water.

Spotted Eagle population in the Western Palearctic

Poland		15-30 pairs (1984)[30]	Decreasing (?) due to destruction of breeding habitats.
Finand		2? pairs (1985)[10]	
USSR	*Estonia*	approx. 12 pairs (1976)[11]	
	Latvia	approx. 10 pairs (1983)[34]	
	Lithuania	rare (1975)[35]	
	Central Russia	1000-1500 pairs (1974)[3]	In an area of 270,000sq.km
Romania		5 pairs (1981)[2]	
Yugoslavia		<5 pairs (1982)[19]	

Spotted Eagle juvenile, pale form. *Photo B. Génsbøl/Biofoto*

Lesser Spotted Eagle

Aquila pomarina

Distribution

Apart from a small area on the south side of the Caspian Sea the whole distribution of the nominate race is shown on the map. In addition, the Lesser Spotted Eagle breeds in India and Burma as the race *A.p. hastata*. This is very similar to the nominate race but the young birds lack the characteristic white markings on the upperside of the wings.

Population estimates

The table on p. 203 shows a population figure of around 1300 pairs for most of the European sites, but it is not possible to give an estimate for the total population in the Western Palearctic. This is mainly because there are no figures for most of the Soviet part of the distribution range. Evidently the population passes through the Middle East during migration. Here in the autumn of 1983 roughly 141,000 birds of this species were counted at Tel Aviv. If half of these are young birds the remainder suggest a total Western Palearctic population of the order of 30,000–35,000 pairs. It is therefore very likely that the number of breeding pairs in some of the countries involved has been much under-estimated. Furthermore, the Soviet population is very dense and the distribution may cover a greater area than known.

The under-estimate in many countries is perhaps associated with the fact that, during the breeding season, the Lesser Spotted Eagle leads a very secluded existence.

Population trends

During the 1800s and the beginning of the 1900s the species suffered severe persecution from shooting, egg-collecting and so on, which resulted in a serious reduction in the population. In addition, the outposts in north-west Germany and Austria were forsaken.

Today the situation is much stabilized and the populations appear to be good and healthy. In general, the Lesser Spotted Eagle, like the Buzzard, seems to have become adapted to cultivated areas. Some pessimists fear that destruction of ideal habitats may have a negative influence on the size of the population.

In certain areas, however, the population appears to have a surplus, leading to slow expansion, including a spread westwards into East Germany.

Migration

The Lesser Spotted Eagle is a long-distance migrant wintering in the East African savanna from Sudan to Transvaal. Some have been reported from further west (Chad and Cameroon) and a few may remain in the Balkans, Asia Minor or Egypt. The autumn movement starts in August and extends through to mid-October in Europe. As a soaring migrant the birds are heavily concentrated at short water crossings and the autumn total over the Bosporus, far and away the most important site, may reach 19,000 in a year (1971). Many fewer pass east of the Black Sea (736 birds in 1976).

The return passage reaches Suez, Israel and Lebanon in March and April but this species is definitely not one of the Eilat 'specials'. Spring counts at the Bosporus indicate peak passage in April but numbers are far fewer than in autumn. A small passage between Cap Bon (Tunisia) and Sicily has also been recorded with about 70 seen in the first half of May 1975. Western European vagrants have been reported from the Low Countries, France, Spain and Portugal but not from Britain. Records from Sweden and Denmark are quite regular, most seem to be birds over-shooting the breeding range in the spring.

Habitat

Breeds either in the inner parts of forests with marshes, meadows and large clearings or on the edge of smaller forests with damp areas in the vicinity, sometimes nesting in damp alder woodland. In the Caucasus and Balkans the species also breeds in dry mountain forests up to 1800 m or even 2200 m. When foraging the species usually uses the territory's wet areas, but is also often seen in grassland. Overwinters on savanna.

Voice

Used more than is usual for raptors. The call most often heard is very similar to that of the Spotted Eagle but with a somewhat higher pitch: a melodious, rhythmical *dip-dip-dip*.

Breeding

It is believed that the species normally breeds for the first time when the adult plumage is acquired, at an age of four years. The pair is very tied to the territory and the birds appear to remain together for many years.

Lesser Spotted Eagle young almost ready to fly. *Photo B-U. Meyburg.*

Spotted Eagle – adult in a faded plumage, when it is easy to confuse with Lesser Spotted Eagle. *Photo B. Génsbøl/Biofoto.*

Arrival at the breeding grounds in Poland and the Baltic is on 6–27 April, in East Germany 10–15 April. The courtship display is seen immediately after this. Using his voice sedulously, the male circles round and then falls in an impressive stoop.

The nest, placed in a tree, often high up (average 15 m), is built by both sexes. In Poland and East Germany the 2 (1–3) eggs are laid in late April to early May and incubated by the female only for 38–41 days per egg. Young are fledged after 51–58 days and independent after a further 20–30 days.

The situation regarding clutch size is worth noting. Two eggs is by far the commonest (83 per cent) and two chicks hatch in 75 per cent of the nests. But never more than one chick is reared successfully.

The reason is that up to the age of six weeks the chicks are very aggressive towards anything that moves in the close vicinity. This leads to the larger chick incessantly attacking the smaller which therefore does not survive. So the production of young is low in relation to the clutch size – in Slovakia 0.76 (from a sample of 17) and in the Soviet Union 0.6 (from a sample of 35). This is, however, sufficient to maintain the population.

In some localities, to encourage the population, the smallest chick has on several occasions been removed and reared by man or by another raptor species. At an age of six weeks when the chicks' aggression has disappeared the fostered chick is replaced in the nest and two young become fledged (see page 201).

Food

Varied, mainly depending on what is available locally. Most often small mammals, mainly field voles, common voles, northern voles, water voles and bank voles, secondarily wood mice. Less commonly this species catches mice, various shrews, brown rats, sousliks, hamsters, as well as leverets and rabbits.

The next most important food consists of amphibians, particularly common and field frogs.

Birds are normally a less important part of the food. The Lesser Spotted Eagle takes ground-nesting birds and their chicks: larks, pipits and wagtails. Reptiles are taken in varying numbers, but are normally not an important source of food. The insects caught are mostly beetles and grasshoppers, and, in the winter quarters, termites.

Three separate investigations, two Soviet and one Czech, with respectively 1777, 1362 and 82 prey animals, show variations from place to place. In the three investigations the prey consisted respectively of: mammals 54, 79 and 85 per cent; amphibians 42, 15 and one per cent; birds 4, 6 and 13 per cent. Reptiles were only recorded in the two Soviet investigations, with one per cent in each. Insects were not included in the investigations.

The large difference in the number of amphibians doubtless reflects different degrees of wetness in habitats.

Lesser Spotted Eagle – adult with prey. *Photo B-U. Meyburg.*

Foraging methods

There are three different methods: circling at a height of 30–50 m, hunting from a tree or post and wandering along the ground. The last-named is often used by both species of spotted eagle, which have developed long legs with fewer feathers on the tarsi, particularly in the Lesser Spotted Eagle.

Lesser Spotted Eagle population in the Western Palearctic

East Germany	approx. 80 pairs (1985)[36]	Good stable population. Tendency to move west.
Poland	approx. 80 pairs (1985)[36]	Stable.
USSR *Estonia* *Latvia*	? 50 pairs (1976)[11] 10 pairs (1983)[34]	After big decrease now appears stable.
Czechoslovakia	300 pairs (1988)[43]	Stable.
Hungary	150 pairs (1988)[40]	
Yugoslavia	approx. 40 pairs (1982)[19]	
Romania	40–50 pairs (1977)[42]	Formerly one of Romania's most numerous raptors.
Bulgaria	?	Marked decrease (1971)[1].
Greece	around 70 pairs (1983)[84]	Locally decreasing due to deforestation.
Turkey	30–50 pairs (1982)[19]	
Algeria	1–2 pairs (1982)[19]	

Booted Eagle

Hieraaetus pennatus

Distribution

In addition to the distribution shown on the map the Booted Eagle also breeds to the east in a very narrow belt to Manchuria and, completely isolated, in South Africa. It has no races.

Population estimates

There are no figures for the Soviet population so it is not possible to give an estimate for the whole of the Western Palearctic. For Europe, excluding the Soviet Union, the figures (*see* table on p. 206) suggest a total population of the order of 10,000 pairs with Spain as the dominant country.

Population trends

In general, there has been a considerable decrease in the population during the last two centuries.

Today the species is mainly threatened by changes in habitat, particularly tree-felling, by shooting and, in some areas, poisoning.

The species is not directly endangered but in several countries the populations are so small as to give rise to concern. The ability of the species to survive in an area seems to depend upon the extent to which the habitat has been preserved. It is very selective in its choice of nest sites and does not fit in with modern forestry.

If the species is to survive there must also be respect for the protection laws that have been introduced.

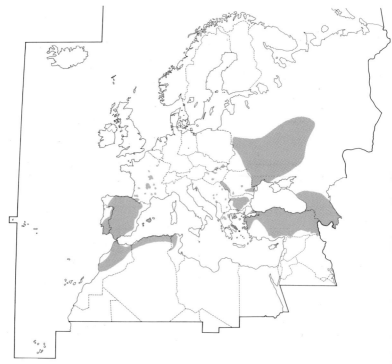

Booted Eagle, dark phase. *Photo W. Wagner.*

Migration

A typical migrant with winter quarters in Africa, mainly in Ethiopia, Sudan, Mali and southwards.

The main migration routes pass through the Caucasus, Bosporus and Gibraltar, with the approximate autumn maximum figures respectively 475 (1976), 525 (1971) and 15,100 in the period late August to early October, with a peak 10–26 September.

The spring migration is seen at the Bosporus and Gibraltar from early March to early May, with a peak between late March and early April.

Within Europe there are some records from outside the breeding range including Sweden, Denmark, Germany, Belgium, Netherlands and Italy. As with other eagles these are

likely to be young, pre-breeding birds and they are mostly seen in the summer or autumn.

Habitat

The preferred habitat is undulating hilly country or mountainous areas where open woodland alternates with thickets and open country. The favourite breeding site is a warm, dry oak wood on a slope. Less commonly it may also breed in coniferous forests.

Breeding

The age at which the Booted Eagle breeds for the first time is not known, nor is the period during which the pair remain together. It is, however, probable that the sexes meet in last

Booted Eagle, pale phase. *Photo P. Petit.*

Booted Eagle. *Photo K. Karel.*

year's territory and resume the partnership.

The display flight is seen immediately after the territory has been occupied. It is of the Buzzard type with impressive dives.

Both sexes take part in building the nest which is placed in a tree at a height of 6–16 m. The 2 (1–3) eggs are laid in mid-April to late May and are incubated, mainly by the female alone, for 36–38 days. The chicks remain in the nest for 50–60 days and are independent after about a further 14 days.

Normally only one chick survives.

Food

Varied, depending upon what the territory offers in the way of reptiles, mostly large lizards; birds, mostly small and medium-sized such as larks, sparrows, starlings, thrushes, doves and poultry; and small mammals, particularly sousliks but also hamsters, rats, moles, stoats and young rabbits. Insects are also caught, normally only as a supplement, but there is a record of them accounting for twenty per cent of the prey. Nests are also plundered, e.g. in heron colonies.

Foraging methods

The Booted Eagle hunts at a great height, stooping to its prey or, like a Kestrel, dropping down from a height of 20–30 m.

Birds are usually taken in hawk fashion, that is when flying low over the ground. Hovering is only rarely seen.

The species may also hunt from a perch, for instance in a forest clearing, and it sometimes wanders about on the ground in search of insects.

In the winter quarters it has been seen to hunt flying termites.

Booted Eagle population in the Western Palearctic

Spain	around 9000 pairs (1982)[19]	Stable or perhaps slightly increasing.
Portugal	130–150 (1982)[19]	Stable.
France	max. 239 pairs (1984)[92]	Now probably stable after a decline.
Poland	1–10 pairs (1984)[80]	Probably stable.
USSR	?	Locally said to be decreasing (1977)[1]. Expanding to the north and north-west (1979)[1].
Czechoslovakia	3 pairs (1988)[43]	Immigrated in the 1960s. Decreasing.

Hungary	max. 10 pairs (1988)[40] Immigrated in 1949.	
Yugoslavia	approx. 50 (1982)[19]	
Albania	possibly breeding (1981)[2]	
Greece	roughly 250 pairs (1983)[84]	
Romania	<5 pairs (1977)[42]	As late as 1966[1] the species was reckoned as relatively common.
Bulgaria	few (1971)[1]	
Turkey	100–500 pairs (1982)[19]	
Cyprus	2 pairs (1982)[19]	
Tunisia	>200 pairs (1982)[19]	
Algeria	abundant (1982)[19]	
Morocco	500–1000 pairs (1982)[19]	

Booted Eagle pale phase. *Photo P. Petit.*

Bonelli's Eagle

Hieraaetus fasciatus

Distribution

In addition to the distribution shown on the map, Bonelli's Eagle also breeds eastwards through Iran and India to southern China. An isolated population in Indonesia forms the race *H.f. renschi*.

There is some disagreement about the status of this bird in Africa south of the equator. Some regard the birds as a separate species *H. spilogaster*, others as a race of the present species, *H.f. spilogaster*.

Population estimates

An estimate of the total population cannot be given as too many areas have not been fully investigated. In Europe, however, there appear to be around 775–900 pairs (*see* table on p. 210), with Spain the dominant area.

Population trends

For decades Bonelli's Eagle has been much persecuted and this has led to a drastic reduction in the population. As the table shows the trend is still negative throughout most of the area.

The species is protected in the whole of the European breeding range but apparently this is not very effective.

In addition to illegal shooting the reduction in population has been due to nest raiding (collection of eggs and chicks), disturbance by tourists, possibly to poisoning and to food shortages caused by myxomatosis in the rabbit population.

Although Bonelli's Eagle is evidently not threatened with extinction in Europe the general situation gives cause for anxiety. Apart from Spain the populations in almost all the other countries are disturbingly low.

Migration

Essentially a non-migrant, the adults remaining near the nesting area throughout the year. Young birds disperse and there are frequent records 50 km or more from the nearest breeding sites in southern France and in Spain. There are a very few records of birds crossing the Mediterranean at Gibraltar. Vagrants have been recorded north to Belgium, Holland, Germany, Denmark and Finland, but none have been found in Britain.

Habitat

Within the Western Palearctic this bird is associated with the transition zone between subtropical desert and more rainy temperate country with maquis as the characteristic vegetation. Within this habitat the species lives mainly in open mountainous regions and for breeding requires a steep cliff face.

It hunts mainly in areas with bushes or along the edges of cultivated land.

Outside the breeding season Bonelli's Eagle prefers wet areas, such as river estuaries, marshland and small lakes.

Breeding

The age at which this species breeds for the first time is not known but the birds have a full adult plumage when 3–4 years old. Pair formation is apparently for life.

Preparations for breeding start early, so nest-building may take place in November–December. Display flights are seen at the same time. As in the Buzzard these involve repeated dives.

The 2 (1–3) eggs are normally laid in mid-February to early March and are incubated, mainly by the female, for 37–40 days.

Although a clutch of two is by far the commonest only one third of the breeding attempts produce two fledged young.

Bonelli's Eagle female shading chicks. *Photo J. Robert/Jacana.*

Food

Primarily medium-sized mammals and birds, secondarily reptiles (lizards). In south-west Europe the principal prey consists of rabbits, jackdaws and red-legged partridge. Mammals taken also include hares, rats and desert rats; birds mainly doves, herons, gulls, waders, ducks, moorhens, larks and also other raptors. Birds are caught mainly in August–April (80 per cent of the prey), mammals in May–July, the period when the rabbit population reaches its peak.

Foraging methods

A rapid and dexterous hunter. It mostly catches birds as they fly up, but like a hawk it can also chase them over long distances, even through bushes and trees. It often flies the same route every day.

It may also hunt from a perch and exceptionally has been seen wandering about on the ground searching for prey.

Bonelli's Eagle population in the Western Palearctic

Spain	611–699 pairs (1987)[98]	Decreasing, often killed illegally.
Portugal	30–40 pairs (1982)[19]	Violent decreasing – reason unknown.

Bonelli's Eagle juvenile taking off from a branch. *Photo B. Gensbøl/Biofoto.*

Adult Bonelli's Eagle. *Photo R. Nardi.*

France	50 pairs (1982)[19]	Reduced 70–75 per cent since the 1930s. Stable in some years in spite of illegal shooting. Now violent decrease in Southern France. Reason unknown.

Italy
    Mainland
    Sicily
    Sardinia
	15–30 pairs (1982)[19]
	very rare (1981)[2]
	approx. 10 pairs (1981)[2]
	10–20 pairs (1981)[2]
		Apparently still in decline, is protected but illegal shooting still continues.

Greece	roughly 60 pairs (1983)[84]	Largest population in Crete and the larger Aegean islands.
Albania	?	No recent information.
Turkey	50 pairs (1982)[19]	
Cyprus	10 pairs (1985)[5]	Decrease from about 50 pairs in 1950s.
Israel	19–20 (1982)[19]	Extermination close, due to poisoning with thallium sulphate (1–2 pairs in 1971). Thereafter re-establishing.
Tunisia	40–50 pairs (1982)[19]	Formerly common. Apparently in decline.
Algeria	frequent (1982)[19]	
Morocco	500–1000 pairs (1982)[19]	

Osprey

Pandion haliaetus

Distribution

The Osprey is one of the cosmopolitan raptors. It breeds in North and Central America, North and East Europe, in some Mediterranean countries, in large parts of Asia east to the Pacific Ocean, sporadically in Africa, and along the coasts of most of Australia and of many of the islands to the north.

As is usual with a species covering such a large area the Osprey has evolved a number of races. The nominate form *P.h. haliaetus* covers the largest area, namely Europe, Africa, breeding grounds on the Asiatic mainland and islands in the Pacific southwards to and including Taiwan. The Philippines, Indonesia and further east to New Caledonia, extending to northern Australia, have *P.h. melvillensis*. This race is replaced in the rest of Australia and in Tasmania by *P.h. cristatus*. The largest

part of the North American mainland is covered by *P.h. carolinensis*, while birds on the Bahamas, Cuba and the Yucatan Peninsula belong to the race *P.h. ridgwayi*.

Population estimates

The available information (table on p. 222) shows a total population for the Western Palearctic of around 5500 pairs, Fenno-Scandia having a dominant position.

Population trends

As late as the nineteenth century the Osprey was a common breeding bird in most of Europe. The species lives very openly and is therefore vulnerable to persecution. When the great anti-raptor campaign began the result was a rapid decrease in the populations of this species with extermination in many countries: Great Britain (1910), Ireland (start of the 1800s), Switzerland (1911), West Germany (end of 1800s), Italy (1956), Austria (1930s), Czechoslovakia (mid-1800s), Hungary (end of 1800s), Greece (1966), Yugoslavia (1950s), Romania (1960s), and Denmark (1916). Some countries have subsequently attempted breeding and a fresh colonization has taken place in Scotland.

Today the Osprey breeds in northern, eastern and central Europe, in Scotland, the western part of the Mediterranean area, the Middle East and island groups in the Atlantic Ocean. The densest populations are in Sweden and Finland, with a total of about 3000 breeding pairs which represents approximately 60 per cent of the area's breeding population.

The table on p. 222 also shows that successful breeding varies from area to area.

The Mediterranean population is

Osprey – adult. *Photo M. W. Grosnick/Ardea.*

close to extinction, the central European population continues to decrease and so does the Soviet. On the other hand, the position is slowly improving in northern Europe.

This last point is very important. The fact that this population thrives well here suggests the possibility of expansion to other areas, assuming an overproduction of young, to places where the species is lacking or doing less well. The success of the majority of European pairs is to be welcomed but it should not lead to a relaxation of efforts allowing this development to continue. The considerable increase in leisure time around inland lakes also disturbed the birds. Experience in the United States has shown that

213

the species is more sensitive to poisoning of the environment than most raptors.

Migration
European-breeding Ospreys almost all winter in Africa south of the Sahara. A few remain in the Mediterranean and North Africa, but these may include the small local breeding population.

Migrating Ospreys are capable of sustained flapping flight and show none of the concentration exhibited by soaring species at such sites as the Bosporus. The birds are equally capable of traversing seas as deserts, and passage takes place across the full breadth of the Mediterranean. Autumn passage starts from mid-August and most leave Europe in September or October.

Most western European birds winter in Africa between the Sahara and the Equator and the population travelling further south most probably comes from the Soviet Union. The few recoveries so far reported of Scottish birds are from the west coast of Africa; Norwegian and Swedish birds mainly from north of the Gulf of Guinea, and Finnish birds from there across to Eritrea. Thus the overall direction of movement of British, Swedish and Norwegian birds is south-south-west, but Finnish birds move rather more southwards. Many young birds remain over their first summer in Africa, few penetrating further north than the Mediterranean. Adults start the return journey at the beginning of March and most reach their breeding areas by the end of April. Second-year birds move much later and then wander around the breeding grounds, since they would certainly not have time left to settle and breed that year.

Both on passage and during the winter, as during the summer, Ospreys need to have access to areas of water to feed. Within southern Europe, lakes, reservoirs, rivers and ponds are regularly visited on passage and many ringing recoveries are reported from birds shot by fishermen. In Italy there is hardly a suitable site from which a ringing recovery of a Swedish or Finnish bird has not been reported. Within Africa the wintering areas may vary from year to year, dependent upon the extent of the autumn rains.

Within Britain the Osprey remained a regular passage migrant even when the breeding population was extinct. It rebuilt from the settlement of such passage birds, and there have since been more than a dozen recoveries of birds ringed in Sweden and one from Finland. As the Scottish population has built up, sightings of passage birds have become more and more frequent in southern Britain. There are many reservoirs, even within suburban areas, where passage Ospreys are regularly seen, particularly in the autumn.

Habitat
Being so specialized as regards diet the Osprey requires that its breeding site should have a plentiful supply of medium-sized fish which live close to the surface in clear, unpolluted water. Whether this is fresh, brackish or salt is not so important.

In the northern part of the Palearctic region the species mainly lives during the breeding season near to lakes surrounded by woodland and quiet rivers. To a certain extent it is also seen in coastal areas with skirting

Osprey – adult. *Photo B. G. Backström.*

forest, shallow water and moderate winds, where the birds can find their prey. In the Mediterranean the birds are tied exclusively to the sea. During migration Ospreys may also frequent small areas of water rich in fish. In winter they normally live close to the coasts and large rivers in Africa.

Voice

Heard almost exclusively during the breeding season, when performing the display flight, when disturbed at the nest and to keep in touch with its mate. The calls are very varied but are usually whistling and whining screeches produced rhythmically, either slowly or rapidly.

Breeding

Ospreys breed for the first time at an age of 3–5 years. The birds are very faithful to their chosen territory, which leads to the pairs remaining together for life.

On the day of his arrival in the territory the male starts a display flight, partly to indicate that the nest site is occupied, partly to attract the female's attention. The female usually arrives later than the male.

The male starts his display by reaching a considerable height, often over 300 m. This is followed by some fluttering wing beats, with the body for a moment brought to an almost vertical position with the head up. The bird then tips over and dives for about 10 m, flutters up to the previous height, again taking up the vertical position, tips over and dives and so

Osprey pair at nest. *Photo D. England/Ardea.*

Ospreys mating. *Photo Sailler/Jacana.*

on. In a variant of this performance the bird does not regain height after diving, but gradually drops down and finally lands on the nest. During the ceremony he screeches the whole time, a penetrating *pyeb-pyeb-pyeb*, rapidly repeated with 15–18 screeches per ten seconds.

The nest is normally placed at the top of a tree, more rarely on the side branches; the tree is usually a fir, but others may be used. Both sexes take part in building the nest. Before egg-laying the male is the more assiduous in bringing nest material, but it is mainly the female that builds. As is common in raptors, Ospreys continue to add material to the nest throughout the breeding period, but after the start of incubation it is mainly the female that performs this task.

In northern, eastern and central Europe, Ospreys almost always build in trees, sometimes also on electric pylons. In southern Europe, however, it is common for the nest to be placed on a cliff up to 130 m above the sea. Nests in trees are normally at a height of 11–30 m, and in marshy areas in Scandinavia often only 3–10 m high. Nests on the ground are known, for instance, on islands in the Red Sea. In recent years artificial nest sites for Ospreys have been created by building platforms in trees or on stages in lakes. This is done when there are no suitable trees un an otherwise excellent habitat.

Once a nest has been built it is used year after year and is only deserted after repeated disturbance.

The clutch consists of 3 (1-4) eggs. In central Europe egg-laying starts in mid-April, in the north in late April to early May. In the Mediterranean area it takes place in mid-March and in the Red Sea as early as December.

The individual eggs are normally laid at two-day intervals.

Incubation is mainly by the female. The male only relieves her when she has to tear apart the prey he brings home. The eggs are incubated for 37-41 days, most often 38.

The male is responsible for feeding the family right up until the chicks are fledged.

The food is normally brought directly to the nest and divided into bits for the young until they are 5-6 weeks old.

The young are fledged at an age of 7-8 weeks, but the family remains around the nest site for quite a time. Two months after fledging a young bird has been seen to be fed at the nest. During this period the young emit a high begging screech, with 30-40 calls of klee-klee-klee.

During recent years there has been a Swedish investigation of the production of young. In the years 1971-73 they were, on average, 1.48 young from every clutch started and 2.01 for each successful clutch. As already mentioned the Swedish population is apparently doing well. The production figures are, therefore, sufficiently large, in spite of disturbances. In recent years the pressure from shooting has been much reduced, the spe-cies now being protected almost everywhere. The use of several poisons has also been forbidden and this has produced a better situation than in the 1950s and 1960s.

Food

This well-adapted raptor feeds primarily on fish, but when prevented from doing so by ice, rain, fog or cloudy water it will turn to other food such as small mammals, mainly small rodents, birds, reptiles, amphibians, crustaceans or beetles.

The actual fish species taken is dependent upon what is easily available. When an individual fish species is abundant in the area it will be caught as prey.

An investigation of the prey at five nests in Mecklenburg showed the following: pike 40 per cent of total, roach 20 per cent, common bream 12 per cent, perch 11 per cent, silverbream 4 per cent, and crucian carp 3 per cent. The remaining 10 per cent of the total 386 fish were divided among 13 species.

The daily consumption of food has been estimated on the basis of how often the male brought prey to the female. During the breeding season this happened on average 1.7–1.8 times per day. For a clutch with two chicks this happened 3.6 times per day and for three chicks 4.6 times. During the rearing period each individual received 800–830g of fish per day. Adult birds on migration seem to catch approximately two fish per day, and require a total of about 500g of fish.

An investigation of 496 food sources showed that these fish measured 7–57cm, with the small ones by far the commonest. Of 271 prey fish, 75 per cent weighed up to 200g, 17 per cent from 201–500g, 7 per cent a

Osprey – adult tearing prey. *Photo A. Christiansen/Biofoto.*

good 500 g, while the remaining one per cent consisted of one fish weighing 700 g, two at 1000 g, and one at 1500 g.

Foraging methods

Ospreys normally search for prey by hovering at a height of 20–30 m. When prey is seen the bird dives with half-folded wings. Just before it reaches the water it stretches the talons forwards and strikes the water in a splash, sometimes almost disappearing beneath the surface. The catch is carried away in the talons, most often head forward, and usually to a favourite feeding place in a tree. During migration such a place is selected when the bird halts for a while in a particular location. If the fish is too large for the bird to manage it is normally dropped. There have been confirmed cases where an Osprey has drowned because the claws have become embedded in the scales or bones of the fish.

Young birds start to fish as soon as they are fledged, but they sometimes fail because they lack experience. The same applies to the old birds when waves prevent them from accurately assessing the position of the fish. On such days, therefore, they fish mainly in quiet bays and inlets.

Pp. 220–21: Examples of Osprey fishing technique. Not the same individual in every picture. *Photo J. B. Olsen.*

Osprey population in the Western Palearctic

Norway	27 pairs (1974)[1]	Stable.
Sweden	approx. 2000 pairs (1981)[9]	Stable or slowly increasing. Locally there are reports of decrease, probably due to disturbance at the breeding sites.
Finland	1000 pairs (1986)[79]	After decline stable the last 20 years.
Denmark	4–6 pairs (1986)	Increasing.
East Germany	120 pairs (1985)[37]	Stable.
Poland	30–40 pairs (1984)[80]	Little breeding success, apparently due to scarcity of suitable nesting trees. However, apparently stable.
USSR	about 2000 pairs (1983)[6]	Decreasing. Lack of nesting trees. Artificial platforms tried.
Estonia	about 20 pairs (1976)[11]	
Latvia	about 30 pairs (1983)[34]	
Lithuania	about 20 pairs (1971)[12]	
Britain	43 pairs (1986)[45]	500–1000 pairs in last century. Exterminated 1910, but in 1954 a pair appeared in Scotland. With colossal public interest the population has slowly increased. Only in the Scottish Highlands.
Spain	10–15 pairs (1982)[19]	Marked decrease. No longer breeds on the mainland.
Portugal	2 pairs (1987)[45]	Close to extermination, due to persecution and poisoning of the environment.
France	13 pairs (1985)[96]	Threatened for many years. Now only breeds in Corsica – and one pair on mainland.
Turkey	1–5 pairs (1982)[19]	
Cyprus	10 pairs (1982)[19]	
Algeria	10–15 pairs (1983)[85]	
Morocco	>18 pairs (1983)[85]	
Canary Islands	8–10 pairs (1976)[1]	
Cape Verde Islands	about 50 pairs (1969)[1]	Almost extinct due to persecution (1984)[92]. Seen on almost all islands (1982)[97].
Egypt	150–250 pairs (1982)[19]	Of which 45 pairs in Sinai. Population threatened. The Raptor Congress in Thessaloniki in 1982 invited the government to protect the most important colony.

Gyrfalcon
Falco rusticolus

Distribution

As shown on the map this species is tied to the most northerly parts of the Western Palearctic. The distribution is circumpolar.

There is considerable difference of opinion as regards races. Some maintain that the range of colour types is too wide for a division into races to be established, others that there is sufficient uniformity locally for this to be reasonable. G. Dementiev suggests six races: the nominate race, Fenno-Scandia and eastwards to the Kanin Peninsula, a dark phase that is the smallest in the species; *F.r. intermedius*, further east to the Yenisei area, slightly larger and paler, mainly a grey phase but some are white; *F.r. grebnitzkii*, eastwards to the Bering Sea, also a little larger and again with grey and white phases; *F.r. obsoletus* (Labrador Falcon), southern part of the North American range and southern Greenland, a dark phase, the darkest of all with a grey phase; *F.r. candicans* (Greenland Falcon), a white phase north of *obsoletus*; *F.r. islandus*, a grey phase.

Population estimates

Not easy to record for it lives too secretly. During recent years basic investigations have suggested that the species is not as scarce as was thought. In Norway in the middle

223

1970s the total population was estimated at 10–12 pairs, but it is now 200–500. In Sweden and Iceland the figures have been adjusted upwards by about 100 per cent.

According to the latest estimates the total number of breeding pairs in the Western Palearctic, excluding the Soviet Union, is 600–1000 (*see* table on p. 227).

Population trends

The species appears to have declined earlier than other raptors, probably as a result of the high frequency of nest-raiding. For hundreds of years the Gyrfalcon has been the most prized bird for falconry.

In the present century the southern distribution limit appears to have retreated northwards, surely because of a climatic change and also as a result of persecution.

In spite of continuous nest-raiding the different populations appear today to be stable. Environmental poisoning does not seem to affect this stationary species that lives in remote areas.

Migration

The Western Palearctic populations of Gyrfalcons are basically sedentary, although some wandering does occur. Further to the east Russian birds move southwards more frequently and to a greater extent: this is indicated by the broadening of the winter range shown on the map. There is no evidence that Icelandic birds leave the country, however, Greenland birds may travel southwards and regularly reach Iceland in some numbers. It is birds from this population that are

Gyrfalcon juv., Greenlandic grey phase. (Identical with Icelandic.) *Photo F. Wille/Leica.*

Gyrfalcon – adult, white phase (Greenland). *Photo W. Wille/Leica.*

just about annual visitors (in very small numbers) to Britain and Ireland – they are very much more frequent in the west than the east. White Greenland birds have been recorded as far south as Portugal, Spain and Northern Italy.

On the Continent the birds which do move south are mostly youngsters, and movement is more pronounced in years with poor populations of northern gamebirds. Away from the mountains one or two are seen annually in southern Sweden. The species is now recorded every year in Denmark. Vagrants which have reached France, Switzerland and Austria may have come from the more mobile Russian stock. The species is much prized by falconers and some records far from the normal range could be of escaped individuals.

Habitat

Prefers open arctic country with sufficient food and breeding sites.

There are three main types of habitat: 1) tundra, where this is interspersed by rivers with slopes or cliff faces, 2) rocky coasts especially near large seabird colonies, 3) mountain regions beyond the tree limit, with steep cliffs.

Migrating and dispersing birds like to move out to coasts or to marshland, steppes or cultivated land.

Voice

Heard, perhaps exclusively on the breeding grounds, usually as a hoarse, sonorous, very deep and rhythmically repeated *krery-krery-krery.*

Juvenile Scandinavian Gyrfalcon. *Photo P. J. Tömmeraas.*

Breeding

Probably first breeds at 2 years.

The male starts active defence of the territory as early as January or the beginning of February, and if she has not overwintered there the female arrives mid-February to early March.

Display flights are seen at the start of the breeding season. The birds rise up to a great height and dive down towards the nest, screeching loudly.

The nest is placed on an inaccessible cliff face with a sheltering overhang, in forest tundra also in trees, sometimes in the old nest of a Rough-legged Buzzard. The 3–5 (2–7) eggs are laid in early April to mid-May, mainly in mid- to late April, and are incubated mainly by the female for about 35 days. The chicks remain in the nest for 49–56 days and are still dependent upon the parents for at least a further 30 days.

The number of breeding pairs varies according to the food supply, generally depending upon the number of grouse. Thus, in an area in Alaska, three pairs bred in one year, twelve pairs in another. The average number of young per successful pair is around 2.5.

Food

In inland areas the main prey consists of grouse and ptarmigan, accounting for up to 92 per cent by weight. However, local variations occur. In years with numerous rodents, such as lemmings and sousliks, these may also be important.

Several small investigations all confirm the dominance of grouse. One in the Soviet Union (Kola Peninsula) shows considerable variation: 408 birds, 262 mammals, 4 fish, 2 amphibians and 26 insects. Prey was mostly birds, accounting for 91 per cent by weight. Of these, 68 per cent were grouse, 9 per cent gulls, 5 per cent ducks, 3 per cent divers, 3 per cent waders, 2 per cent auks and about one per cent small birds. (The

9 per cent by weight of mammals consisted entirely of small rodents.)

Foraging methods

In general, this is from a well-placed perch where the bird waits for prey to appear. It sweeps low over the territory, using every bit of cover, and tries a surprise attack. If the prey flies up it is normally struck to the ground from a slightly higher position, and then seized in flight.

This species also searches the countryside at a height of 7–20 m. Birds are often caught after a chase, but this may continue over several kilometres. A much used tactic is to hunt birds on the wing. Birds such as owls, skuas and gulls try to rise up above the falcon. When the prey is sufficiently tired the Gyrfalcon reaches them by a rapid ascent.

In winter the bird is often seen hovering over willow scrub, flushing grouse. Two birds often hunt together.

With its slow wing-beats the Gyrfalcon may appear clumsy but this is an optical illusion. In level flight it can catch a Peregrine, and as already mentioned prey is often caught in a direct aerial chase.

Gyrfalcon population in the Western Palearctic

Iceland	approx. 200 pairs (1987)[98]	Decreasing up to about 1930. Now stable but fluctuating in relation to grouse stocks. In spite of protection not increasing, may be due to nest plundering from falcon robbers.
Norway	200–500 pairs (1980)[64]	Apparently stable.
Sweden	100 pairs (1981)[9]	Southern breeding sites deserted. Now apparently stable.
Finland	30 pairs (1985)[10]	Earlier threatened by extinction due to egg-collecting and falcon robbers. Now stable.
USSR	rare (1951)[1]	Apparently decreasing (1977)[1].

Juvenile Scandinavian Gyrfalcon. *Photo P. J. Tömmeraas.*

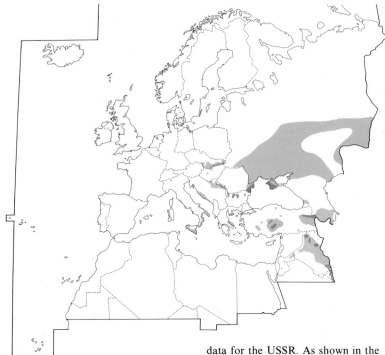

Saker Falcon
Falco cherrug

Distribution
In addition to the Western Palearctic distribution shown on the map, this species breeds eastwards through forest and steppe in large parts of central Asia as far as China.

There are two races, the nominate in the Western Palearctic and *F.c. milvipes* in central Asia, with a rust-red band on the upperparts and a more prominent pattern on the underparts.

Population estimates
This cannot be given for the Western Palearctic as a whole as there are no

data for the USSR. As shown in the table on p. 230 the European population, excluding the Soviet, is 130–170 pairs.

Population trends
In decline because of shooting, collection of young for falconry and possibly environmental poisoning. Many young birds are caught for falconry in the winter quarters in the Middle East.

The species has not, however, suffered the population collapse seen in the Peregrine. This is perhaps because its prey, mainly sousliks, has not suffered from environmental poisoning to the same extent.

Migration
Migratory (Russian birds) and a partial migrant. A few overwinter as

far north as Austria and Czechoslovakia. However, as shown on the distribution map, the true winter quarters are in the Mediterranean area, Caucasus, and the Middle East as well as East Africa.

Russian birds are normally away from the breeding grounds from late September or early October to March and early April, Romanian often only in December and January. Long-distance migration is mainly by young birds.

In the autumn migration small numbers are seen at the Bosporus (maximum 13 in 1971). Spring migration has been recorded at Cape Bon in Tunisia, of the order of 25 birds.

Seen as a rare visitor north of the breeding range, most often in southern Poland, East and West Germany. Scandinavia is also visited, e.g. Halland in Sweden, November 1900.

Habitat

For breeding, the species prefers forest steppe, particularly where forest alternates with fields, meadows, uncultivated areas or reed-beds. It is also found breeding in steppe country or on mountain spurs. For breeding sites there should be a plentiful supply of diurnal small mammals, in Europe represented by sousliks.

Outside the breeding season the species is often seen near rivers, marshes, sea bays and other habitats with plenty of birds.

Voice

May be very noisy at the breeding site. The voice is similar to that of the other large falcons, usually hoarse, rhythmical screeches which may vary in speed, length and tone.

Breeding

Probably breeds for the first time at

Saker Falcon at nest. *Photo A. Limbrunner.*

an age of 2–3 years, but one-year-old birds have been seen at a nest. The pair remain together for much of the year and also long after the young have become independent. The partnership often appears to be life-long.

The display flight is seen at the start of the breeding season. With the wings stiff and the tail spread out, the birds fly up to a great height and dive down towards the nest, screeching loudly.

In the Western Palearctic most pairs nest in trees, usually in old raptor nests, but a few choose steep cliff faces.

In Central Europe the 3–5 (2–6) eggs are laid in mid- or late March to early April and are incubated for around 30 days, mainly by the female. The chicks remain in the nest for 45–50 days and become independent after a further 30–45 days.

Food

Primarily sousliks, but Saker Falcons also take other small mammals, such as desert rats, field voles, moles, lemmings, marmots, hamsters, as well as a few hares, stoats and hedgehogs.

They also catch birds, mainly ground-nesting species, in a broad spectrum from small birds such as larks up to the size of herons and bustards. About 30–50 per cent of bird prey has been recorded during the breeding season, but this is not general. Sousliks are normally completely dominant.

Secondary foods taken include reptiles (lizards), amphibians (frogs) and several insects.

Foraging methods

Most frequently hunts from a perch high up. When prey is sighted the bird attacks from low down, taking the prey by surprise, like a Goshawk.

It may also search the terrain from a height of 10–20 m, in between hovering. Less commonly it sometimes walks on the ground, looking for beetles.

Saker Falcon population in the Western Palearctic

Austria	extinct? (1981)[2]	Has apparently never been numerous. Last known breeding record 1973[66].
Czechoslovakia	c. 25 pairs (1988)[43]	Stable or perhaps slightly decreasing.
Hungary	about 50 pairs (1988)[40]	Nests are strictly watched owing to threats from eggs and young robbers.
Yugoslavia	about 15 pairs (1982)[19]	
Romania	roughly 20 pairs (1981)[2]	Marked decrease.
Bulgaria	30–50 pairs (1977)[1]	
USSR **Moldavia** **Crimea**	rare (1983)[6] about 20 pairs (1983)[6] 5–6 pairs (1983)[6]	Seems to be decreasing in the European part, stable in the Asiatic. More than 1000 pairs estimated for the whole USSR.
Greece	exterminated? (1982)[19]	
Turkey	10–150 pairs (1982)[19]	
Iraq	?	
Cyprus	1 pair (1982)[19]	

Saker Falcon juvenile. *Photo K. Karel.*

Lanner Falcon
Falco biarmicus

Distribution
In addition to the breeding range shown on the map, the Lanner Falcon is distributed throughout large areas of Africa.

There are several races including the following: *F.b. feldegii*, Europe to eastern Turkey; *F.b. erlangeri*, Morocco to Tunisia, the palest and smallest race; *F.b. tanypterus*, Libya to Jordan, slightly larger than *erlangeri* and occasionally darker.

Population estimates
According to the available information (*see* table on p. 234) there are 150–200 pairs in Europe. There is disagreement on the validity of these figures. Pessimists estimate that there are only a few pairs remaining in Europe.

Population trends
A considerable reduction from around 1960. The reasons are not known, but are probably environmental poisoning (comparable to the Peregrine), persecution and nest raiding.

At the moment the species is perhaps Europe's most threatened raptor.

Migration
Non-migratory, although in certain cases the young may wander. Thus, there are seasonal movements from the highlands to the lowlands.

Only a few are seen north of the breeding range, including northern Italy, south-east France, Czechoslovakia, Spain and Portugal.

Habitat
In North Africa the species typically breeds in semi-desert, desert and dry savanna country. In Europe the breeding places are in rocky areas with steep cliffs, thus in Sicily they are usually where cliff faces rise above extensive areas of fields and meadows. Also found nesting on coasts.

Lanner Falcon – adult with chicken. *Photo P. Steyn/Ardea.*

Voice

Very similar to that of the other large falcons. Often rhythmical hoarse screeches varying in speed, length and tone.

Breeding

Not very well known. The age at which the birds breed for the first time has not been investigated.

The pair probably remain together for life and live close together throughout the year.

The nest is usually placed on a cliff face or in a tree. Here the pair may take over an old nest, most often from another raptor or a crow. In Sicily the 3–4 (2) eggs are laid in late February to mid-March, in the Balkans probably somewhat later, and are incubated by both sexes for 32–35 days. The chicks remain in the nest for 44–46 days, and are independent after a further 28–42 days.

Food

Mainly small and medium-sized birds, ranging from larks to mallard. The latter are, however, too large for the bird to fly with.

Normally small mammals, reptiles and insects only form a supplement to the diet, but may take over the main role in areas with few birds.

An investigation in Sicily of 73 prey animals collected at nests gave the following results: jackdaw 23, Lesser Kestrel 12, rock dove 7, skylark 2, rock partridge 2, Kestrel 2, corn bunting 2, Italian sparrow 2, plus several species with one speci-

men each. In addition, there was one rabbit and one rat, at least 3 lizards, one common toad and one carabid beetle.

Foraging methods

Usually tries a surprise attack, flying at low level to catch birds at the moment they fly up. This falcon is not always fast enough to catch flying birds.

The male and female often hunt together in the following way: the female flies along a cliff face using every form of concealment. The male follows at a distance, waiting for the prey to be flushed. When this happens the male strikes.

In desert regions the Lanner Falcon typically hunts bird flocks which visit water-holes to drink.

Lanner Falcon population in the Western Palearctic

Italy	100–150 pairs (1982)[19]	Marked decrease. 20–40 pairs in Sicily.
Yugoslavia	about 20 pairs (1982)[19]	Decreasing.
Albania	?	Has bred in the past. No recent information.
Bulgaria	?	Possibly breeds in south-west.
Greece	30 pairs (1983)[84]	Decreasing considerably.
Turkey	about 20 pairs (1982)[19]	
Cyprus	1 pair (1982)[19]	
Syria	?	Possibly breeding irregularly (1979)[1].
Israel	10–20 pairs (1982)[19]	Exterminated locally due to use of thallium sulphate (1979)[1].
Egypt	10–500 pairs (1982)[19]	
Libya	?	Should be common.
Tunisia	200–250 pairs (1982)[19]	
Algeria	frequent (1982)[19]	
Morocco	>1000 pairs (1982)[19]	

Peregrine Falcon

Falco peregrinus

Distribution

As a form of protection for the species many countries do not provide precise information on its distribution. Thus, the map only shows the distribution in approximate terms. Apart from this region the Peregrine breeds in large parts of Asia, Africa, Australia and America.

There are several races, of which the following are relevant: the nominate race is in most of Europe and eastwards to the Yenisei region; *F.p. calidus* in the tundra areas from the Varanger Peninsula in Norway eastwards to the Lena, is slightly larger, paler and more blue on the upperparts; *F.p. brookei* from the Mediterranean area to the Caucasus is smaller than the nominate race, darker on the underparts and with rust-coloured markings on the nape; *F.p. madens* is in the Cape Verde Islands.

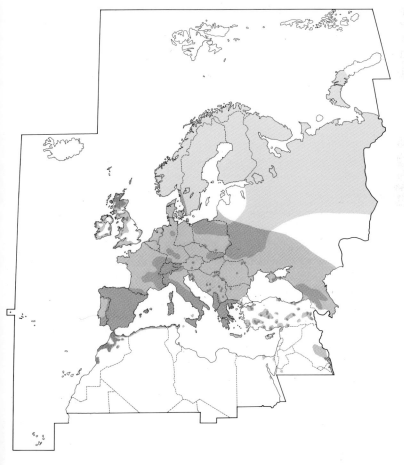

Peregrine Falcon adult female at the nesting cliff. *Photo B. Génsbøl/Biofoto.*

Population estimates

For the Western Palearctic as a whole the figures in the table on p. 240 give a breeding population of the order of 7000 pairs.

The accuracy of the individual figures varies considerably from very exact to rough estimates. In any case the latter is the case for the figures from the Soviet Union, Spain (2) and Morocco (in all 4000 pairs).

Population trends

For two centuries the Peregrine has been subjected to its nests being raided by egg-collectors and falconers and to shooting by sportsmen, pigeon breeders and gamekeepers. According to the energy expended on these activities the species has suffered large or small declines in certain localities. As a species, however, the Peregrine has managed to survive.

From about 1950 the situation had become very serious, largely because of environmental poisoning. In the highly industrialized countries of the northern hemisphere the next two decades witnessed an unusual total collapse of an otherwise vigorous population. The breeding populations were, in some places, reduced by over 90 per cent.

At first the reasons for this were not apparent. At the beginning of the 1960s it was found, particularly by British investigators, that the decline was due to the use of poisons, especially DDT.

In the following years many countries forbade DDT and other environmental poisons, or their use was restricted, and gradually the decline was halted.

As the table shows the species has been re-established in certain of the badly affected countries, such as Great Britain, Ireland, West Germany, Switzerland and Finland.

It is remarkable that in Sweden there was no sign of a real improvement, in spite of a very energetic protection programme and the introduction of captive-bred birds to help the population.

During the period concerned the populations in the Mediterranean countries did not suffer the same fate, evidently because they had a smaller dose of poison. On the other hand, there are now other problems in southern Europe. Shooting continues to be widespread, but the greatest threat seems to be from falcon robbers.

There has been a renaissance of falconry, and large numbers of young Peregrines are stolen today. It is reckoned that from Italy alone at least 200 young are smuggled annually into West Germany. A check on 30 nests in southern Italy and Sicily showed that these only produced two chicks in all. The rest had been taken by falcon robbers.

A population cannot tolerate such a large toll, and as shown in the table the general picture in southern Europe is one of decline.

Migration

Southern European populations are essentially sedentary with some of the younger birds wandering. British and Irish birds are probably more mobile but there is only a single foreign recovery (N. Ireland to Portugal). Central European adults are probably resident but young birds regularly move quite long distances, and 70 per cent of first year recoveries were further than 100 km from the nesting site.

As can be seen from the map, northern populations are wholly migratory. Most Scandinavian birds move south and west with recoveries in Spain, France, Britain and intermediate areas. The crash in population is reflected in the numbers now seen each autumn at Falsterbo – generally less than 10 compared with 110 in 1942.

Further to the east, from Finnmark through into Siberia, the race *F.p. calidus* is a long-distance migrant with some birds wintering in Central Europe and the Mediterranean but others crossing the Sahara. The presence of local breeding African Peregrines obscures this picture, but the much larger migrants have been recorded as far southwards as Cape Province. Most migrants are in the east, but *F.p. calidus* has been recorded as far west as Senegal and Guinea.

Habitat

This is not particularly specialized. There are two principal requirements: a good basic food supply, that is, plenty of birds, and a safe nesting site. In the Western Palearctic the nests are mainly on steep cliff faces, both on the coasts and inland. Mainly in low-lying areas in central and eastern Europe the nests may be placed in a

tall tree or, in northern Sweden, Finland, northern Russia and Estonia, where there are no steep cliffs, on the ground in an inaccessible marshy area.

Peregrines prefer open country for hunting and undisturbed access to the nest. They therefore avoid extensive areas of dense forest.

Voice

Mostly heard at the breeding site where, for instance, any disturbance is met by a rhythmical hoarse *grey-grey-grey* screech.

Breeding

Rarely seen at the nest as a one-year-old. Most breed for the first time at an age of 2–3 years. The pairs appear to live together for life.

Where the climate allows, the pair live in or near the territory throughout the year. Scandinavian breeding pairs arrive in March–April.

The display flight is seen at the start of the breeding season. The birds soar together at a great height and then the male usually dives towards the female. She turns on her back and they touch one another's talons. During the flight they may also just touch each other's breast feathers or 'kiss' with their beaks.

Where possible the nest is placed on a cliff face or high up in a tree in the old nest of a raptor, heron, stork or crow, rarely on the ground in an inaccessible marsh (mainly in the Baltic, Finland and northern Soviet Union).

In the British Isles, central Europe and Fenno-Scandia the clutch of 3–4 (1–6) eggs is laid in late March to

Peregrine Falcon – adult female at the nest site. *Photo B. Génsbøl/Biofoto.*

late April and incubated by both sexes for 29–32 days per egg. The chicks remain in the nest for 35–42 days and are independent after about a further two months.

In northern Europe the production of young was very low in the 1950s and 1960s. British investigations before 1950 showed 2.53 young per successful pair against 2.09 in 1971, that is, before and after the environmental catastrophe. Apart from artificial doubling of the clutch and exchange of eggs, Swedish Peregrines typically produced 1.2–1.4 young per breeding pair, which is not enough to prevent a decline in the population. On the other hand, Finnish birds have done well in recent years, producing 2.4–2.5 young per breeding pair.

Food

Almost exclusively birds from the size of a goldcrest to a heron, with a large range of species. In Great Britain 132 species have been recorded, in central Europe 210. The main source depends upon the habitat.

An investigation in central Europe of 6410 collected food remains showed that the commonest species taken were: domestic pigeons 32 per cent, starlings 19 per cent, various thrushes 10 per cent, lapwings 8 per cent, corvids 6 per cent, skylarks 5 per cent, chaffinches 3 per cent and black-headed gulls 3 per cent.

In closely inhabited areas domestic pigeons were the main prey with a share fluctuating between 20 and 30 per cent. In other places such prey was not taken, or if so only in small numbers; in Finland, for example, only 0.2 per cent out of 1075 prey animals. Here the main prey consisted of: ducks, 21 per cent; waders excluding lapwings, 20 per cent; and lapwings, 11 per cent. In the Scottish highlands grouse were predominant and on the Scottish coast sea birds were. In certain localities corvids may account for up to 85 per cent.

Small mammals, reptiles and insects accounted for only 0.1–0.6 per cent of the prey. However, in tundra regions field voles and lemmings are caught in large numbers in years when they are plentiful.

Foraging methods

Often catches birds in flight. Apparently hunting from a perch is the commonest method. The bird sits high up and watches. Sooner or later prey passes below it and the falcon immediately stoops, as is so typical of this species. The angle may be oblique and the wings slightly folded, or vertical with fully folded wings.

The prey usually sees the danger and when the falcon strikes it tries an evasive manoeuvre. Owing to its enormous speed (up to 380 km per hour) the falcon cannot change direction as rapidly as the prey and many sorties therefore fail. The hunt often continues as a direct chase.

In a desperate attempt to save itself the hunted bird may fold its wings together and allow itself to fall to the ground. If the falcon cannot hunt the prey again in flight it usually gives up.

From the perch the Peregrine may also see prey high up in the air. Rapid fliers such as pigeons, ducks and waders will then try to escape by horizontal flight, while birds that hover, such as owls, herons, gulls and corvids carry out a rapid spiral ascent to keep above the falcon.

Finally, the Peregrine may seek suitable prey by soaring or flying in a straight line over the countryside.

Peregrine Falcon population in the Western Palearctic

Sweden	approx. 25 pairs (1987)[21]	Decreased from about 1000 pairs in 1900, 350 pairs in 1945 to the present figure close to extinction. At first this was due to persecution, latterly to environmental poisons. Captive-bred birds are released.
Norway	50–100 pairs (1984)[90]	Now increasing after decreasing considerably.
Finland	approx. 70 pairs (1985)[10]	1000–2000 pairs in 1940s, 90 pairs in 1960s, 35 pairs in 1970, 20 pairs in 1975. A certain amount of re-establishment now going on. Production of young is good.
USSR	1000 pairs (1983)[65]	Decreasing. Southern areas deserted. Exterminated in the Baltic (1983)[6].
Poland	0–5 pairs (1984)[80]	Formerly a widespread breeding bird. A breeding record in 1980.
East Germany	5 pairs (1985)[87]	In 1939: common; 1960: 80 pairs; 1968: 14–21 pairs (only 2 young); 1979: 1 pair.

Peregrine Falcon – adult with a cuckoo in the talons. *Photo Hisato Okamoto.*

West Germany	>130 pairs (1986)[24]	About 400 pairs in 1950. Decline now halted, due to energetic protection.
British Isles	1100 pairs (1986)[24]	Increasing after a considerable decline in 1950s and 1960s. Now over the 1940 level. 300 pairs in Ireland, 800 in Great Britain.
France	600 pairs (1986)[24]	Decrease of 80 per cent since 1950s. Now increasing.
Switzerland	100 pairs (1986)[24]	After collapse of the population only one pair in 1971. Now surprisingly rapid re-establishment due to special protection measures.
Austria	5–8 pairs (1977)[48]	Decreasing considerably.
Italy	430–550 pairs (1986)[24]	Mostly threatened by nest robbers. Estimated that 90 per cent of the nests are plundered annually. Sardinia: 110–130 pairs.
Spain	1700 pairs (1986)[45]	Decreasing owing to robbing of nests, shooting by pigeon keepers and environmental poison (?) 1960–85: estimated 1225 young removed from nests.
Portugal	20–30 pairs (1982)[19]	Decreasing.

Peregrine Falcon/Barbary Falcon

Czechoslovakia	1 pair (1988)[43]	Marked decrease since mid-1960s.
Hungary	exterminated (1988)[40]	Apparently never numerous. Last breeding about 1960.
Yugoslavia	40 pairs (1982)[19]	Apparently never common.
Albania	?	No recent information. A few breeding birds in 1930s.
Romania	<5 pairs (1981)[2]	Apparently never numerous.
Bulgaria	very rare (1979)[1]	Apparently never numerous.
Greece	150 pairs (1983)[84]	Decreasing.
Turkey	100–300 pairs (1982)[19]	
Cyprus	5–10 pairs (1985)[5]	Breeds in various palces since 1960s.
Malta	1 pair (1982)[50]	
Tunisia	>200 pairs (1982)[19]	incl. Barbary Falcon.
Algeria	common (1982)[19]	incl. Barbary Falcon.
Morocco	>1000 pairs (1982)[19]	incl. Barbary Falcon.
Cape Verde Islands	very rare (1982)[13]	

Barbary Falcon – adult. *Photo C. J. Andersen/Biofoto.*

Barbary Falcon
Falco pelegrinoides

Distribution
This species is not well known, primarily because it is often confused with the Peregrine Falcon. For a long time regarded as a race of the Peregrine to which it is very closely related.

Apart from the Western Palearctic area there are a few known breeding places in Africa on the borders of Algeria, Mali and Niger. The species also breeds in Asia from Iran to Tien-Shan.

There are two races: the nominate in the Western Palearctic and *F.p. babylonicus* in Asia, which is larger with more rust colour on the crown and nape.

Population estimates
It is difficult to estimate the size of the population because it is sometimes confused with the closely related Peregrine, which breeds in the same area.

At one time the Barbary Falcon, particularly *F.p. babylonicus*, was regarded as uncommon or rare. However, mainly on the basis of falconry birds, the two races are estimated to have a population of some hundreds of pairs (1982)[65].

Migration
There is little information but this is apparently a species that wanders. Old birds are seen in the breeding area throughout the year and are probably non-migratory.

Habitat
Usually found in barren areas, particularly in semi-deserts with areas of cliff. It also breeds near rivers, e.g. the Nile, and along the coast including northern Africa.

Breeding
Not completely known. Pairs consisting of non-migratory birds remain

243

together throughout the year and probably form a life-long partnership.

The nest is placed on a cliff ledge or on a building, and the 3 (2–5) eggs are laid in March to early April.

Food

Almost exclusively small and medium-sized birds, with pigeons and ducks as the upper size limit.

In North Africa the main prey consists of sandgrouse and small doves. Bats are also caught occasionally.

Foraging methods

Very similar to the Peregrine. Appears, however, to be even faster and more agile.

Barbary Falcon – adult male. *Photo C. Frahm/Biofoto.*

Barbary Falcon population in the Western Palearctic

Israel	50–80 pairs (1982)[19]	Breeds west of the Dead Sea and south to Eilat.
Egypt	?	Breeds in Sinai, along the Red Sea and the Nile.
Libya	few? (1976)[1]	
Tunisia	53 pairs (1975)[1]	
Algeria	common? (1982)[65]	Local falconers know many breeding sites, but it is not clear whether they always differentiate between Peregrine and Barbary Falcons.
Morocco	common? (1982)[65]	Local falconers know many breeding sites, but it is not clear whether they always differentiate between Peregrine and Barbary Falcons.
Mauretania	?	Nests recorded on the coast possibly confused with Peregrine Falcon (1962)[1].
Canary Islands	?	Status not clear. Seen on many of the islands but very few nesting records (1979)[1].

Eleanora's Falcon

Falco eleanorae

Distribution

Only breeds in the Western Palearctic, thus the whole distribution is shown on the map.

Population estimates

In 1978 H. Walther[71] estimated the total population at 4400 pairs with a possible range of 2000–7000 pairs. The uncertainty is partly due to the fact that all the colonies are not counted in a given year, and hitherto unknown colonies are still being found. At the moment scarcely 100 colonies are known. About 65 per cent of the total population is in the Greek region.

Population trends

The trends are not uniform (*see* the table on p. 248). Some places have recorded a decline, e.g. Canary Islands, others an increase, e.g. Majorca.

Although, like the Peregrine, the species catches small birds, it does not appear to have been affected by environmental poisoning. It is thought that this is because for most of the year Eleanora's Falcon feeds on insects, and only catches small birds which may contain poison during four months of the year. The problem of poison is not very great because the prey consists largely of insectivorous birds such as hoopoes and golden orioles.

At one time, in the Greek area, the nestlings were used as human food. Fortunately this practice appears to be on the wane. On the other hand, disturbance by tourists is a growing problem.

As regards egg collectors and falcon robbers the species is at a disadvantage because it nests in colonies, making collecting easier. However, the danger from falconers is probably not very great, as Eleanora's Falcon is rather unsuitable for falconry.

Migration

A migratory bird with winter quarters in East Africa, Madagascar and

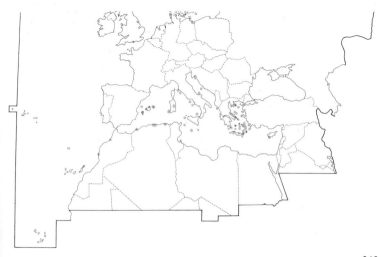

islands in the Indian Ocean. New reports on overwintering flocks in the southern Aegean Sea require further documentation.

It is thought that the migration goes from the Mediterranean to the Red Sea and then on to the winter quarters. Even North African birds probably use this migration route. Thus, the Canaries population first travels 1000 km to the north-east, then 3500 km eastwards through the Mediterranean, and a further 6000 km south to Madagascar.

The autumn migration starts in October and the breeding grounds are deserted by early November. By late November the winter visitors have been recorded in Madagascar. The breeding sites are occupied again from late April, continuing in the Mediterranean in May–June.

During the summer, small flocks are often seen far from the breeding grounds, for instance catching insects in inland mountainous areas.

In Europe the species is rarely seen outside the Mediterranean area. There are, however, observations from Great Britain, Poland and, most surprisingly, Sweden, indluding Øland: two birds were seen in 1983 (summer).

Habitat

The species breeds in colonies usually on isolated uninhabited islands in the Mediterranean and North Atlantic. It may also breed on larger inhabited islands where there are inaccessible cliff faces.

Eleanora's Falcon – dark phase with prey. *Photo A. Limbrunner.*

The preferred habitat outside the breeding season is little known.

Voice
A rapid, rhythmical *ke-ke-ke* when disturbed at the nesting site. This is not so hoarse as in the larger falcons, nor so high-pitched and sonorous as, for example, in the Hobby.

Breeding
Female breeds for the first time at an age of two years, occasionally at one year; males start at an age of three years. The partnership may be life-long.

Lives in colonies, normally with 5–20 pairs, but up to 200 pairs have been recorded. Apparently never found as a solitary breeder.

The rearing of the young is based on autumn-migrating small birds. The breeding season starts late, the eggs being laid from mid-July. Display flights are seen in the first part of the season, the birds performing impressive dives and making mock attacks on one another. There is also a form of social behaviour in which the whole population evidently go hunting insects together.

The nest is placed on the side of a cliff, among large boulders, in small caves, between bushes or lying free. The 2–3 (1–5) eggs are incubated by both sexes for about 28 days per egg. The chicks remain in the nest for 35–40 days and are independent after about a further 15 days.

Food
Highly specialized during the breeding season. Lives primarily on small birds migrating by night, which are caught on passage from Europe to the winter quarters in Africa.

Several prey species have been recorded, but certain may be dominant locally. At one breeding site in the Aegean Sea: willow warbler, red-backed shrike, whinchat and white-throat. In Morocco, woodchat-shrike, whitethroat, nightingale and redstart. In the two localities the total number of species caught was respectively 52 and 37.

Outside the breeding season, Eleanora's Falcon apparently only catches insects: beetles, grasshoppers, dragonflies, butterflies and flying ants.

Foraging methods
The technique for catching birds depends on outside factors. In the Aegean Sea hunting takes place at dawn, when the nocturnal migration ceases. Here the falcons typically form a front line at a height of 800–1000 m, with perhaps 10–20 birds at intervals of 100–200 m. They hover facing a normally strong wind, and wait for the migrating birds to fly towards them. The prey is attacked and caught in a powerful stoop, so the hunt is very effective. Only 50 per cent slip through such a phalanx.

The number of birds on autumn migration is very large so from the biological viewpoint the effectiveness of this method is not critical.

Another technique has been recorded at a Moroccan breeding site. On account of the longer distances involved here the small birds from the north arrive throughout the day, and the falcons hunt all day. Strong winds only occur rarely so usually the falcons hunt low over the water. Here, too, this is very effective. The migrating birds are probably tired, and at this height they cannot escape by diving without falling into the water.

Insects are caught in flight by stooping or by simply chasing them. The falcons may also hover and catch insects on the ground.

Eleanora's Falcon population in the Western Palearctic

Canary Islands	approx. 60 pairs (1971)[1]	Decreasing (1976)[1].
Morocco	90 pairs (1986)[79]	Increasing.
Algeria	>100 pairs (1982)[19]	
Tunisia	60 pairs (1982)[19]	
Spain	>300 pairs (1982)[19]	Last available estimate says 300 pairs (1977)[27]. However, Majorca alone has about 320 pairs (1981)[69]. Here the species is increasing.
Italy	480 pairs (1982)[19]	Of which 120–150 pairs are to be found on Sardinia.
Yugoslavia	about 12 pairs (1982)[19]	
Greece	2500 pairs (1982)[19]	Some uncertainty about the figure, which is the best estimate between the extremes 1120 and 4550 pairs.
Cyprus	110–120 pairs (1983)[4]	
Turkey	30–50 pairs (1982)[19]	

Eleanora's Falcon – adult pale phase. *Photo A. Limbrunner.*

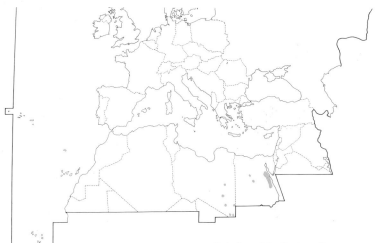

Sooty Falcon
Falco concolor

Distribution
Poorly known. Apart from the distribution shown on the map the species may well be found in other areas. Outside the Western Palearctic, breeding places are only known in Arabia and on the coasts of the Red Sea in Sudan and Ethiopia.

Population estimates
On the basis of observations in the winter quarters the total has been estimated at around 20,000 (1982)[65]. Today only a few of the breeding places are known. It is thought that the unknown sites may be in the interior of Arabia, and to a lesser extent in the desert regions of North Africa. In 1982[19], 30–50 pairs bred in Israel.

Migration
A migrant with winter quarters south of the equator, mainly in Madagascar but also on the African mainland and on islands in the Indian Ocean.

It is found in the breeding area up to October–November and in its winter quarters from November to May. The spring migration, however, appears to begin in March–April.

Habitat
Breeds in very dry and warm treeless areas, often true deserts. It also lives on rocky islands.

Breeding
Not well known. The species usually lives in colonies of up to 100 pairs, but these are more loosely formed than those of Eleanora's Falcon. It is also found breeding solitarily. Pair formation appears to take place in the winter quarters.

The nest is placed in a cave or crevice in the rocks and under bushes. The 2–3 (4) eggs are laid in late July to late August.

Food
Very similar to that of Eleanora's Falcon. It too has found a special ecological niche, feeding its young on birds during the autumn migration.

In general, the prey ranges in size between a warbler and a hoopoe,

Sooty Falcon adult in flight and on a lookout perch. *Photos Y. Eshbol/Bruce Coleman.*

together with various shrikes.

At a breeding site on the Red Sea in Ethiopia between mid-August and mid-September, that is, early in the migration season, the commonest species was blue-cheeked bee-eater, followed by bee-eater, golden oriole and hoopoe.

In the winter quarters it feeds almost exclusively on insects, mostly locusts, ants, termites and dragonflies. It also catches bats.

Foraging methods
Like the Eleanora's Falcon, the species may hunt for birds in groups, but it is more common for a couple of males or the pair to forage together.

It usually hunts the migrating birds in the twilight or at dawn and then very low over the terrain.

Hobby

Falco subbuteo

Distribution

As shown on the map the Hobby breeds in much of the Western Palearctic. To the east it extends in a very broad belt through Asia to the Pacific Ocean

The Chinese population forms a special race, *F.s. streichi*, the rest of the breeding range being covered by the nominate race.

Population estimates

In general, the figures given for the individual countries rest on estimates. During the breeding season the Hobby leads a very secluded existence and so is difficult to record. There is, therefore, no doubt that in the coming years greater knowledge will enable the information given to be much amended.

There is no data for large areas (*see* table on p. 255) so an estimate for the whole of the Western Palearctic is not possible. The material available sug-

gests a total breeding population for Europe, excluding the Soviet Union, of the order of 15,000–20,000 pairs.

Population trends

There is no clear picture. There may apparently have been a general decline at the end of the 1800s to a lower level, based perhaps on changes in habitat in the form of new agricultural methods, draining and changes in the appearance of the forests towards a denser type.

The species did not suffer any collapse of the population in the 1950s and 1960s based on the use of environmental poisons. This is probably because its food consists largely of insects. However, in certain localities there have been reductions in populations during these years due perhaps to these poisons.

In certain countries human perse-

cution has been a factor in the reduction of populations.

As shown in the table on p. 255 there has been considerable variation in the estimates, with mention of reductions, stability and increases. This is probably because, in certain localities, the population fluctuates from year to year, due to changes in the availability of food caused, for example, by weather conditions.

Migration

The Hobby is essentially a long-distance migrant, with the European breeding populations wintering in Africa. However there are some winter records as far north as Central Europe. In Africa most winter south of 10°S, but there is recent evidence that some may also be in West Africa.

Although the Hobby is a strong flier, up to 300 have been seen in an

Adult Hobby. *Photo G. K. Brown/Ardea.*

Adult Hobby. *Photo L. Jonsson.*

autumn at Gibraltar, but the bulk of the passage takes place over a broad front. The autumn movement starts in late August and is over by mid-October – when birds are already reaching the southern wintering areas. Return passage starts in March and continues through April, with the arrival of adults on the breeding grounds from April in the south to the end of May in the north. Records of birds in the distinctive first summer plumage are rare in the central and northern parts of the breeding range, and those seen are generally found in July and August: probably many of these youngsters remain south.

In Britain Hobbies are most con-spicuous in the autumn months of August and September, when birds may make regular visits to feed on roosting hirundines. Some such rec-ords may be of unsuspected locally breeding Hobbies, but many are prob-ably of passage birds.

Habitat

During the breeding season the Hobby prefers sheltered areas with plenty of insects and small birds, typically in damp meadows, extensive marshes and heathland. For nesting, the species often uses an old corvid nest, usually placed in a small wood. However, large forests are also used, where they are broken up by clearings

253

and fields. It seems that the Hobby prefers woodland with a sandy soil.

Voice

The commonest screech is a wryneck-like *kew-kew-kew* used, for instance, as communication between the sexes; it is very high-pitched and sonorous.

Breeding

Normally breeds for the first time at an age of two years, a few females at one year. The pair may remain together for several years, but it is not known how often this occurs. Pair formation seems to take place in the winter quarters or during migration, for the birds may arrive at the breeding grounds in pairs.

The display involves mutual soaring flights during which the male dives towards the female, or with delivery of prey when the male catches prey and dives to deliver it to the female. She turns on her back and seizes it in flight.

No falcon builds its own nest. The Hobby uses in particular old crow nests, usually placed in a fir tree.

Egg-laying starts late: in central Europe in mid-May at the earliest, most often in June; in Scandinavia most frequently in late June, and even July clutches are known. The 3 (1–4) eggs are incubated for 28–31 days, almost exclusively by the female. The young are fledged after 28–34 days and independent 30–40 days later.

The Hobby is often said to have its nest plundered, particularly by crows. According to German investigations this may happen to almost half the population in an area. The breeding success of the species is dependent upon weather conditions. One wet summer only a single pair was re-corded as having one young successfully launched.

Recent Swedish investigations show the production of young as 1.81 per pair and only a limited loss of complete clutches (4 out of 26).

Food

Mainly small birds and insects, occasionally bats, various small rodents and shrews, moles and young rabbits, exceptionally also reptiles.

More than 70 bird species have been recorded as prey, mainly the commonest forms from open country. An investigation in central Europe showed: swallows 30 per cent, skylarks 19 per cent, house martins 9 per cent, house sparrows 6 per cent, swifts 5 per cent, linnets 3 per cent, starlings 3 per cent, greenfinches 3 per cent, tree sparrows 3 per cent and chaffinches 3 per cent. These ten species therefore accounted for more than 80 per cent, and the two first-named alone almost 50 per cent.

The maximum catches were birds of the size of cuckoos, hoopoes, greater spotted woodpeckers and mistle thrushes.

In general, insects appear to account for about 50 per cent of the food, but with considerable local and individual differences. Large flying insects predominated. However, the spectrum is considerable: cockchafers, dung-beetles, stag beetles, glow-worms, cabbage white butterflies, dragonflies, mayflies, ants, craneflies etc.

Foraging methods

A very rapid and skilful hunter. When catching birds the species usually uses a surprise attack, flying low over the ground or suddenly appear-

Juvenile Hobby with dragonfly being torn apart in the air. *Photo J. B. Bruun/Biofoto.*

ing from behind buildings, hedges etc. These tactics seem to explain how the Hobby can catch birds as fast as swallows and swifts.

Insects are caught during slow, searching flights with short chases.

Hunting from a perch is also used, for example, for mammals. However, it is probable that most prey of this type is stolen from Kestrels.

Hobbies are also seen hunting insects on the ground.

Hobby population in the Western Palearctic

Denmark	>10 pairs (1982)[15]	Common at the end of the 1800s. Since then decreasing to the present level, close to total extinction. Decrease may be due to climatic factors and changes of habitat.
Norway	few pairs (1987)[79]	New colonisation. 18 breeding pairs recorded since 1956.
Sweden	approx. 1000 pairs (1981)[9]	Position not clear.
Finland	approx. 2000 pairs (1985)[10]	Decrease? Population possibly halved since 1930s.
USSR *Estonia* *Latvia*	? approx 500 pairs (1976)[11] common (1983)[34]	About 2500 pairs in a 270,000 sq. km area in central Russia. Probably increasing thanks to protection (1977)[1]. Commonest falcon in Latvia.
Poland	2300 pairs (1984)[80]	Stable?

Hobby

East Germany	400 pairs (1985)[67]	Decrease in the 1960s and early 1970s very marked[36, 52]
West Germany	950–1450 pairs (1982)[22]	Local reduction of 50 per cent in 1950s and 1960s. Schleswig-Holstein fluctuates between 100 and 200 pairs (1981)[59].
Holland	1000–1100 pairs (1979)[53]	Increasing in the last 20–30 years. Big annual fluctuations.
Belgium	about 65 pairs (1977)[76]	Decreasing.
Luxembourg	6–8 pairs (1981)[94]	
Britain	approx. 300 pairs (1986)[18]	Increasing.
France	1500–2300 (1984)[92]	Considerable decline, locally up to 80 per cent.
Switzerland	155 pairs (1981)[73]	Apparently stable.
Austria	few (1974)[3]	Apparently stable (1977)[48].
Italy	100–300 pairs (1982)[50]	Halved since 1940s, due to shooting and perhaps poison.
Spain	around 5000 pairs (1982)[19]	Probably decreasing.
Portugal	min. 300 pairs (1982)[19]	Stable.
Czechoslovakia	300 pairs (1988)[43]	Trend unknown.
Hungary	600–700 pairs (1988)[40]	Stable?
Yugoslavia	200 pairs (1982)[19]	Decreasing?
Albania	?	
Romania	100–120 pairs (1977)[42]	
Bulgaria	few (1971)[1]	
Greece	>100 pairs (1982)[19]	Decreasing (1983)[84].
Turkey	500–1000 pairs (1982)[19]	
Lebanon	?	Scattered breeding records (1968)[1]. Perhaps disappeared (1974)[1].
Israel	50–70 pairs (1982)[19]	
Tunisia	20–30 pairs (1982)[19]	
Cyprus	max. 5 pairs (1985)[5]	

Algeria	Irregular breeder (1982)[19].
Morocco	500–1000 pairs (1982)[19]

Adult Hobby. *Photo J. Elmelid/N.*

Red-footed Falcon
Falco vespertinus

Distribution
This is shown on the map. From this area the breeding range extends eastwards in a broad belt through the Soviet Union to the region around the Lena.

Population estimates
According to the figures given in the table on p. 262, there are 800–900 pairs in Europe excluding the Soviet Union. In 1982[65] T. Cade estimated the world population at 20,000 pairs.

Population trends
During the present century there has been, at any rate locally, a considerable reduction in the population; in Hungary this was probably due to changes in habitats. In the 1920s and 1930s there were, in suitable localities, colonies of 500–600 pairs. Today, 'large colonies' in Hungary have a maximum of 50 pairs. The decline is possibly due to the fact that eastern Europe forms the western limit of the species. Fluctuations are common in border populations.

At the present time it is difficult to discern a clear trend. This may be due to the fluctuations that occur in the supply of food. It can perhaps be taken as a positive sign that, during recent years, the species has occurred more frequently to the north and west of the breeding range than was the case only a few years ago.

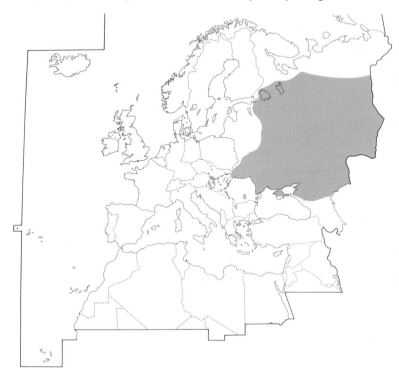

In the present century it has been characteristic that the species has had sudden, short-term sorties to the west, far beyond the true breeding range. Thus, it has been recorded in France, West Germany, East Germany, Finland, Sweden and Denmark (Bornholm 1974)[72].

In Sweden the species possibly now breeds annually (1981)[9]. There have also been breeding records on the edge of the true breeding range in the Baltic and Poland.

Migration

This species is a full-scale long-distance migrant with the whole population wintering in southern Africa – mainly in Zimbabwe, Botswana, Namibia and Angola. During the winter very large nocturnal roosts may be formed, and the birds will normally feed and move in parties.

Autumn passage starts early and the main passage, which is over the eastern Mediterranean, takes place from mid-September to early October. By the end of the month few remain in Europe and many have reached the wintering grounds. Return passage commences in March and many pass much further to the west in spring than autumn, with records of flocks of up to 5000 in Nigeria. A substantial regular passage has been reported from the North African coasts of Algeria and Tunisia from mid-April to mid-May.

Most vagrant records from western Europe are during the spring with regular sightings (often of small groups) during May in south-east England in most recent years. Every few years very substantial numbers of birds are seen in western Europe, and extra-limital breeding may result from these 'irruptions'.

Red-footed Falcon – adult male. *Photo L. Jonsson.*

Habitat

During the breeding season the Red-footed Falcon prefers grassy and wooded steppes, but is also commonly seen in large areas of upland marsh, in river valleys and in forest clearings. It will, however, only settle in these types of country if there is a plentiful supply of food, particularly insects.

In European latitudes the species is most often seen while foraging inland over areas of wetland.

Red-footed Falcon juvenile on lookout post. *Photo B. Génsbøl/Biofoto.*

Voice

When breeding in colonies this species is very talkative. It often emits a rapid, rhythmical *kew-kew-kew*, softer and weaker than the corresponding voice in the Hobby and Kestrel.

Breeding

May breed when one year old, but it is not known how common this is. The pair only remains together for one breeding season.

The species normally breeds in colonies where the nests are typically placed in rookeries. Where food is scarce it also breeds solitarily.

The display flight is very like that of the Kestrel, with mutual soaring and the male diving towards the female. When the male is alone in the air he stoops, screaming loudly, towards the female on the nest.

The 3–4 (2–6) eggs are laid from mid-May to early June and incubated by both sexes for roughly 28 days per egg. The chicks remain in the nest for 27–30 days and are independent after only 7–14 days more.

There are no up-to-date investigations on the production of young.

Food

Mainly insects, particularly various species of grasshoppers, beetles and ants, supplemented by dragonflies, mayflies, wasps, bumblebees, crane-flies, butterfly caterpillars and spiders. In the winter quarters many termites are caught.

The young are fed primarily on vertebrates: lizards, fledged chicks of small birds (those recorded include blackcap, skylark, red-backed shrike and golden oriole), various amphibians, small rodents and shrews.

Adult birds are only rarely caught in flight.

Foraging methods

The Red-footed Falcon hunts from a perch, or an electric cable, a tree stump or a tree, with brief chases after the prey.

It also flies low over the terrain, either gliding or hovering, or hunts on foot. Insects are often torn apart in the air.

The species normally hunts in two periods: in the morning and late in the afternoon. The latter period of hunting may extend far into the evening.

Red-footed Falcon juvenile killing prey. *Photo B. Génsbøl/Biofoto.*

Red-footed Falcon – immature female. *Photo B. Génsbøl/Biofoto.*

Red-footed Falcon population in the Western Palearctic

Czechoslovakia	0–50 pairs (1988)[43]	Irregular breeder.
Hungary	1500 pairs (1988)[40]	Decreasing, especially west of the Danube. 2000–2500 pairs in 1957.
Austria	5–10 pairs (1977)[48]	Breeds at Lake Neusiedler, where population has probably never been larger than today.
Yugoslavia	approx. 80 pairs (1982)[19]	Only breeds in Serbia.
Romania	100–120 pairs (1977)[42]	Decreasing.
Bulgaria	few (1974)[3]	
USSR	?	About 400 pairs in 270,000 sq. km area in central Russia (1979)[1].

Merlin

Falco columbarius

Distribution

As the map shows this species breeds in the northern part of the Western Palearctic. From there the breeding area extends eastwards, mainly through conifer forests and forest tundra into Asia and North America.

There are ten races, of which the following are relevant: *F.c. subaesalon* in Iceland and the Faeroes is darker and somewhat larger than *F.c. aesalon* in the rest of the Western Palearctic and eastwards to the region around the Yenisei. Here it is replaced by the paler, somewhat larger *F.c. insignis*. The still paler *F.c. pallidus* is found in south-western Siberia and northern Kazakstan. The last two species are winter visitors in the south-eastern part of the Western Palearctic. The nominate race is in North America.

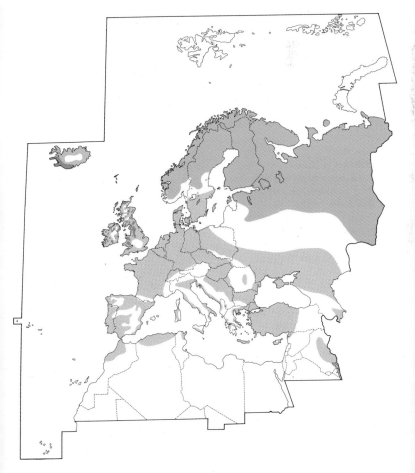

Merlin – adult female. *Photo D. Green/Bruce Coleman.*

Population estimates

During the breeding season the species lives a secluded life and is therefore difficult to record. So the figures given in the table on p. 268 should be regarded as very rough estimates.

As there are no data from the Soviet Union it is not possible to give an estimate for the whole of the Western Palearctic. For the remainder of the area (Europe excluding the Soviet Union) the breeding population can be estimated as of the order of 10,000 pairs.

Population trends

During this century, the Merlin has suffered a continuous decrease, apparently on account of changes in habitat. In addition, it was much affected by environmental poisons in the 1950s and 1960s. This was almost certainly because the species feeds nearly exclusively on birds which to a great extent accumulate poisons such as DDT.

In certain localities there has been persecution on the breeding grounds and in the winter quarters, while in many areas an increase in tourism has also raised problems.

After the considerable decrease due to poison there is now a general trend towards stability or a slight re-establishment.

Migration

Most Merlins are migrants moving south, to a greater or lesser extent, of their breeding areas for the winter. A very few Scandinavian birds and some British, Irish and Icelandic ones remain at or close to the breeding grounds. However these often move down from the hilly moorland breeding areas to warmer coastal or valley sites, where there are still small birds in winter for them to prey upon.

There are a dozen records of Icelandic ringed birds in western Britain and Ireland. Specimens referable to the Icelandic race *F.c. subaesalon* have been found in Norway, the Low Countries and France; these have to be treated with caution as northern Scottish and Faeroese birds may be very similar. The autumn passage through Fair Isle (Shetland) takes place from mid-August to the end of October (peak mid-October). Return passage, involving many fewer birds, is in April and May.

Most of the British and Irish ringing recoveries are within 100 km of the natal areas, but a minority move into France and there is one recovery from northern Spain. The birds from Fenno-Scandia are recovered in winter south to France, Spain and Italy and most show a south-south-west or south-west direction of movement. Autumn passage is mostly in October, returning in March and April, but the most northerly breeding areas are not re-occupied until late May.

As a strong-flying species, the Merlin's passage is not concentrated at the short sea crossings and so the annual autumn peaks for the Scandinavian sites are only 100–200. The occurrences of vagrant Icelandic birds in Greenland and Spitzbergen, and of a bird of the American race in the Outer Hebrides, provide good evidence for the Merlin's ability to cross wide areas of sea.

Merlin – adult male on the nest. *Photo D. Green/Bruce Coleman.*

Merlin – adult female. *Photo P. Klaesson & B. O. Olsson.*

Habitat

In areas with plenty of small birds, Merlins breed in or near open country, such as high moorland, heaths, forest tundra, in the mountains in the birch zone, at the edges of open conifer forests and on treeless coastal stretches. In Scandinavia the species most frequently breeds in birch country, in Britain mainly in extensive areas of heathland.

The winter is spent in areas of marshland, meadows and cultivated land where the tree cover is not too dense.

Voice

Normally only heard at the nest. Usually a rapid, very high-pitched *yee-yee-yee*, very like that of the Kestrel. The voice is used as a warning and when attacking.

Breeding

Females often seem to breed for the first time at an age of one year, males at two years. Apparently pair formation usually only lasts one season.

The nest is placed either on the ground (in the British Isles 75 per cent) or in trees (commonest in Scandinavia), usually in an old rook nest. More unusually the species may also nest in woodpecker holes and large nest boxes.

In Scandinavia the 3–5 (1–7) eggs are laid in late May to mid-June, in the British Isles from early May, and are incubated by both sexes for 28–32 days (26 days per egg). The chicks remain in the nest for 28–32 days and are independent after about a further 30 days.

A British investigation based on 84 clutches showed an offspring production of 3.21 per successful pair. In Scandinavia there was considerable variation in breeding success from year to year. In Norway success was correlated with good and bad rodent years, in spite of the fact that Merlins do not catch many rodents.

Food

Mainly small birds, particularly species from open country. In many areas, meadow pipits predominated (up to 90 per cent). Other commonly occurring prey included song larks, various finches and thrushes, wheatears, whinchats, dunlins, redshanks, lapwings and snipe.

A Swedish investigation has shown that, to a considerable extent, Merlins feed their young on nestlings of small birds and recently fledged young (mostly warblers).

The species also catches small mammals, such as field voles, lemmings, mice and shrews, making, according to a Norwegian investigation, about five per cent of total prey. In good rodent years the share of this type of prey may rise to ten per cent.

A relatively small number of insects, such as dragonflies, beetles and butterflies, are also caught.

Foraging methods

Hunts over open country. Likes to perch in an elevated position on the lookout. When prey is sighted the bird flies very low, at about one metre, and there is a surprise attack. If this is unsuccessful it starts a long chase. However, the greatest success is with a surprise attack when the prey does not manage to react to the danger.

The prey is usually struck on the

Merlin – adult female with young lark. *Photo D. Green/Bruce Coleman.*

ground or at a very low height. Thus in 343 hunts the prey was taken on the ground in 278 cases, 49 times in the air and 16 on a branch or similar.

Sometimes two birds hunt together, often the male and female.

Merlin population in the Western Palearctic

Iceland	?	Very common in the north, few in other regions (1979)[1].
Faeroes	<10 pairs (1981)[78]	Decreasing.
Sweden	approx. 5000 pairs (1981)[9]	Seems to be decreasing.
Norway	very common (1971)[62]	Marked decrease (1974)[3].
Finland	2000 pairs (1985)[10]	Possibly halved since the 1930s. Decreasing?
USSR *Estonia* *Latvia*	few (1961)[1] about 1600 pairs (1967)[11] few (1983)[34]	
Britain and Ireland	600–800 pairs (1976)[47]	About 100 pairs in Ireland (1976)[1]. After considerable decrease due to persecution, disturbance and environmental poisons now stable or slightly increasing.

Kestrel – adult female. *Photo A. Linderheim/N.*

Kestrel

Falco tinnunculus

Distribution

Breeds in the extensive areas shown on the map and in much of Asia and Africa.

There are several races of which the following are relevant: the nominate race in the Western Palearctic and eastwards to north-eastern Siberia, *F.t. canariensis* in the western Canary Islands, *F.t. dacotiae* in the eastern Canary Islands, *F.t. neglectus* in the northern Cape Verde Islands, *F.t. alexandri* in the south-eastern Cape Verde Islands and *F.t. rupicolae-formis*, smaller and more brightly coloured, in Egypt, northern Sudan and Arabia.

Population estimates

It is not possible to give an estimate for the whole of the Western Palearctic, as data are lacking for large areas.

Kestrel – adult male. *Photo K. Bjerre.*

For Europe, excluding the Soviet Union, the information available suggests a total of the order of 270,000–340,000 breeding pairs. The Kestrel is, therefore, the area's commonest raptor.

Population trends

In the 1800s there seems to have been a reduction in the populations, probably caused by more intensive cultivation and draining, so that today the number of breeding pairs is at a lower level.

In many places in the Western Palearctic there was a significant decline in the populations in the 1950s and 1960s. This is the period when environmental poisoning was a very serious problem. It is typical that, at any rate in northern Europe, there has in recent years been a certain recovery. On the other hand, the trend has been adverse in southern Europe, due to environmental poisons (?), shooting and changes of habitat.

In certain localities the population can fluctuate considerably (in Schleswig-Holstein by 400 per cent), as a result of changes in rodent stocks. In addition, many Kestrels die in severe winters. This is reflected in the following year by a marked decrease in the number of breeding pairs.

Migration

Northern populations (especially in the east) are fully migratory, including a substantial trans-Saharan element, but southern ones may be almost wholly sedentary. The British birds show a variable amount of movement, the young ones seeming to move furthest.

Like other falcons the Kestrel migrates over a broad front but, since it is a common species, the numbers seen at migration stations may reach 500 or more annually in Scandinavia. The wide north-to-south range of breeding may account for the very extended migration seasons. Autumn passage lasts from mid-August to November and the return starts in February in the south and continues into early June in the north.

Ringing recoveries show that a few British birds move into France and Iberia. Young birds move further than adults and the northern ones further than southern; nonetheless, due to the proximity of France, most of the birds found abroad are from England. Post-fledging dispersal (July and August) of British birds does not seem to be oriented. However, the recoveries of Dutch birds in Suffolk within a month and Norfolk within six weeks of fledging, and a Luxembourg-ringed nestling over 1100 km away in Co. Clare (Ireland) two months later, shows how far and fast these movements may be.

In Britain most of the wintering birds originate from the Low Countries and Fenno-Scandia. Many of the winter recoveries of Finnish-ringed birds come from the Mediterranean area, east to the Balkans, but most Scandinavian returns show movements south or south-west into France and Iberia. The wintering population in trans-Saharan Africa, mostly from Russia, far outnumbers the local populations. There are recoveries of European birds in Mauritania, Li-

Kestrel – sub-adult male. *Photo R. J. C. Blewitt/Ardea.*

beria, Ghana and Nigeria, showing that western birds may move very long distances too. However, the extensive ringing at Cap Bon (Tunisia) showed that the spring birds leaving Africa, in the middle of the Mediterranean coast, were mostly from Russia. The furthest east of their recoveries was at Kemerov (86°E).

Habitat

A widespread species. The preferred habitats for breeding include cultivated steppes, uncultivated grassy areas, heathland, wet areas, dunes, stretches along motorways, airports and large and small towns. The two principal requirements are open country with a good population of small rodents, and adequate nesting sites, often in an old tree, on a cliff face or building, or in a nesting box.

In Denmark a characteristic habitat is a small wood or group of trees surrounded by open country, using a rook's nest for breeding.

Outside the breeding season Kestrels live in a variety of habitats in open country.

Voice

Often rather talkative in the breeding season. Mostly a rhythmic high *kik-kik-kik* – female a little lower than male.

Breeding

Breeds at an age of one year. In a population of non-migratory birds the pair remains together throughout the year and apparently forms a lifelong partnership, while migratory birds evidently change partners more frequently. However, pairs can be seen migrating together.

Display flights are of two types. The male makes short dives towards the sitting female, who ducks and takes up a position with raised tail, or the male chases the female during mutual circling.

As is typical for falcons the birds do not build a nest themselves. They take over the old nest of another species, most often of a crow, or they use a building, for example a church tower, silo, water tower, industrial building, ruin, bridge or large agricultural building, electric pylon, nesting box or hollow tree. In areas without trees, mostly on islands, they will also nest on the ground.

The Kestrel chooses a nest in a tree, either at the edge of woodland, in a small wood or in a free-standing tree.

Although very adaptable in the choice of a nest site, the population may suffer if nothing suitable is available.

The eggs may be laid from late April to June, those in towns from early to mid-April, but the timing often varies considerably from year to year. The clutch of 3–6 (1–9) eggs is incubated by the female for 27–29 days per egg. The clutch hatches within a period of 3–5 days. The chicks remain in the nest for 27–32 days and are independent after about a further 30 days. Normally the family then breaks up but there are instances when the young have remained in the territory throughout the winter.

Dutch investigations on 413 clutches showed a loss of 43 per cent from the eggs being laid until the young flew from the nest, mostly when the whole clutch was deserted, the male not bringing sufficient food. In Norway and Finland considerable variation has been recorded in the production of young in good and bad rodent years, Norway having a variation of respectively 3.7 and 1.9 chicks per breeding pair.

Food

Mainly small mammals, particularly field voles. The species also catches, but only as a supplement, small birds, reptiles, amphibians, insects and molluscs. Birds can be more important when the numbers of rodents are insufficient, and in southern Europe insects and lizards form a significant part of the diet.

Among the small mammals the basic prey consists of common voles and field voles, followed by water voles and bank voles. House mice and wood mice are also taken regularly, but in much smaller numbers. More occasionally, Kestrels catch rats, shrews, moles, weasels and bats. In certain localities further east in Europe other rodents play an important role.

Bird prey consists primarily of nestlings and fledglings of passerines from open country, mainly starlings,

Kestrel – juv. with mouse. *Photo D. Nill.*

Kestrel – adult female hovering. *Photo J. Elmelid/N.*

house sparrows, skylarks, various finches and buntings, pipits and thrushes, secondarily the chicks of gulls, waders and gallinaceous birds. The maximum size of prey would be adult lapwings and turtle doves, but normally the species takes considerably smaller prey.

The principal insects taken are large beetles, such as cerambycids, dung beetles and cockchafers, as well as grasshoppers and crickets.

Several investigations of the food have all shown the dominance of small rodents. At the start of this century a sample in northern Germany of 516 stomachs revealed remains of 642 small rodents, mainly field voles, one young rat, one leveret, 3 shrews, 20 birds (skylarks, house and tree sparrows, goldfinches and wrens), 9 lizards and one slowworm. There were also insects in 125 of the stomachs. Rodents accounted for 95 per cent of the vertebrates, birds 3 per cent and reptiles one per cent.

A smaller Corsican investigation demonstrated the difference between northern and southern Europe. Here, mammals accounted for 59 per cent, reptiles 30 per cent and small birds 11 per cent. There were also many insects.

Foraging methods

Very frequently hovers at a height of 10–40 m, and also hunts from a post, electric pylon or similar. The species is not well adapted for catching birds in flight. When this happens it is usually the result of a surprise attack. It also wanders about on the ground, searching for insects, earthworms and snails.

Kestrel population in the Western Palearctic

Denmark	1500–2000 pairs (1978)[84]	Big decrease at start of this century due to intensive farming. Now apparently stable.
Sweden	approx. 3000 pairs (1981)[9]	Scania: about 500 pairs. Possibly decreasing.
Norway	?	Common in the south, few in north (1974)[3].
Finland	1500 pairs (1985)[10]	Decreased considerably, associated amongst other things with harsh winters.
USSR	?	About 3500 pairs in a 270,000 sq. km area in central Russia. Here slightly increasing due to protection (1977)[1].
Poland	1000–2000 pairs (1984)[80]	Decreasing.
East Germany	2500–5000 pairs (1985)[87]	Mecklenburg: about 600 pairs (1979)[52]. After Buzzard the commonest raptor.
West Germany	41,000–90,000 pairs (1982)[22]	Local decreases of 75 per cent since 1930s. Schleswig-Holstein: fluctuates between 300 and 1000–1300 pairs, depending upon food supply (1981)[59]. Rhineland 1500–1800 pairs (1982)[88].
Holland	5000–6500 pairs (1979)[53]	After a big decrease a certain improvement in recent decades.
Belgium	about 750 pairs (1977)[76]	Big fluctuations.
Luxembourg	2000–2500 pairs (1971)[3]	Figures seem rather high.
Britain and Ireland	>100,000 pairs (1976)[47]	Fluctuations associated with food supply. Commonest raptor in Britain.
France	42,000–57,000 pairs (1984)[92]	Fluctuations associated with food supply and severe winters.
Switzerland	?	Now stable after decrease in 1960s. Locally the commonest raptor (1980)[25].

Kestrel

Austria	?	Population small but apparently stable (1977)[48].
Italy	2000–8000 pairs (1982)[19]	Considerable decrease. Sardinia: 2000–8000 pairs (1977)[41]. Common in Sicily (1977)[46].
Spain	approx. 30,000 pairs (1982)[19]	Commonest raptor after the Lesser Kestrel. Decreasing due to shooting, habitat changes and environmental poisoning.
Portugal	1000–1500 pairs (1982)[19]	Decreasing for same reasons as in Spain.
Czechoslovakia	7000 pairs (1988)[19]	Trend unknown.
Hungary	3500 pairs (1988)[40]	After big decline due to poison, now improving.
Yugoslavia	common (1982)[19]	
Albania	?	
Romania	240–300 pairs (1977)[42]	Decreasing markedly.
Bulgaria	?	Decreasing rapidly but still the country's commonest raptor (1974)[3].
Greece	approx. 3000 pairs (1982)[19]	Commonest raptor (1983)[84].
Turkey	500–5000 pairs (1982)[50]	
Cyprus	approx. 200 pairs (1982)[5]	Common (1983)[85].
Israel	1000–2000 pairs (1982)[50]	Very numerous before 1950, then a big decrease due to thallium sulphate poisoning. Now re-establishing (1979)[1].
Egypt	1000 pairs (1982)[19]	
Tunisia	600 pairs (1982)[19]	
Algeria	common (1982)[19]	
Morocco	>1000 pairs (1982)[19]	Commonest raptor.
Canary Islands	?	Commonest on some islands (1986)[5].
Madeira	very common (1986)[5]	
Cape Verde Islands	very common (1982)[13, 35]	

Lesser Kestrel

Falco naumanni

Distribution

In addition to the distribution in the Western Palearctic (*see* map) the Lesser Kestrel breeds eastwards, mainly on the steppes and in half-deserts, to the Altai, and in areas still further east.

Population estimates

This cannot be estimated for the Western Palearctic as a whole. Europe, excluding the Soviet Union, has a population of the order of 60,000 pairs.

Population trends

The table on p. 281 shows that there has been a significant decline in the population. The reasons for this cannot be exclusively due to environmental poisons, persecution and habitat changes, although these have had a certain influence.

It seems probable that pesticides and modern agricultural methods have reduced the number of insects so that there has been a steady reduction in the bird's population.

This reduction is also probably due to climatic conditions. The population has, in fact, undergone significant fluctuations. In periods 1830(?)–50, 1885–1915 and 1940–55 the species reached a peak in population and distribution. The periods outside these were characterized by a decline.

With climatic conditions in view it can be noted that the Lesser Kestrel

today breeds irregularly in Poland, Czechoslovakia and Hungary, areas which formerly had a true breeding population.

Local declines may be due to changes in ecological conditions in the vicinity of the colonies, for the species normally forages within a distance of one kilometre from the breeding site.

Migration

Basically a trans-Saharan migrant, although a few of the old birds winter in the southern part of the breeding range (North Africa, southern Spain and Turkey). Autumn passage out of Europe takes place in August and September. The migrants return as early as mid-February in the southern part of the range but elsewhere not until April.

This species is very seldom seen on autumn passage and is thought to make a broad-front, high altitude flight southwards to cross the Mediterranean and Sahara non-stop – about 2500 km. In winter it is found in savanna areas from West Africa across to the Red Sea and down the whole eastern part of the continent. A census of the communal winter roosts in 1967 provided a figure of 157,000 in South Africa, outnumbering all the other falcons. The birds that far south are more likely to be

Lesser Kestrel – adult female. *Photo B. Génsbøl/Biofoto.*

from the eastern populations. These wintering birds arrive from October onwards, and return in March, when western European birds are already as far north as the Mediterranean.

This species is more often seen, in small flocks, on spring migration. The vagrant records north of the breeding area (Britain, Ireland, Denmark and Sweden) are from both spring and autumn. Several of the British sightings have been of late birds in October or November.

Habitat
Prefers steppes and semi-deserts, country where the vegetation does not completely cover the ground, so that the bird can catch food without difficulty. The species also requires a cave for its nest, either in cliffs, slopes, trees or buildings. It often forms colonies in towns.

The foraging habitat must also lie close to the breeding site, for normally it catches food at not more than one kilometre from the nest.

It spends the winter in open areas in a nomadic existence, hunting for suitable food, either solitarily or in flocks.

Voice
This differs considerably from that of the Kestrel, consisting partly of hoarse *tske-tske-tske* calls, and partly of harmonious wader-like *vivivi*. The voice is much used in the colony and in the winter quarters, when living as a flock.

Breeding
Lesser Kestrels breed for the first time when 1–2 years old. Pair formation only lasts a single season. They breed in colonies, not uncommonly

Lesser Kestrel – adult female. *Photo B. Génsbøl/Biofoto.*

with 100–200 pairs. The species may also breed solitarily.

It seems that the male arrives in the breeding grounds first. He starts immediately to search for a nest site, such as clefts or caves in cliffs or slopes, niches in buildings and lofts, roof cavities and hollow trees. Nesting boxes are also used.

The display, which is similar to that of the Kestrel, starts when the female arrives. The eggs are laid in mid-April in the Mediterranean area, in late April in the Balkans and in early May in central Europe. The clutch of 3–5 (2–8) eggs is incubated by both sexes for 28–29 days per egg. The chicks remain in the nest for 28 days.

Lesser Kestrel – adult male with insect. *Photo B. Génsbøl/Biofoto.*

Food

Mainly insects with grasshoppers and beetles as the most important element. In spring, when grasshoppers are not present in sufficient numbers, the birds catch a number of small mammals, primarily small rodents. As secondary prey they take various reptiles (lizards and small snakes). In the winter quarters flying termites form an important part of the diet.

An Austrian investigation carried out in the breeding season (on 23,980 prey remains) showed the following distribution: field crickets 40 per cent, mole crickets 28 per cent, green grasshoppers 12 per cent, a beetle species 8 per cent, bush crickets 4 per cent and cockchafers 3 per cent. These 6 insect species accounted for 95 per cent of the prey in respect of weight. Mammals were recorded as scarcely 4 per cent by weight (various small rodents and insectivores) and birds as scarcely one per cent (skylark nestlings).

Foraging methods

As the list of prey suggests, this raptor does not require a great display of strength. It hunts from a perch or, now and again, by hovering. When prey is sighted on the ground the falcon hovers downwards, only stooping from a height of 30–100 m.

Flying insects are seized in the talons and sometimes eaten in the air.

Lesser Kestrels can also be seen walking about on the ground in search of prey.

Lesser Kestrel – adult male with grasshoppers. *Photo A. Limbrunner.*

Lesser Kestrel population in the Western Palearctic

Portugal	min. 300 pairs (1982)[19]	Decreasing.
Spain	< 50,000 pairs (1982)[19]	Decreasing markedly due to habitat changes and environmental poisoning. About 100,000 pairs in 1960s.

Lesser Kestrel

Gibraltar	15 pairs (1980)[32]	
France	15 pairs (1982)[19]	
Italy	200–400 pairs (1982)[19]	Decreasing. Sicily: only a few small colonies (1977)[46]. Sardinia 200–400 pairs (1977)[41].
Austria	4–7 pairs (1978)[1]	Decreasing markedly. 280 pairs in 1960.
Yugoslavia	few (1982)[19]	Decreasing.
Albania	?	Recorded as breeding, but numbers unknown (1974)[3].
Greece	>2000 pairs (1982)[19]	Decreasing markedly in certain places due to poisoning (1974)[3]. In addition, prevented from breeding in old houses (1983)[84].
Bulgaria	rare (1979)[1]	Formerly very common.
Romania	rare (1979)[1]	Formerly common, in any case locally.
USSR	?	Common in Ukraine, Crimea and Caucasus (1951)[1].
Turkey	500–2000 pairs (1982)[19]	Locally common (1979)[1].
Cyprus	15 pairs (1982)[19]	
Syria	?	Decreasing. Still quite a few breeding sites (1982)[65].
Lebanon	?	Decreasing. Still quite a few breeding sites (1982)[65].
Israel	300–500 pairs (1982)[19]	Considerable decrease (from 2000–2500 pairs) due to poisoning.
Tunisia	<100 pairs (1982)[19]	
Algeria	rare (1982)[19]	
Morocco	>1000 pairs (1982)[19]	

Steppe Eagle juvenile. *Photo B. Génsbøl/Biofoto.*

Identification of flying raptors

Apart from field ornithologists most people find considerable difficulty in identifying raptors. An individual species may show differences from bird to bird in the appearance of the plumage. There may be variation in the proportions from individual to individual and between the sexes. A stiff breeze can radically alter the profile of a flying raptor. The bird is often a considerable distance away and the conditions for observation are sometimes poor, as for example when seen against a grey sky.

Identification is based on three main elements: the appearance of the plumage, the proportions of the bird's body and the characteristics of flight.

Plumage

Of these three elements the plumage is the most basic. Several species show considerable individual differences and the colour patterns may also be useless for identification. Nevertheless, there are some species which are easy to identify from their plumage. These are, for instance, Osprey, Short-toed Eagle, Booted Eagle (pale phase), adult White-tailed Eagle and Bonelli's Eagle, young Golden Eagle, Egyptian Vulture, Kite and Black-winged Kite.

In the identification of the individual species the following expressions are used for the different age stages. Juvenile plumage (juv.): the bird's first fully feathered plumage. Immature plumage (imm.): the stage between the moulting of the juvenile plumage and the acquisition of the adult plumage. Lastly, adult plumage (ad.).

In addition, the drawings may provide a more accurate indication of age, e.g. 2 yrs. This means that the bird's plumage is shown in its second calendar year. A bird designated as 2 yrs in June is therefore about one year old.

Proportions

There are difficulties in assessing differences in proportions. It is plain that, compared to a Buzzard, a Kestrel has both narrower wings and a longer tail. However, to record that a Rough-legged Buzzard has longer wings than a Buzzard requires experience. The observer must have seen a certain number of individuals of both species, and most will be on uncertain ground when trying to judge from the slenderness of the wings and the length of the tail whether the bird seen is an Imperial Eagle rather than a Golden Eagle. Such a judgement requires much experience.

Flight characteristics

Experience is also required when it comes to noticing the differences in flight of individual species. Many Buzzards must be seen before the observer realizes that an actively flying Honey Buzzard moves its wings in a different way. Generally speaking there should be a systematic approach to the problem. The observer cannot be said to know his raptors until he is capable of distinguishing these slight differences in flight pattern.

Each species has a typical way of

holding its wings when soaring and when gliding. It is important to stress that this refers to the 'typical' mode. Deviations from this are common, possibly only for short periods and often under particular weather conditions. Furthermore, the way the wings are held when gliding depends upon the flight speed.

Aberrant individuals

The identification of raptors is a difficult field, even for the expert. The distance away of the bird will often prevent the accurate identification of a species, and aberrant individuals may also be confusing so that identification is impossible. Thus the ornithologist who can cover all the detailed points is scarcely credible.

Attempts at simplification

In the following review of the species the idea has been to render the difficult points as simple as possible. This does not mean that the subject has thereby become simple. It does, however, mean that the number of characteristics is restricted to what I find necessary for an accurate species identification. So, some detailed descriptions of plumage will not be found. As an example of this principle I should mention that in the section on the Kite there is a total of ten recognition characteristics covering plumage and proportions. Without going into great detail it would be possible to give ten more characteristics, but there are not necessary. The species can be easily identified from the first-named ten, to add the next ten would be confusing.

The Kite is, of course, an example of a species that is easy to identify. It is much more difficult, for example, to distinguish between an Imperial Eagle and a Steppe Eagle, and under each of these it has been necessary to cite over 30 different characteristics associated with plumage and proportions.

Analyses

As will be seen, the text cannot be used to learn everything about raptors. This must be learned from other sources. Species that are easy to identify can be dealt with by a rapid overall assessment, but more difficult ones must be judged in relation to the three elements already mentioned, namely plumage, proportions and flight. Here it is very necessary to know the points that are of special importance in the identification of an individual species.

Detailed drawings

The artist has attempted to provide a completely accurate picture of the bird's appearance, so that, generally speaking, the drawings may show characteristics not mentioned in the text.

Arrangement of species

In a work of this nature it is best to present the species on the basis of their common characteristics. So the following arrangement has been used:

buzzards	kites	hawks
eagles	harriers	falcons
vultures		

Upperside

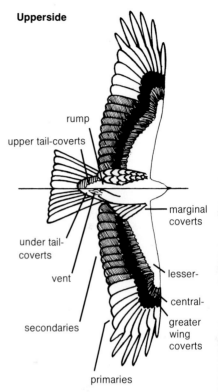

rump

upper tail-coverts

marginal coverts

under tail-coverts

vent

lesser-

central-

secondaries

greater wing coverts

primaries

Underside

Plumage characters

This section of the book assumes that the reader has a knowledge of certain technical terms, particularly those used to describe parts of the plumage. The above diagram of a Black Kite shows these terms.

Buzzard

Buteo buteo

General impression: standard buzzard type. A medium-sized, very broad-winged and relatively short-tailed raptor with a large, rounded head.

Proportions: the relation between the wing breadth, tail length and the large head positioned close to the front edge to the wings gives the Buzzard a very compact appearance.

Plumage: this is one of the species in which the plumage shows great variation, making identification based on plumage difficult. However, most individuals have the normal type of plumage, in which the upperparts are dark brown, the underparts with the body and wing-coverts are more or less dark, dark markings at the wing joints and wing tips (B 1), dark rear edges to wings and tail (E 2) and, in contrast to all this, a pale area on the outermost primaries (E 3).

Within this basic pattern there are transitional phases to darker or paler birds. The darkest (E) has blackish-brown underparts (but is distinctly pale on the wing primaries). The palest phase has very pale underparts (A). The variations on the upperparts are not so marked as those on the underparts. But pale birds sometimes also have pale areas on the back and root of the tail and may be as pale as the bird in drawing L.

Races: there are several races within the Western Palearctic. Two of these, *B.b. vulpinus*, Steppe

Buzzard, breeding to the north and east, and *B.b. menestriesi* from the south-eastern area can often be distinguished in the field. The Steppe Buzzard is generally smaller and has slightly narrower and more pointed wings than the nominate race, and has more contrast on the underparts. Thus, as seen on the drawings F, G and H, the pale areas on the primaries are distinctly larger and the secondaries also appear paler. This provides more contrast to the black rear edge of the wings. The tail is yellowish-white, pale red-brown or cinnamon-coloured.

The Steppe Buzzard occurs in three distinct phases in which the body and wing-coverts are almost a uniform red-brown (H), grey-brown (G) or (uncommonly) almost black (F). Apart from these typical birds there are 'multi-coloured' ones, very similar to the nominate race, in which the race sometimes cannot be identified in the field.

B.b. menestriesi resembles the Steppe Buzzard but is larger (generally larger than the nominate race). The plumage is typically rust-red.

Young birds: when conditions for observation are good it is often possible to determine the age of Buzzards in the field. The best character is the tail pattern. Old Buzzards usually have a distinct broad and sharply defined band at the edge of the tail (E 2).

Young birds lack this. This character is best seen when the birds are soaring and the tail is spread. In general, the young birds are paler than the old ones. They often have the underparts distinctly marked with longitudinal stripes; dark birds also have longitudinal stripes on the characteristic pale breast. Very pale birds cannot be aged with any certainty, but they just appear to be young.

Young Buzzards also have a more diffuse dark pattern on the rear edge of the wing and darker, more coarsely patterned secondaries, but this character requires considerable experience. There are often only small differences from the old birds.

Flight: in the typical soaring flight the wings are held slightly raised (Q) and pressed distinctly forwards (P). When gliding the wings are held almost flat (R). However, it is also seen with the hand more drooping (like a Honey Buzzard), but then usually with a very distinct angle between arm and hand, so that the outermost serrated primaries are very clearly seen. In gliding the arm is held obliquely forward, the hand obliquely backwards, so the wings form a distinct angle. The wing beat is very stiff and not particularly deep.

Characteristic behaviour: now and again hovers when hunting.

Buzzard I – adult (w. 113–128 cm)

A

B

1

C

D

E

3

2

F Steppe Buzzard   **G** Steppe Buzzard   **H** Steppe Buzzard

Likelihood of confusion: in northern Europe one of the main problems is to distinguish between the Buzzard and the Honey Buzzard. Even though there are several distinguishing characters for the two species, in practice there are often difficulties in identification. In silhouette the Honey Buzzard appears to have a smaller head, more slender neck and the head extended forwards so that the beak is seen. The Honey Buzzard also has a longer tail, which appears convex when folded, with rounded corners, and often a slight fork, most typically in the young birds. The wings are also longer, narrower at the base and with the hand more rounded than in the Buzzard.

Separation of the two species on a basis of silhouettes may be difficult where young Honey Buzzards are concerned. These are typically more like Buzzards. The wings are relatively shorter than in the old birds, with a broader arm and narrower hand. Individual young Honey Buzzards also have a shorter tail and so in conjunction with the juvenile wing shape may to a considerable extent show the proportions of a Buzzard.

In soaring flight the Honey Buzzard generally holds its wings flat, while the Buzzard's are clearly raised, lifted and pressed forwards. In gliding flight it is typical that the Honey Buzzard has drooping hands whereas the Buzzard holds its wings flat. There are transitional stages, for example, a Buzzard often glides with drooping hands. Apart from its smaller wingspan the Buzzard is characterized by the more distinct angle between arm and hand, and by the outer primaries appearing more clearly as 'fingers'.

In active flight it is also typical that the Honey Buzzard lifts its head so that the breast becomes convex, and that like the kites it often turns the tail on its own axis. For the trained observer the wing movements also differ. The Honey Buzzard has distinctly deeper, softer and more elastic wing beats than the Buzzard. Under good conditions the observer will, in spite of all these details, generally use the plumage characters to separate the two species. Thus, it is typical that most old Honey Buzzards have a 'watered' pattern on the underparts. Note that in the Buzzard the pattern on the wings is evenly arranged as narrow bands.

All old Honey Buzzards have a distinct dark rear edge to the wings and tail, in contrast to the Buzzard.

These clearly contrast with the surrounding areas of plumage.

While young Buzzards, to a considerable extent, resemble the old, the plumage of young Honey Buzzards is less characteristic. The secondaries are usually dark and cross-banded and the rear edges to the wings and tail lack the striking dark bands.

On the other hand, many young Honey Buzzards (around 60 per cent in Scandinavia) have a characteristic yellowish-brown or red-brown colour on the body and wing-coverts, which is a good field character. The dark type (roughly 20 per cent in Scandinavia) may, at difficult angles, be distinguished from dark Buzzards by their pale greater wing-coverts, which appear as a diffuse pale band on the underwings. Note that dark Buzzards (nominate race) always have a pale area on the breast (drawing E on p. 287).

For other likely points of confusion see Rough-legged Buzzard (p. 290), Long-legged Buzzard (p. 292) and Short-toed Eagle (p. 322).

Buzzard II

I juv.

Buzzard

J juv.

K juv.

L juv.

N juv.

M juv.

O ad. Steppe Buzzard

Q soaring

R gliding

P ad.

289

Rough-legged Buzzard

Buteo lagopus

General impression: a typical buzzard, particularly when soaring, so a broad-winged raptor with a full tail and a large broad head. Larger than a Buzzard.

Proportions: wings and tail relatively longer than in the Buzzard. In low flight over open country these proportions have a certain resemblance to the larger harriers.

Plumage: typical old birds have very pale underparts with black on the wing tips, at the base of the hands (C 1), on the belly (C 2), throat, and front of breast, and a distinct dark rear edge to the wings. Between the dark on the breast and belly there is a characteristic pale band. The white tail with a broad dark distal band (C 3, F 3) is a completely decisive identification character. In adult birds the sex can be distinguished. The male (A) has 3–4 (5) bands on the underside of the tail, 4–5 on its upperside (F). In addition, the underside of the secondaries has numerous cross-bands and dark lesser wing-coverts, and the breast is dark with a relatively pale belly marking. The adult female (C) somewhat resembles the young birds. The underside of the wing-coverts is pale, the secondaries often with distinctly fewer cross-bands. The belly marking is darker and the breast paler than in the male, the tail normally with only one broad distal band, now and again with a narrow band proximal to it.

Young birds: similar to the female but with less contrast. Typically they have very pale secondaries (D 4) without distinct distal bands, pale wing-coverts, pale throat and front of breast and a diffuse distal band on the tail (D 5). The upperparts have a paler head, front of back, wing-coverts (E 6) and primaries (E 7). After the first moult, when about one year old, immature males may show a tail like an old female. At an age of two years the birds have a full plumage.

Variants: pale birds without the dark belly marking (B) are seen, but rarely.

Flight: soars with the wings pressed slightly forwards, as in the Buzzard, but raised somewhat higher (G), often like a harrier. In active flight the wing beats are slow and elastic, unlike the very stiff beats of a Buzzard. When gliding the wings are slightly raised (H).

Characteristic behaviour: often hovers. Sometimes seen flying low over open country.

Likelihood of confusion: seen flying low over the ground, the Rough-legged Buzzard has a striking resemblance to a large harrier; if the white tail is seen to a Hen Harrier, and otherwise to a Marsh Harrier. However, the differences are so great that this confusion is soon lost. Large, very long-winged individuals, only observed superficially, may also resemble a medium-sized eagle.

The real chance of confusion is between this species and a pale Buzzard or Honey Buzzard. Thus, a white tail base is seen in pale Buzzards but unlike that of a Rough-legged Buzzard it lacks the well-defined black distal band. Individuals of the eastern Buzzard race, the Steppe Buzzard, may resemble a Rough-legged Buzzard in the tail pattern. Here the size will be a help. The Steppe Buzzard is smaller than the nominate race of Buzzard and thus clearly smaller than a Rough-legged Buzzard. If there are difficulties in seeing the characteristic tail then the relatively longer wings of the present species should help in identification. Similarly, when in flight, the more elastic wing beats and the raised wings of the Rough-legged Buzzard should be good clues to identification.

On confusion with the Long-legged Buzzard *see* p. 292.

Rough-legged Buzzard (w. 120–150 cm)

B ad.

C ad. ♀

A ad. ♂

1

2

3

3

D juv.

4

7

6

5

E juv.

3 →

G soaring

H gliding

F ad. ♂

291

Long-legged Buzzard

Buteo rufinus

General impression: in silhouette, a typical buzzard, that is a medium-sized, very broad-winged raptor with a large, broad and rounded head and a full tail.

Proportions: very similar to the Rough-legged Buzzard in size and proportions and distinctly larger than the Buzzard, with longer wings and a long tail (about the same as the width of the wing).

Plumage: as is typical for buzzards, the Long-legged Buzzard also varies in appearance from individual to individual, with very dark to very pale birds. However, the species has the following good recognition characters: the head and foremost part of the breast are often very pale (C 1), in contrast to the dark belly and rump (C 2). In addition, most have a pale tail which is a good field character (E 3). In very pale individuals with full plumage the dark rear edge of the wings is clearly seen (C 4). The underparts all have striking white on the primaries, often in contrast to the black markings at the joint between arm and hand or to the dark wing-coverts.

The upperparts are often characterized by four characters: pale head (E 5), pale tail (E 3), a pale area on the primaries (E 6) and red-brown wing-coverts in contrast to dark secondaries (E 7). There are three colour phases: pale, red and dark. There are all sorts of possible transitions between the first two, but the third is generally a pure dark form.

In this the tail (D) is marked with cross-bands. This dark form generally breeds only in the Volga region and eastwards, but is seen on migration in the Middle East.

Young birds: the two pale phases can be distinguished by the 9–12 transverse stripes on the pale tail. This character is rather difficult to discern in the field. As is usual in buzzards, the black rear edge to the wing is more diffuse or only just indicated in the young birds. The primaries are often darker and the dark belly marking not so well developed. The species has a full plumage when about two years old.

Flight: very similar to that of the Rough-legged Buzzard, that is, with very slow elastic beats. In soaring flight the wings are held slightly forwards, as in the Buzzard, and compared with the latter a good field character is that the wings are raised still higher (G), and so are very similar to the Rough-legged Buzzard.

Characteristic behaviour: often hovers.

Likelihood of confusion: in profile and in flight the Long-legged Buzzard much resembles the Rough-legged Buzzard. In certain cases the plumage of the two species is also similar. The Rough-legged Buzzard can, however, always be recognized by the broad, outermost tail band. Only very exceptionally, however, will the two species occur in the same area. The pattern of the red-brown Steppe

Buzzard, a race of the Buzzard, resembles that of the Long-legged Buzzard to the point of confusion. The Steppe Buzzard is, however, distinctly smaller and does not raise the wings so high when soaring. To a considerable extent the present species with its relatively long wings somewhat resembles an eagle. So there are no great problems when the Steppe Buzzard and Long-legged Buzzard are seen together. Normally it is a good field character that the Long-legged Buzzard's belly is dark in contrast to the surrounding pale areas. Most old Steppe Buzzards have a uniformly coloured body and uniformly coloured wing-coverts on the underside, with very pale wing feathers with broad, blackish markings at the tips. Young Steppe Buzzards may be very pale, but neither these nor the old have the dark belly markings of the Long-legged Buzzard. This is not particularly well marked in the young of the present species. The Steppe Buzzard may well have a dark area on the underparts, but this is usually seen on the breast, that is, higher up than in the Long-legged Buzzard. Normally, the latter's head is also paler and the upperparts have more contrast. Thus, there is a contrast between wing feathers and wing-coverts. Here, the Steppe Buzzard shows almost uniformly coloured upperparts, with the exception of the pale areas on the head and the pale tail. In addition, the tail often has several weakly-marked cross-bands, whereas old Long-legged Buzzards are entirely pale.

A ad.

B ad.

D ad.

C ad.

1

2

4

E ad.

6

7

5

← 3

F juv.

G soaring

H gliding

Honey Buzzard

Pernis apivorus

General impression: a medium-sized, very broad-winged and long-tailed raptor, the size of a Buzzard.

Proportions: in comparison with a Buzzard, note a slender neck and a small dove-like head (e.g. C 1), which extends beyond the front edge of the wings, and a long tail about as long as the wing breadth or more. When folded the tail is convex and often rounded. Old birds have narrower wings than the Buzzard, due to a narrower arm, although the hand is more rounded. The wingspan is a little greater than that of the Buzzard.

Plumage: this varies so much that it cannot always be used in identifying the species. Typical individuals (B, C, D and E) can, however, be identified by the striking patterns on the underwing and the body's mottled pattern (C 2). Individual variations extend from pale (A) to very dark (F).

It is especially the underparts that vary, particularly the colour and pattern of the head, body and wing-coverts. But as can be seen in illustrations A to F, the appearance of the wing feathers is generally the same in old birds whether they belong to dark or pale individuals; these feathers are very pale with a conspicuous black edge to the wing (F 3) and usually with two narrow bands more proximally on the wing. The cross-bands on the tail are also useful characters (B 4).

The upperparts are a very uniform dark colour (G) and on the whole only show minimum variation.

Sex differences: adult birds: **male** – slate grey head; **female** – usually brown head, in some cases with grey around eyes. Furthermore males have fewer bands on wings (F), these bands also being more irregularly distributed than in the females. Thus there is a greater distance between the broad band on the back edge of the wings and the next.

The same sex-difference is found relating to tail features (cannot be seen on drawings, where all birds have been drawn with 'male-tails').

Normally the males can also be distinguished by the banding on the upper primaries and upper secondaries (G7).

Young birds: differ in proportion, often being more like a Buzzard. Thus the arm is sometimes broader, the hand narrower than in old birds, and the wingspan less.

The plumage differs on several points from that of old birds. It is important that the secondaries are grey to greyish-black and cross-banded (J 5) irrespective of whether the birds are dark or pale. However, young birds without this character may occur. Furthermore, the young birds lack the conspicuous dark edges to the wings which is so characteristic of old Honey Buzzards. It is less striking that the young birds have several, most often four, not particularly conspicuous tail bands (L 6). The tail may be shorter but this is not common; it is often slightly

forked. The rear edge of the wing is S-shaped. A wing with this appearance *may*, however, also be seen in old birds. Furthermore, the wing tips are distinctly darker than in the old birds. As in the case of the adults there are also several types of plumage in the young birds, from dark to very pale. In the darkest type (around 20 per cent) the underparts (head, body and wing-coverts) are blackish-brown, but the commonest form (about 60 per cent) is a characteristic red-brown colour on the underparts, a good field character compared with the Buzzard. For many young birds (the common type plus most of the pale) it is typical that the breast has longitudinal stripes (N). On the upperside the young birds have slightly paler tips to the greater wing-coverts. Apparently, birds with a pale head are most often young. In the completely pale individuals there is a dark pattern near the eyes, suggesting that the bird has spectacles. At close range one sees quite clearly that the young birds, like those of the Buzzard, have a yellow cere. In old birds this is blue-grey. Honey Buzzards acquire a full plumage at an age of about two years.

Flight: in comparison with the Buzzard the wing beats are deeper and more elastic. In soaring flight the wings are held straight out from the body, in contrast to the Buzzard which presses its wings forwards. Also in soaring flight the rear edge of the wing has a less distinctive S-curve than the Buzzard, on account of the more rounded head. In soaring flight the wings are

Honey Buzzard I – adult (w. 135–150 cm)

A

B

C

↑ ↑
1 2

↑
4

D

E

F

♂

← 3

G

↑
7

H soaring

gliding

295

Adult Honey Buzzard *Photo D. Skjelle*

held flat (H), in gliding more arched (I) with the hands almost drooping. In slow gliding the rear edge of the arm forms an almost straight line (F), a character only seen in old Honey Buzzards. In the Buzzard it is curved.

Likelihood of confusion: *see* Buzzard (p. 286). Pale Honey Buzzards may be confused with Rough-legged Buzzards, but they never have the latter's striking tail pattern. Pale individuals of Buzzard and Honey Buzzard may have patterns similar to those of the pale phase of Booted Eagle. These will, however, never have the Booted Eagle's dark wing feathers. Compared with dark individuals of Buzzard and Honey Buzzard the dark wing feathers of the Booted Eagle are also a decisive character (dark phase). The combination of dark wing feathers and three pale innermost primaries will never be seen in the buzzards, which always have large or small areas of white on the primary feathers.

In the Booted Eagle the three innermost primaries are not particularly prominent. If colours cannot be seen the sharp corners to the Booted Eagle's tail are a good recognition character. Furthermore, in soaring flight the Booted Eagle holds its wings flat, unlike the Buzzard which holds them slightly raised. The upperparts of the Booted Eagle are completely different from those of the buzzards.

K

← 5

J

6
↓

M

L

N

O

Golden Eagle
Aquila chrysaetos

General impression: a very large eagle whose well-proportioned silhouette, easy and effortless flight may lead to an under-estimate of the size.

Proportions: smaller than the White-tailed Eagle, but larger than the Imperial Eagle and the Steppe Eagle, with very long, broad wings. Unlike those of the Imperial Eagle these are not rectangular, but with a distinct S-curve. The head is powerful and extended forwards, the tail is full and long and about the same as the wing breadth.

Plumage: Adult: at a distance of more than 500 m the old bird appears dark. At closer quarters it will be seen that the wing feathers on the underside have paler cross-bands at the base. The same applies to the tail feathers (A 1), a characteristic also present on the upperside (E 1). In some cases however, birds with a uniformly dark tail are seen. There is a pale area on the upperside of the wing-coverts (E 2). In all plumages the nape and crown are pale, varying between yellow and pale brown (E 3).

Young birds: in fairly good conditions these are not difficult to identify. There is a characteristic large, white area at the base of the wing feathers in both the upper- and underside (C 4), varying somewhat in size from bird to bird, and a white tail with a striking dark outermost band (C 5). On the upperside of the wings such white areas may, in some cases, be lacking. The white areas dwindle with age (D). The birds acquire a full adult plumage at an age of 5–6 years.

Flight: thanks to an easy and effortless flight pattern, with deep, powerful wing beats and full command even in a strong wind, the size of this species is often under-estimated. When soaring the wings are slightly raised (F) and pressed a little forwards so that the front edges form a curve (A). In gliding the wings are also held in the open V, as long flight is slow. With increasing speed they flatten out (G).

Likelihood of confusion: on account of the tail pattern and under poor conditions for observation the young birds may be confused with a Rough-legged Buzzard. However, the difference in size is considerable.

In Scandinavia there may be confusion with the White-tailed Eagle, but apart from the differences in proportions and plumage the flight patterns are also quite different. While the Golden Eagle is essentially elegant in the air, the White-tailed Eagle is a heavy and rather clumsy bird with stiff wing movements. The Golden Eagle has soft, deep wing beats. Furthermore, when soaring the White-tailed Eagle holds its wings flat or just slightly raised, not in the open V of the Golden Eagle.

There may also be confusion with the Steppe Eagle as the old birds of both species are dark. In its proportions the Steppe Eagle differs in being slightly smaller, with more rectangular wings, the head scarcely extended so far forwards and the tail shorter, often almost wedge-shaped. The plumages of the two species also differ. The Golden Eagle has a distinctly pale crown and nape, a pale area on the most central wing-coverts on the upperside, and a two-coloured tail. Also the wing feathers on the underside are only pale at the base, whereas in the Steppe Eagle they are greyish with distinct cross-bands with only the rear edge dark. At a distance the Golden Eagle appears uniformly dark on the underparts, while even at a long distance the Steppe Eagle appears to have a black body contrasting with the rather grey underwings with black tips. Normally the Steppe Eagle has pale areas on the upperside of the hands. These can, however, be replaced by weaker markings with pale shafts to the primaries. Furthermore, when soaring the Golden Eagle slightly raises the wings, whereas the Steppe Eagle holds them flat or even slightly drooping, as seen in the spotted eagles.

For possible confusion with the Imperial Eagle *see* p. 300.

Golden Eagle (w. 204–220 cm)

A ad.

B juv.

C imm.

D imm.

E ad.

F soaring

G gliding

Imperial Eagle
Aquila heliaca

General impression: a large eagle, almost as large as the Golden Eagle. Depending upon age there are several different plumages.

Proportions: relatively long and broad wings and these, unlike the Golden Eagle, have the front and rear edges almost parallel (A and I). This does not apply to the young birds. The very powerful head protrudes beyond the front edge of the wings, the tail is full and fairly long, almost as long as the wing breadth.

Plumage: adults. The adult plumage is very dark (blackish-brown). In sharp contrast to this is the pale yellowish colour on the upperside of the head and on the nape (I 1), the pale shoulder feathers (I 2) and the greyish-white vent (A 3). The tail is greyish with darker cross-bands and with a broad dark edge, a character which together with the pale rump gives the impression of a two-coloured tail. The same character is also seen on the upperside, but is most striking on the underside where it is visible from a great distance (A 4). In good light the species shows a contrast on the underside, as in the Spotted Eagle, of very dark wing-coverts with paler grey wing feathers.

Races: old birds of the Spanish race (I) have a very distinct pale area on the upperside of the arm's front edge (the lesser wing-coverts).

Young birds: in their first plumage the juveniles differ considerably from the old birds. The total impression is of a very pale bird, with pale yellow-brown feathers on the head and most of the body and on the lesser and more central wing-coverts, both on the upper- and underside (E 5 and L 5).

The breast and the upper part of the belly have fairly dense dark brown longitudinal stripes. At a distance this may look like a dark breast band. On the underside the greater wing-coverts and wing feathers are dark with pale tips. This is seen as a narrow whitish band in the middle of the wing and a broader one on its rear edge. A corresponding band is found at the outermost edge of the dark tail. These white rear edges are not seen at a distance and because of this the young birds appear more slender than they really are. Another decisive character is the uniformly silver-grey colour of the innermost three primaries (F 6). In certain cases this extends to the lesser wing-coverts giving a slightly paler area, somewhat reminiscent of a young Steppe Eagle. However, this area is not in the same place and is not nearly so striking as the sharply patterned wing band of a Steppe Eagle.

On the upperside the contrasts correspond to those on the underside. However, the greater and central wing-coverts have pale tips, producing two pale wing bands (L 7). There is a large whitish area on the rear of the back and on the rump (L 8). The pale area on the wing, formed by the three pale primaries, is also seen very distinctly on the upperside (L 6).

The next plumage stage, the immature, is acquired when the bird is about three years old. The moult, however, is continuous so that there are innumerable different transitional plumages, some of which are very variegated. The throat, the upper part of the breast and the lesser wing-coverts are moulted first. The other contour feathers and wing-coverts moult next, so that the plumage gradually becomes darker. The juvenile characters are longest retained on the most central wing-coverts and on the rear of the back. The pale band on the upperside of the wing may persist but less distinctly.

The Imperial Eagle has its full adult plumage at an age of five years.

Flight: an elegant bird in the air, but scarcely as elegant as the Golden Eagle, although old birds in particular can appear slender and elegant. The wing beats are powerful and well-executed. When soaring the wings are held flat (G), or in certain cases slightly raised and at a right angle from the body, so not pressed forwards as in the Golden Eagle. In rapid gliding flight the wings often have drooping hands (H).

Likelihood of confusion: in Europe confusion is most likely with the Golden Eagle. Old Imperial Eagles have slightly narrower wings, with parallel front and rear edges, giving them a more rectangular appearance. So

Imperial Eagle I (w. 190–210 cm)

A ad.

B ad. (Spanish race)

4

3

C imm. (3 yrs)

D imm.

F juv.

5

6

E juv.

G soaring

H gliding

the rear edge of the wing does not have the S-curve of the Golden Eagle. However, the two species can be incredibly similar to one another. The Imperial Eagle's tail is scarcely as long and full. Among the differences in plumage it is important to mention that the Golden Eagle has a pale area (yellow-brown) on the upperside's wing-coverts and that, seen from below, the Imperial Eagle's tail is distinctly two-coloured. This impression is strengthened by the pale vent. Old Golden Eagles also have a two-coloured tail but this is only seen under really good conditions of observation.

The Imperial Eagle's pale crown and shoulder feathers are striking, but pale shoulder feathers may also be seen in the Golden Eagle, although they are less conspicuous. All in all, the two species are very similar. This applies both to their majestic proportions and flight and to their plumage.

In soaring flight the Imperial Eagle normally holds the wings flat, but may hold them raised, whereas the Golden Eagle soars with slightly raised wings. Confusion with the Steppe Eagle, Spotted Eagle and Lesser Spotted is discussed under these species.

Steppe Eagle
Aquila nipalensis

General impression: a large, powerful and broad-winged eagle, with proportions and mode of flight that are reminiscent of the spotted eagles.

Proportions: as in the Imperial Eagle, the wings in this species have parallel front and rear edges. The head is scarcely as large, but markedly extended forwards, and the beak is smaller. The tail varies in length and shape, usually a little shorter than in the Imperial Eagle and often with a tendency to become wedge-shaped. Thus, in its proportions it resembles a large Spotted Eagle, but in relation to the latter the wings and particularly the head are longer. The head is more protruding and less rounded, the beak larger. In very young Steppe Eagles and Imperial Eagles the proportions are closer to one another. However, the Imperial Eagle has a larger more protruding head, a more powerful neck and a larger beak.

Plumage: at a distance the old birds show a characteristic contrast on the underparts, having a uniformly dark body, with greyish underwings in which only the tips are dark. At closer quarters the lesser and central wing-coverts (to a varying extent) are also dark, and the wing feathers are greyish with very characteristic cross-banding (A 1). The tail has the same character. The upperparts appear uniformly dark blackish-brown. There is usually also a conspicuous pale area on the innermost primaries (K 2) and in about 75 per cent of the birds a pale marking on the back (K 3). In addition, the rump, nape (K 4) and throat are slightly paler.

Young birds: very young Steppe Eagles (juveniles) like young Imperial Eagles often have a somewhat convex rear edge to the wings, forming an S-curve. In comparison with the adults the tail often seems to be slightly longer. In many cases the young will therefore appear better proportioned than the old birds, and the plumage clearly paler. Thus, the whole of the head, body and the lesser and central wing-coverts are yellow-brown (J 5 and M 5). In contrast to this the secondaries and tail feathers are very dark but with pale tips, so producing a pale rear border. This may, however, be difficult to see against a blue sky. The white greater wing-coverts which form a band on the underside of the wings is in sharp contrast to the remainder of the plumage (J 6). The three innermost primaries are slightly paler than the other wing feathers and they also have close cross-banding.

The contrasts on the upperside correspond with those on the underparts except for the white upper tail-coverts, and the dark greater wing-coverts with their pale tips which form a narrow pale band at the transition between the wing-coverts and the flight feathers.

The pale area on the three innermost primaries is rather more distinct than on the underside, but these feathers are not pale silver-grey (M 8) as in the Imperial Eagle. In rare cases young Steppe Eagles may have the rear of the back completely pale as in the Imperial Eagle.

J imm. (4 yrs?)

ad.
(Spanish race)

1

2

8

5

7

6

L juv.

K imm.

Steppe Eagle I (w. 174–260 cm)

A ad.

B ad.

1

D soaring

E gliding

C ad.

The birds only start to acquire the adult plumage at the second moult. The head, neck, breast and belly gradually become darker. The same applies to the lesser and central wing-coverts and the back. Because there is great individual variation in the pattern of moulting there are numerous different transitional plumages (F, G, H and I), with a range of variation which is possibly even greater than in the Imperial Eagle.

In the transitional plumages most Steppe Eagles retain the underside's distinct wing bands, either completely or partially (G, H and I). Thus, birds which have almost attained the definitive plumage continue to show the pale area on the greater wing-coverts. This character may, however, be lacking. Dark birds may cause problems on account of their similarity to the Imperial Eagle. At this stage in the development of the full plumage, immature Steppe Eagles will have acquired the adult proportions and at close quarters the transverse striping on the flight feathers can also be seen. The dark rear edge of the wings and the pale base of the primaries will also be specific. Also, immature Imperial Eagles have a cream-coloured crown.

Flight: the wing movements appear somewhat heavy and stiff. The Steppe Eagle does not fly with the 'carried through' wing beats used by the Imperial Eagle. It normally soars on flat or slightly drooping wings (D), extended at right angles from the body, so not pressed forwards as in the Golden Eagle. When gliding the wings form an angle at the base of the hand (E), very like the Spotted Eagle.

Likelihood of confusion: compared with adult Imperial Eagles this is a more stoutly built, more broad-winged and short-tailed bird, with a less protruding head and beak.

The plumage differs in having a dark head, possibly a little pale on the nape, in having greyish flight feathers with conspicuous dark cross-bands, and in not having a two-coloured tail. At a distance this gives the Steppe Eagle a characteristic contrast between the almost black body and the paler underwings. Here the Imperial Eagle appears more uniformly dark, that is, apart from the two-coloured tail and the pale crown. In good light the Imperial Eagle may often show a black body and central and lesser wing-coverts, in contrast to the otherwise grey underwings.

Young Imperial Eagles are more difficult to distinguish from young Steppe Eagles, partly because the differences in proportions are not so distinct as in the old birds. Young Imperial Eagles are generally pale yellow-brown. The Steppe Eagle's white greater wing-coverts on the underside are very typical. These extend as a white band under the wings, and will be visible either completely or partially in almost all the juvenile plumages. Here the Imperial Eagle has only a narrow band, which in most cases will be difficult to see. Another important difference is the pattern on the three innermost primaries. Here the Imperial Eagle's silver-grey forms a pale wedge in the otherwise dark flight feathers, while the Steppe Eagle's are only slightly paler and cross-banded and at the most appear as a pale, translucent area, far less intense than in the young Imperial Eagle. It is also characteristic that in the latter the breast has distinct longitudinal stripes, something which at a distance has the appearance of a breast band. Moulting Steppe Eagles may show a similar character but a dark throat.

The uppersides of the two species are more similar when young, except for the Imperial Eagle's pale inner primaries and pale area on the rear of the back and rump. Here the Steppe Eagle only has the upper tail-coverts white, but in very many cases it can also have a pale area at the rear of the back. In transitional plumages it may be difficult to distinguish the two species for both can appear very variegated. As a rule the young Imperial Eagle will either have the typical primaries pattern or the adult's pale crown and nape, and the two-coloured tail. In most cases the Steppe Eagle retains at least part of the wing band on the underparts. This may, however, be completely lacking. If the flight feathers have not yet been moulted to the adult's characteristic greyish tone with cross-bands, the plumage may resemble that of the adult's or that of an Imperial Eagle with an almost complete adult plumage. In such a case the plumage will, however, lack the pale crown and nape and the two-coloured tail of the Imperial Eagle.

Steppe Eagle II

Steppe Eagle

G imm. (ca. 3 yrs)

F imm. (ca. 4 yrs)

H imm. (2–3 yrs)

I imm. (2–3 yrs)

6 5

J juv.

K ad.

4

3

2

L imm. (3–4 yrs)

5

7

8

M juv.

305

Tawny Eagle
Aquila rapax

General impression and proportions: very similar to the Steppe Eagle, the plumage often resembling that of a young Imperial Eagle.

Plumage: very variable but not fully investigated. The only common character seems to be a pale area on the hand, with or without cross-bands, varying in both extent and intensity (B 1, C 1, D 1 and E 1). This may be restricted to a mere trace on the three innermost primaries. In addition, a pale dorsal area is very common (C 2, D 2 and E 2). The North American Tawny Eagle (*belisarius*) often appears to be pale yellowish. The plumage becomes markedly bleached (especially in pale birds?) by the sun. In the juvenile plumage (D) this passes in the first year from red-brown to a whitish-cream colour (E). New, unbleached feathers are differently coloured, often a red-lead colour (E 3).

The variation not only occurs in dark and pale forms. Drawing B shows a dark bird with the front of the body particularly dark. The birds may be completely dark on the underparts and lack the pale area on the rear of the back. Note also that the cross-banding is different from that of the other *Aquila* species. Furthermore, the whiteness on the back may, for example, vary independently of the bird's age.

Flight: very similar to that of the Steppe Eagle.

Likelihood of confusion: pale birds are mostly like a juvenile Imperial Eagle. The similarity is so marked that it may not be possible to separate the two. However, the pale area on the upperside of the wings may be less marked. In addition, the Imperial Eagle has a tendency to raise its wings slightly when soaring.

In comparison with juvenile and immature Steppe Eagles, the Tawny Eagle lacks the pale band on the underwings. The length of the gape also differs. In the Steppe Eagle this reaches the rear edge of the eye, in the Tawny Eagle only to the middle of the eye. The Tawny Eagle has a yellow iris, the Steppe Eagle dark brown, occasionally yellow-brown.

Dark Tawny Eagles can be confused with Imperial, Steppe, Spotted and Lesser Spotted Eagles. There will, however, always be a combination of detailed characters which excludes each of these species.

Black Eagle
Aquila verreauxii

General impression: a very large, dark eagle.

Proportions: compared with the Golden Eagle this species has a relatively longer tail and longer wings. The wing base is very narrow and the rear edge of the wing has a distinct S-curve.

Plumage: Adult: very dark. The back is black, in contrast to the white innermost on the primaries, the outermost lesser wing-coverts (B 1), the rump and rear of the back (B 2) and two white bands on the back (B 3). These bands may be separated from the white rear of the back, forming a characteristic V.

On the underside the body and wing-coverts are black, in contrast to greyish-white cross-banded primaries (A 1) and grey secondaries.

Young birds: The rump and rear of the back are white with dark markings, in contrast to a black tail. Dark centres on the wing-coverts on the upperparts give a speckled appearance. The belly is brownish-yellow with dark longitudinal stripes. The wing-coverts are paler than in the adults.

The head is brownish-yellow or golden, the nape and uppermost part of the back are red-brown, the cheeks dark.

The adult plumage is acquired gradually from the second to the fifth year. In the immature plumage it is characteristic that the tibial feathers are pale.

Flight: light and effortless. Active flight is rarely seen. In soaring the wings are raised very high (E).

Likelihood of confusion: Unlike the juvenile Imperial Eagle, young Black Eagles lack the pale three innermost primaries and have a dark front to the breast (immature Imperials may also have this). They differ from juvenile Steppe Eagles in having a different ground colour (Steppe Eagles are normally but not always more red-brown) and in lacking the distinct white band on the underside of the wings.

Tawny Eagle (w. 172–185 cm)

A

Tawny Eagle/Black Eagle

B ad. ←1

C ad. ←1 2

D juv. ←1 2

E juv. ←1 2 3

Black Eagle (w. 225–245 cm)

A ad. ←1

B ad. 1 3 2

C juv.

E soaring

D juv.

Lesser Spotted Eagle

Aquila pomarina

General impression: a medium-sized to small species with the characters typical of the spotted eagles. Compared with the Spotted Eagle the Lesser Spotted Eagle is a paler, browner bird.

Proportions: distinctly long-winged with parallel front and rear edges to the wings (most marked in the adults). The head is buzzard-like. The tail is two-thirds to three-quarters of the wing breadth (*see also* Spotted Eagle). On average the wing measurements are only about four per cent less than those of the Spotted Eagle, so size can only be used in identification in extreme cases.

Plumage: Adult: the plumage is so characteristic that it can usually be used in identification. On the underside the wing-coverts are paler warm red-brown (A 1) than the darker secondaries (A 2). The reverse is true of the Spotted Eagle. Good conditions are needed for this to be seen. Another excellent criterion for distinguishing the larger species are the pale wing-coverts on the upperside (C 3) and the pale wing markings which occur in all adults (C 4, F 4 and G 4). However, they vary in extent and strength and may be more diffuse than in drawing C (*see also* Likelihood of confusion). Other important plumage characters, not species-specific, include the pale tail-coverts on both the upper- and undersides.

Young birds: as drawing I shows the underside's contrast between wing-coverts and flight feathers may be less than in the adults. The upperside is also darker but with the lesser and central wing-coverts pale yellowish or red-brown. Normally the young of this species have only one pale wing band on the upperside, however there may be a less distinct one in front of it. Juvenile or immature Spotted Eagles may occur with a single wing band, so this character cannot be used in identification.

The young birds normally have larger and more distinct wing markings than the adults and, more important, they are more distinct than in the Spotted Eagle in which the paler markings are restricted to the feather shaft stripes. Other characters in the young are a narrow pale band on the underside of the wings, a pale rear edge to the wings and tail and a pale marking on the back. At very close quarters a pale nape marking can be seen and this is species-specific. With age the white markings on the wing-coverts disappear and the white areas around the root of the tail normally become reduced. At the same time it is common for a pale marking on the back to persist, and this may even occur in the adults. The full adult plumage is acquired at an age of 4–5 years.

Variants: *see* also under the Spotted Eagle. In rare cases there is no contrast on the underside between the wing-coverts and the flight feathers (K). Examination of drawings A, H, J and K gives an impression of the variation in the contrasts on the underside. There are also atypical individuals with a pale underside, pale head and rear of the back. Some birds, normally adults, lack the pale tone on the upper tail-coverts. Finally, recent investigations suggest that the rare '*fulvescens* variant' may also occur in the Lesser Spotted Eagle.

Flight: *see* Spotted Eagle.

Likelihood of confusion: the surest way of distinguishing adults of the two species of spotted eagle is to observe the contrasts on the underside. In the Spotted Eagle the wing-coverts are darker than the flight feathers (page 311, A 1 and A 2), while this condition is reversed in the Lesser Spotted Eagle (A 1 and A 2 on page 308). Contrasts on the upperside are also excellent field characters. Here, the Lesser Spotted Eagle has pale wing-coverts (C 3) contrasting with darker secondaries (C 5) and a distinct pale marking on each wing (C 4). The Spotted Eagle, on the other hand, is normally uniformly dark on the upperside of the wings and so without appreciable contrast, but usually with a slightly pale marking in the form of some pale shafts on certain of the primaries. However, young Spotted Eagles can be tricky. At a distance the pale markings on the wing-coverts cannot always be discerned but give the impression that the wing-coverts are pale. At

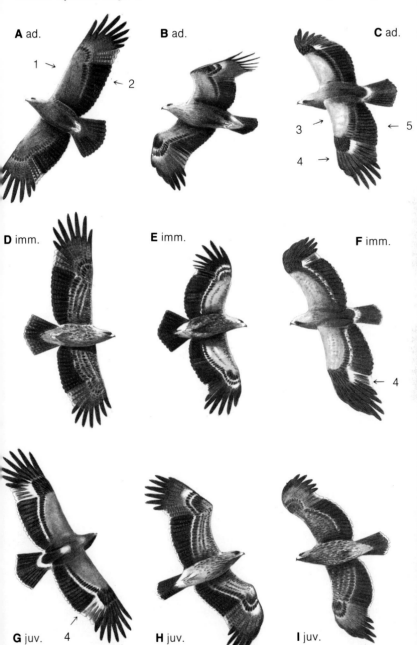

Lesser Spotted Eagle (w. 134–159 cm)

A ad.

1

2

B ad.

C ad.

3

5

4

D imm.

E imm.

F imm.

4

G juv.

4

H juv.

I juv.

the same time the pale feather shaft stripes may, at a distance, look like a pale area of wing. So there may be a faulty identification, for this character is typical of the Lesser Spotted Eagle.

As is mentioned under the Spotted Eagle the silhouette, wing position and flight are only specific criteria in very few cases. The proportions may give a slight clue to identification, but not more. Thus, there are only a few Spotted Eagles that are so broad-winged and

short-tailed (A) that corresponding characters are not seen in the Lesser Spotted Eagle. Similarly, only the very largest individuals of the Spotted Eagle fly so heavily and clumsily that this can be used as a specific identification character. There are, however, better criteria. The Spotted Eagle is normally a very dark, almost black bird, whereas the Lesser Spotted Eagle is distinctly paler and at a distance looks pale brown.

There might, of course,

be confusion with the other dark eagles, such as the Golden, Imperial, Steppe and White-tailed. These four all have the head protruding forwards, whereas the two spotted eagles are in this respect more like a Buzzard. The two first named have such long tails that there should be no problem and, of course, all four are much larger.

For details of plumage differences see under the individual species.

Spotted Eagle
Aquila clanga

General impression: a medium-sized very dark eagle, appearing almost black at a distance.

Proportions: a typical eagle with a more rounded head than the Imperial and Steppe Eagles and scarcely such long wings as these. Adults have broad wings with parallel front and rear edges, a character not so pronounced in the young. There is said to be considerable variation from individual to individual, both in size and proportions.

The species overlaps the Lesser Spotted Eagle in size and only in really large individuals (females) is the size difference so marked that a trained observer can use it as a basis for identification.

It was formerly considered that the silhouette was the best criterion for separating the two species of spotted eagle, but here too there is considerable overlapping. On average the Spotted Eagle has somewhat broader wings, and

therefore, also on average, the tail appears somewhat shorter. In both species the normal length of the tail is two-thirds to three-quarters the breadth of the wings. Older views on how prominent the head appears (it is more protruding in the present species) are invalidated. In the Spotted Eagle the same applies to the rear edge of the wings which should generally have a distinct curve. In Steppe and Imperial Eagles this is a typical character of the young birds.

Plumage: Adult: the Spotted Eagle is most easily recognized from its plumage. On the whole it is a very dark bird. In good light and at a reasonable distance it can, however, be seen that the underside's blackish-brown wing-coverts (A 1) are darker than the greyish secondaries (A 2) and that the under tail-coverts are grey (A 6). On the other hand, the upperside is almost uniformly dark (C), apart from a grey tail root

(C 3) and a not particularly distinct area on the wings formed by the pale shafts of the innermost primaries (C 4). These characters may, however, be lacking.

Young birds: may be recognized first and foremost by the upperside having white tips to the wing-coverts, usually forming a band on the wing. If there are several of these as shown in drawing K (p. 313), that is, 3–4 bands, then the bird can certainly be identified as a juvenile Spotted Eagle. At a distance this species' numerous markings may give the impression of wings with paler coverts (I). In addition, it is characteristic that the young birds have a pale rear edge to the wings and tail, white tail-coverts on the upperside (these are dark or grey in adults), and pale shafts in many of the primaries, while the body is paler towards the rear (H 5).

With age the upperside's markings dwindle and often become a single band (F 5). Now and again, there is a

Lesser Spotted Eagle II

J juv. pale phase

K juv. dark phase

L soaring

M gliding

Spotted Eagle I (w. 155–182 cm)

A ad.

B ad.

C ad.

D gliding

white marking on the back in the transition to the adult plumage, and in most cases pale tail-coverts are clearly seen. The adult plumage is apparently acquired when the birds are 4–5 years old.

Variants: this otherwise dark species can occur with the whole of the underside of the body atypically pale. There are also birds with pale feathers on the head and rearmost part of the back. Old birds without pale under tail-coverts (B) and without the pale area on the upperside of the wings are also seen occasionally. Unfortunately some birds

also lack the contrast between the underside's wing-coverts and flight feathers (J). On the whole there may be so much variation between individuals that it is not really possible to distinguish the two species of spotted eagle in the field. In another completely aberrant variant the bird has a pale head, pale body and pale wing-coverts, only the flight feathers and tail having the normal pattern. Such birds are known as the *fulvescens* variant (L) and were formerly thought to be a separate species (*Aquila fulvescens*).

Flight: the two species have more or less the same type of flight with heavy, deep wing beats. Often the larger species will appear heavier and clumsier than the Lesser Spotted Eagle. In both species, particularly when gliding, the wings are held in the way typical of spotted eagles, with the arms held out horizontally and the hands drooping (M and D). This is not a species-specific character. When soaring, both species hold the wings almost flat.

Likelihood of confusion: *see* under Lesser Spotted Eagle.

Spotted Eagle. *Photo B. Génsbøl/Biofoto.*

E imm.

F imm.

G imm.

I juv.

H juv.

5

J juv.

K juv.

L *fulvescens*

M juv. pale phase

White-tailed Eagle

Haliaeetus albicilla

General impression: a very large and heavy eagle.

Proportions: one of the largest raptors in these latitudes, and larger than the Golden Eagle. The wings are long and very broad with the front and rear edges parallel, and with the hand very full. The head extends unusually far forwards, further than in any other raptor (D 1). Thus, it protrudes as far in front of the wing edge as the tail extends behind the rear edge of the wing (D). The very large, powerful beak is also characteristic. The tail is wedge-shaped, particularly in old birds, very short (A), about half to two-thirds of the wing breadth, and longer in juveniles than in adults.

Plumage: Adult: with its white tail this is a very characteristic bird (A 2). The underparts are dark apart from the head and, to a varying extent, the breast, both of which are pale brown to yellow-brown (A 3). The upperparts are paler, with yellow-brown wing-coverts (D 4) and grey-brown to dark brown flight feathers.

Young birds: in the first, juvenile plumage this is a very dark bird. Under good

conditions the underside shows a pale marking in the armpit (C 5) and a diffuse pale band on the wing-coverts (C 6). The upperparts also have a diffuse pale band on the wing-coverts (F 7). Furthermore, the tail feathers in the otherwise dark tail have pale shafts, apart from the most central, which are completely dark (C 8). In juveniles the tail appears longer on account of the S-shaped rear edge to the wing with its distinct narrowing where it joins the body. The tail is not so markedly wedge-shaped as in the old birds.

The immature plumage is characterized primarily by the pale feathers in the tail (B and E) and on the upperside by the paler fronts of the wings. There is considerable individual variation in the moulting pattern, so the appearance of the tail does not help in age determination. The adult plumage is acquired at an age of 4–5 years, but even then there may be brown feathers in the middle of the tail.

Flight: when seen flying this is a large, heavy bird with slow, stiff but not particularly deep wing beats. In soaring the wings are held flat (G), or possibly

slightly raised and extended almost at right angles from the body. In gliding the wings are held either flat or slightly angled at the root of the hand (H).

Likelihood of confusion: *see also* Golden Eagle. Under poor conditions the White-tailed Eagle can be confused with several of the large raptors, but none of these has the head protruding so far forwards nor the tail so far backwards. These characters are particularly good in distinguishing the present species from the Griffon Vulture and the Black Vulture, both of which have a much protruding head when flying. When the plumage is worn the other large eagles, Golden, Imperial and Steppe, can also be seen with a wedge-shaped tail. However, these show a reasonably marked difference from the juvenile White-tailed Eagle, for the old dark birds always have a pale area on the head or nape where the young White-tailed is dark. Confusion arises most readily with an adult Steppe Eagle but this has a different contrast on the underparts. With its white tail, an adult White-tailed Eagle cannot be confused with other species.

White-tailed Eagle (w.200–240 cm)

A ad.

3

2

B imm.

C juv.

6

5

8

D ad.

4

1

2

E imm.

7

G soaring

H gliding

Pallas's Sea Eagle
Haliaeetus leucoryphus

General impression: a large, well-proportioned, lightly built eagle.

Proportions: for such a large eagle the wings are long and very narrow, with a parallel front and rear edges in the adult. Long neck, very small head with a large beak, and a long tail.

Plumage: Adult: dark (blackish-brown) apart from a striking white band on the tail (A 1), a pale, sandy coloured head, and the front of the breast is a pale cinnamon colour (A 2).

Young birds: at a distance the juvenile's upperparts appear very uniformly brown. Under good conditions, however, it will be seen that the upper tail-coverts, the base of the primaries and the central wing-coverts are slightly paler. The body is a paler brown on the underparts. Here, there is a pale area on the 3–6 outermost primaries (D 3), pale greater wing-coverts (D 4) and pale on the innermost secondaries (D 5). Immature birds (C) have paler underparts than juveniles, a more distinct pale area on the innermost primaries (C 3) and a weakly-marked pale tail band (C 1).

Flight: surprisingly light and elegant, with deep, well-executed wing beats. Soars with the wings flat (G).

Likelihood of confusion: the tail pattern is so distinctive in the adults that, under reasonable conditions, they cannot be confused with other species. The young birds are more like the other large eagles. They are distinguished from the White-tailed Eagle by different proportions and a much lighter flight, from the *Aquila* species by different patterns on the underparts. Note that Imperial, Steppe (young) and Tawny Eagles also have pale innermost primaries. In Pallas's Sea Eagle, however, these have a broad, dark rear edge.

Note also that the juveniles and immature Pallas's Sea Eagles (like other young *Haliaeetus*) have very pointed, dentate secondaries and tail feathers.

Adult Pallas's Sea Eagle.
Photo B. Gensbøl/Biofoto.

Pallas's Sea Eagle (w. 200–250 cm)

A ad.

B ad.

C imm.

D juv.

E ad.

F juv.

G soaring

Bonelli's Eagle
Hieraaetus fasciatus

General impression: a medium-sized eagle, approximately the same as the Short-toed Eagle, often appearing rather like a Honey Buzzard.

Proportions: varies quite a bit in size, from small males only a little larger than a Rough-legged Buzzard to large females the size of a Short-toed Eagle. There is also considerable variation in the proportions. Certain individuals may have very long slender wings, but in general the wings are very broad with a slightly more slender wing base, with the hand a little more slender and rounded. Compared with the Booted Eagle the hand is fuller. The head is relatively small but distinctly protruding (B). The tail is long, a little longer than the wing breadth.

Plumage, Adult: the old birds have such distinct field characters that they cannot be confused. The white body (A 2 and B 2) in contrast with the dark wings is very characteristic. To a varying extent there is also white along the front edge of the wings (A 3 and B 3). Between this and the very pale flight feathers some very dark wing-coverts form a black band on the wing (A 4 and B 4). A good field character is the pale area on the upperparts (E 5 and F 5), visible even at a distance of 1–2 km. This, too, may vary in size and intensity. Finally, the cross-banded tail ends with a broad black outer band.

Young birds: the underside of the typical young has pale red-brown wing-coverts and distinct dark wing tips (D 6). In most individuals the tips of the greater wing-coverts are blackish, forming a narrow band between the flight feathers and the coverts (D 7). This may, however, be lacking or only present on the hand. The upperside lacks the characteristic pale marking of the adults.

While the younger birds in this plumage are very characteristic, no other European raptor showing such a red-brown plumage with dark wing tips, there may be problems with the identification of transitional plumages. Thus, the appearance may be variegated, and completely dark individuals occur, both at this age and as juveniles. When the plumage of the young birds is moulted there will usually be pale feathers on the body, and the characteristic wing band on the underside will normally become more pronounced. After the first moult the outermost tail band starts to appear and after the second, at an age of around two years, there may be a pale marking on the back. The full plumage is acquired at an age of about three years.

Variants: completely dark individuals occur among juveniles and immatures.

Flight: in active flight the wing beats are rapid, elastic and powerful, but not particularly deep. The bird is often seen in a fast glide, which is when it may resemble a Honey Buzzard. In soaring flight the wings are held flat (H), slightly pressed forwards and the tail widely spread.

Characteristic behaviour: an aggressive and agile raptor sometimes reminiscent in behaviour of a Goshawk. In the breeding grounds often seen gliding back and forth over the area.

Likelihood of confusion: there is no chance of this if the reliable characters can be seen. In its pale phase it is true that the Booted Eagle also has a pale body, but its under wing-coverts are all pale and the conditions must be extremely bad for there to be any chance of confusion.

In spite of the big difference in size, but a certain resemblance in proportions, confusion is more likely with the Honey Buzzard, particularly in gliding, when both species have flat, angled wings. However, Bonelli's Eagle has a longer, more angular tail, more parallel wing edges and more incised, 'eagle-like' primaries. Furthermore, the beak is distinctly larger. In proportions and behaviour there is also some resemblance to the Goshawk, and there may be confusion with the dark phase of the Booted Eagle. This is described under the latter species.

318

Bonelli's Eagle (w. 150–180 cm)

A ad.
4
3
2
1

B ad.
3
4
2

D juv.

E ad.
5

C imm.

7
6

F ad.
5

G juv.

H soaring

Booted Eagle

Hieraaetus pennatus

General impression: about the size of a Buzzard, but with more slender wings and a much longer tail.

Proportions: compared with the Buzzard the wings are longer and narrower, when soaring often with almost parallel front and rear edges. The deeply separated primaries give an eagle-like appearance. When the primaries are gathered together the wings may appear pointed. The head is round, not particularly protruding, almost Buzzard-like, but with a more powerful beak. The tail is long, about as much as the maximum wing breadth, truncated or slightly rounded with sharp corners.

Plumage: the pale phase, the commonest, is very characteristic on account of the white belly (C 1) and wing-coverts (C 2). In the dark phase the underside is almost uniformly dark brown but with a pale area on the outermost part of the innermost three primaries (B 3), a character seen in all, independent of phase, and of which there is also a trace on the upperside (E 3). The upperside is the same in all Booted Eagles of all phases, with pale brownish wing-coverts in contrast to the dark secondaries (E 4) and with pale brownish to white tail-coverts (E 5). A kite-like, broad wing band (E 6) gives the upperside a particularly variegated and very characteristic appearance. Seen from in front, a pair of white markings on the front edge of each wing is a good recognition character (F 7).

Variants: birds of an intermediate phase are often seen (D). The areas which are white in the pale phase are apparently always paler than the dark flight feathers.

Young birds: cannot always be distinguished. The pale phases often have a more red-brown head and more red-brown underparts with browner stripes. In the field the dark phase is indistinguishable from the adults.

Flight: in soaring flight the wings are held slightly advanced (C) and flat to slightly drooping (F); the tail is spread and in kite fashion characteristically moves on its own axis. In gliding flight the wing position is angled with the joint well forward, and the wings are held flat to slightly drooping (G). In active flight the wing beats are rapid, elastic, powerful and very deep, often with 4–5 beats followed by gliding.

Likelihood of confusion: on account of a certain similarity in proportions and colour pattern, the dark phase can be confused with the Marsh Harrier. However, unlike the Booted Eagle, the latter is always seen with the wings raised high.

The dark phase may be confused with the Black Kite, particularly on account of a similarity in the uppersides and tail lengths. The differing shape of the tails is a good recognition character. It should, however, be noted that Black Kites show pale on the primaries in the same way as the Booted Eagle (*see also* Black Kite p. 334).

The pale phase of the Booted Eagle has a pattern on the underside very similar to the full plumage of an Egyptian Vulture. The latter, however, is considerably larger, with longer wings and a wedge-shaped tail.

In their transitional plumage Bonelli's Eagles may appear very dark and, particularly at a distance, it may be difficult to distinguish them from the dark phase of the Booted Eagle. The two species may have a very similar silhouette, but probably Bonelli's Eagle is larger and has broader wings with a fuller and more rounded hand. The relatively small head of Bonelli's Eagle, much extended forwards, is however a distinguishing character which can be used even at a considerable distance. At closer quarters it should be possible to see a broad, dark wing band on Bonelli's wing-coverts (underside) and the usually very red-brown to greyish variegated body and the slightly paler secondaries which the species has in all plumages. Identification will be certain if the Booted Eagle's paler secondaries can be seen. With its characteristic pattern the upperside of the present species will always be a good field character.

For possible confusion with the Buzzard and Honey Buzzard, *see* p. 296.

Booted Eagle (w. 110–132 cm)

A dark phase

B dark phase

3

C pale phase

2

1

D intermediate phase

5

4

3

6

E

7

F soaring

G gliding

Short-toed Eagle
Circaetus gallicus

General impression: a medium-sized eagle, usually with a dark head and fore-breast in contrast to paler underparts, and therefore one of the easiest raptors to identify.

Proportions: somewhat larger than the Osprey, with long broad wings, the front and rear edges almost parallel, and a particularly long, full and rounded hand. When not soaring with the wings out at right angles from the body, the joint between arm and hand is very conspicuous. The body is powerful and elongated, the tail as long as the wing breadth or a trifle shorter. The head is broad, rounded and extended forwards.

Plumage: Adult: as already mentioned most Short-toed Eagles have a dark area around the head in contrast to pale underparts (A 1, B 1 and C 1). As drawings A to E show the pattern of the underside varies considerably. Some individuals have a more conspicuous marking than others, the extremes being A and D. However, birds as pale as D are rare. It is also typical that the individual markings form bands on the secondaries and

wing-coverts. At a distance most birds appear greyish-white on the underparts. The tail has several cross-bands, of which the outermost is particularly conspicuous (C 2). These are also found in pale birds but not so markedly (E). The upperparts have dark (blackish-brown) flight feathers in contrast to pale grey to yellow-brown wing-coverts and back, (G 3) and a distinctly banded tail (F 2). Darker birds occur, as in F, and individuals with a white rump and a pale band over the wings are also seen. Apparently there is conformity between the upper- and underparts, so that birds with pale underparts have pale upperparts.

Variants: some individuals lack the dark head (D and E), in autumn about ten per cent. These may be young birds but this is not yet clear.

Young birds: cannot be distinguished in the field, but *see* the last paragraph.

Flight: soars with the wings pressed slightly forwards and held either flat or, in windy conditions, raised (H). In active flight the wing beats are deep, powerful

and elastic. In gliding the wing joint is very distinctly extended forwards and the head turned backwards (I).

Characteristic behaviour: on the breeding grounds but not so frequently on migration this species hovers (B). It can also remain stationary in the air on flat wings. Both types of flight are good recognition characters as they do not occur in other raptors of similar size, apart from the Osprey.

Likelihood of confusion: none very likely. It is true that the Osprey has pale underparts, but its pattern and proportions are completely different. Pale Buzzards may occur with a dark head but here again this species has different proportions and also it flies in a different way, e.g. it soars with conspicuously raised wings. In dark Short-toed Eagles the underside pattern (A) sometimes resembles the typical plumage of a Honey Buzzard, but lacks this species' dark markings on the wing joints. The Short-toed Eagle is also considerably larger, with relatively longer wings and sharp corners to the tail (A 2).

Short-toed Eagle (w. 185–195 cm)

H soaring

I gliding

Osprey

Pandion haliaetus

General impression: a medium-sized raptor with long narrow wings which in gliding flight are held at an angle, so that the bird, seen superficially, resembles a large gull.

Proportions: considerably larger than a Buzzard and with completely different proportions. As already mentioned the wings are very long and narrow, the tail is of medium length, slightly shorter than the wing breadth, the head is relatively smaller but markedly extended forwards and the beak is powerful.

Plumage: the underparts are very characteristic, with the white body, white head and white lesser and central wing-coverts (A 1). The black markings at the wing joint are also distinctive and so are the black greater wing-coverts which lie as a band at the centre of the wings. The females and the young birds have a conspicuous black band over the breast (A 2 and D 2). With their dark brown coloration the upperparts contrast sharply with the underparts. This impression is only broken by the white head (C 3). The conspicuous dark streak through the eye (B 4) is also a good field character, even at quite a distance.

Young birds: distinguished by the paler upperside and its more variegated appearance due to the pale edges of the wing-coverts and contour feathers (D 5). As shown in drawing D these form two pale bands on the wing-coverts. Furthermore, the crown and nape are darker. In the field the underparts cannot be distinguished from those of the adults. At an age of about one year the young can no longer be distinguished from the adults.

Flight: with its long narrow wings held clearly angled when gliding (F), and with very protruding wing joints (C), this is a very characteristic bird when flying. Its appearance is then more like a gull than what is expected in a raptor. However, when gliding it can also resemble a kite. In soaring the wings are sometimes held slightly drooping, as is common in the spotted eagles. In active flight the wing beats are powerful and not particularly deep. It is characteristic that there are long periods of gliding in between the individual series of wing beats.

Characteristic behaviour: hovers over the water when a fish is sighted and when searching for prey. Dives head first into the water.

Likelihood of confusion: not very likely, but *see* under Short-toed Eagle, p. 322. Many Ospreys are unnoticed because the profile of the species, from in front and behind, is so similar to that of a large gull.

A ad. ♀

B ad. ♂

C ad.

D juv.

E soaring

F gliding

Egyptian Vulture
Neophron percnopterus

General impression: a medium-sized raptor with a wing span like the Lesser Spotted Eagle or the largest individuals of the Rough-legged Buzzard.

Proportions: the combination of long, very broad wings, small head and short tail is typical of the vultures, of which the Egyptian is the smallest of the Western Palearctic species. Other important characters are that the head appears pointed due to the long, thin beak which protrudes far in front of the wing edge (A 1) and that the tail is wedge-shaped (A 2) and very short (two-thirds to three-quarters of the wing breadth).

Plumage: the species is easy to identify from its plumage. On the underside the tail, belly and wing-coverts are white (A 3), contrasting with the black flight feathers (A 4). The upperside is almost identical, but not so distinctly patterned. The secondaries are mainly white and the primaries have conspicuous shaft stripes (D 4). Furthermore, the wing-coverts are black at the wing-joints and there is a cloudy area on the innermost greater and central wing-coverts. At close quarters the naked bright yellow area around the beak is visible.

In the first (juvenile) plumage the underside is very dark (C). The upperparts are paler, the flight feathers patterned like those of the adults, but with less contrast (F). The wing-coverts are distinctly paler, and in a completely fresh plumage there is a pair of pale bands which, however, rapidly become worn away. On the upperside the tail-coverts are also pale (F 5).

At the next moult the bird gradually becomes paler on the body, tail and wing-coverts and, as drawings B and E show, the young bird in the transitional plumages is very mottled. The Egyptian Vulture acquires its full plumage at an age of four years.

Flight: often seen soaring on slightly raised or flat wings (G). In rapid gliding flight the hand drops distinctly below the horizontal plane. In active flight the wing beats are very slow, soft and deep.

Likelihood of confusion: not really likely, although at a great distance there is a chance of confusion with a white stork. The pale phase of the Booted Eagle has the same colour pattern on the underparts as an Egyptian Vulture but the difference in size and the shape of the head and tail render identification easy. Under poor conditions for observation the dark juvenile birds might be confused with several species, but at a reasonable distance the distinctly wedge-shaped tail and the pointed vulture head are so striking that there is usually no problem.

Egyptian Vulture (w. 160–170 cm)

A ad.

B imm.

C juv.

D ad.

E imm.

F juv.

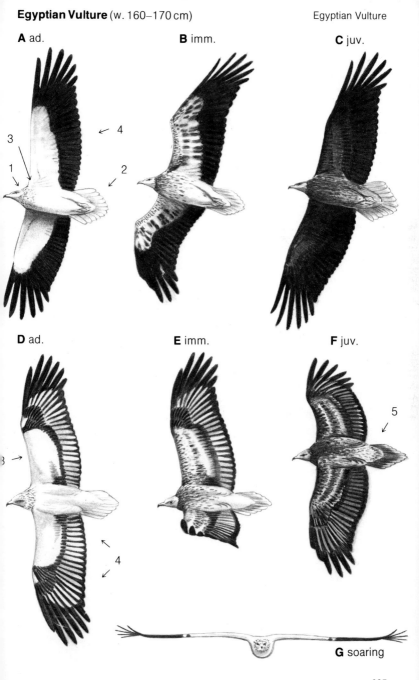

G soaring

Griffon Vulture
Gyps fulvus

General impression: a very large raptor, considerably larger than the large eagles.

Proportions: long, very broad wings with deeply incised primaries, a small very slightly protruding head (D 1) and a short tail, about one-third the wing breadth (D 2). In addition to this and the colossal size it is characteristic that the rear edge of the wings has a distinct curve. This is because the innermost primaries and the secondaries nearest to the body are shorter than the other flight feathers (D 3).

Plumage: Adult: both the upperside and underside are characterized by the contrast between dark flight feathers (E 4) and pale wing-coverts (E 5). The underside has almost white bands on the lesser and central wing-coverts (C 6). The collar is pale but may be difficult to see.

Young birds: in the juvenile plumage the body and wing-coverts on the underside are paler than in the adults (D 7), and without the white bands on the wing-coverts. On the upperside the wing-coverts are slightly darker than on the underside. The collar is brown. Full plumage is acquired at an age of 5–6 years.

Flight: most often seen soaring with the wings raised (A). In gliding flight the hands normally droop (B). In active flight the wing beats are very slow and deep.

Characteristic behaviour: seen soaring for long periods over the same area, e.g. along a cliff face.

Likelihood of confusion: seen superficially the Griffon Vulture resembles a large eagle, but the small head, the very broad wings and the short tail are decisive differences.

In Europe this species can really only be confused with the Black Vulture. However, the latter soars with flat wings with almost parallel front and rear edges, whereas the Griffon Vulture raises its wings to form an open V and has a distinct curve at the rear edge of the wings. There are also considerable differences in plumage. With the marked contrast between flight feathers and wing-coverts there should be no difficulty in identification.

European Black Vulture
Aegypius monachus

General impression: a very large raptor, wing span up to 2.95 m, with very long, very broad wings, a remarkably small head (A 1) and a very short tail (A 2), shorter than half the wing breadth.

Proportions: long, broad wings with deeply incised primaries, a small, very slightly protruding head and a short tail. Apart from this and the colossal size, it is characteristic that the wing edges are more parallel than in the Griffon Vulture, so the rear edge lacks the latter's curve.

Plumage: a very dark bird which at a distance appears black. The only contrast is the pale head (B 1) and the yellow feet. At close quarters a pale brown band may be seen on the underwings' coverts (A 3).

Note the very pointed (toothed) secondaries and tail feathers.

Young birds: even darker than the adults, so they also lack the pale band on the underside of the wings. The head is covered with brown down, the adult having paler areas in between. However, this can only be seen at close quarters. The young do not have the facial mask of the adults. They have a full plumage when about six years old.

Flight: often seen soaring, when the wings are held flat (C) with the tips of the outermost primaries upturned. The flat wing position when soaring is an important field character. When gliding the wings are arched with the hands drooping (D), as seen in the spotted eagles. In active flight the wing beats are slow and deep.

Characteristic behaviour: spends much time soaring to and fro over the same area, and unlike the Griffon Vulture is often alone or in quite a small group.

Likelihood of confusion: *see* under Griffon and Lappet-faced Vulture. At a distance there may be confusion with the Spotted Eagle for both species are very dark.

Griffon Vulture (w. 243–270 cm)

C ad.

← 6

A soaring

B gliding

1

← 3

E ad.

← 3

7

2

F juv.

D juv.

4 →

← 5

A ad.

3 →

B ad.

1

1

2

Black Vulture
(w. 250–295 cm)

C soaring

D gliding

329

Bearded Vulture

Gypaetus barbatus

General impression: a very large raptor with long, narrow, pointed wings, a markedly protruding head (C 1) and a long tail (C 2).

Proportions: in size rather similar to the Griffon and Black Vultures: wing span up to 2.80 m. The other two species, however, have broad wings, a short tail and a very small head, whereas the Bearded Vulture has relatively narrow wings, a long tail, longer than the greatest wing breadth, and a very striking head.

Plumage: the underparts show much contrast, the wings and tail being dark, while the head and body are pale rust-brown, a colour which can be seen from a great distance. The upperparts are uniformly dark greyish-blue. The pale head (F 1) is conspicuous with its 'beard' visible at a very great distance (F 3).

Young birds: easily recognized by the very dark underparts, which do not contrast with the wings as in the adults. The upperparts show more contrast, with paler wing-coverts and a pale area on the back (G 4) and rump (G 5). The head, however, is darker (G 6).

As the bird becomes older, pale feathers appear on the underparts, while the upperside's pale feathers become even paler. With its blackish-brown colour the head appears to mark the transitional plumage for longer than other parts. The full plumage is acquired at an age of about five years.

Flight: often seen soaring with the wings held flat (A). In gliding flight the hand droops (B). In active flight, which is not often seen, the wing beats are slow, soft and elastic.

Characteristic behaviour: often soars over valleys or along the sides of mountains.

Likelihood of confusion: none.

Lappet-faced Vulture

Torgos tracheliotus

General impression: a very large, dark and short-tailed vulture.

Proportions: intermediate between the Griffon and Black Vultures.

Plumage: Adult: the upperparts are brown to dark brown, but palest in birds from the Middle East and Egypt. At close quarters the wing-coverts and body are paler than the rest of the upperparts, with the pale head forming a contrast. The underparts show more contrast. The breast and sides of the body are white with narrow, lanceolate black feathers (A 1). In north-western Africa the birds have white thighs. There are usually two pale bands, one distinct and one more diffuse, on the wing-coverts (A 2). The remainder of the underparts are very dark with dark brown wing-coverts, black secondaries and a black tail. The feathery collar is greyish-brown mixed with dark grey under-down. Birds from the Middle East and Egypt have a greyish-brown head and pale red nape, from north-western Africa a red head.

Note the very pointed, saw-toothed secondaries and tail feathers.

Young birds: those from north-western Africa have the whole of the head, apart from the surrounds of the eye and the cheeks, covered with whitish down. In the first plumage only the forehead, crown and nape are downy, and the thighs are pale brown. After the next moult the down on the head decreases in extent, the underparts become paler and the bands on the wing-coverts start to appear. For birds from the Middle East and Egypt the down on the head cannot be used as a criterion of age, because here the adults also have a downy head. Full plumage acquired at 6–7 years.

Flight: soars on flat wings (C) and flies with powerful, deep wing beats.

Likelihood of confusion: at a reasonable distance the adults can be distinguished from Black Vultures by the patterns on the underparts. Furthermore, the Lappet-faced Vulture shows a certain contrast between the upperside's wing-coverts and the darker secondaries. The juveniles of this species and the Black Vulture are very similar. Young Lappet-faced Vultures from the Middle East and Egypt will, however, be somewhat paler. In addition, the feet are grey in this species, yellow in the Black Vulture.

Only exceptionally do the two species occur in the same area.

Bearded Vulture (w. 250–280 cm)   Bearded Vulture/Lappet-faced Vulture

C ad.

1

2

A   soaring

B   gliding

D juv.

E imm.

1

3

F ad.

4

6

5

G juv.

Lappet-faced Vulture
(w. 255–290 cm)

A ad.

2   1

C soaring

B ad.

331

Kite

Milvus milvus

General impression: a medium-sized raptor with a wing span greater than that of a Buzzard. The tail is very long and deeply forked (A 1).

Proportions: the long wings and the long tail, considerably longer than the wing breadth, give this bird a slender and elegant appearance.

Plumage: the long, rust-red tail is particularly distinctive. The underparts are mainly red-brown, apart from a very conspicuous white area on the hand (A 2). The brownish upperparts show less contrast. A pale band on the central wing-coverts (C 3) is, however, quite striking.

Young birds: the underside of the body (B 4) is distinctly paler than in the adults (A). Thus, there is a contrast between the body and the underside of the wings, only seen at close quarters. Under good conditions for observation the pale tips of the greater and central wing-coverts will be seen to form a pair of narrow bands (B 5). The best chance of identification is found on the upperside which is generally more red-brown. Here the pale tips of the greater wing-coverts form a band over each wing (D 6). There is also a pale band on the central wing-coverts (D 3) which is broader and paler than in the adults. In many cases the tail of the young birds is rust-brown where the adults' is rust-red. This is particularly the case in late summer. The full

plumage is acquired at an age of two years.

Flight: usually soars with the wings slightly raised (E), but in gliding flight the hands are held slightly drooping (G). In active flight the wing beats are deep, elastic and very slow. It is also characteristic that when searching a terrain the bird flies somewhat restlessly. The wings move independently and the tail twists on its axis as the bird manoeuvres. This is an elegant bird in flight.

Likelihood of confusion: mainly only with the Black Kite which is, however, smaller with broader and shorter wings. The two species also differ in flight. The Kite usually has a more harrier-like, easy flight with deeper, more elastic wing beats. There is an important difference in the shape and colour of the tail. In the Kite this is deeply forked and rust-red, whereas in the Black Kite it is not so forked and is grey-brown, although some young birds have a tinge of rust-brown on the uppermost part of the tail. The difference in the forking of the tail is most apparent when it is folded. When spread the Black Kite's tail is only slightly concave or appears truncated. As a result of abrasion it may even be rounded. Even when spread the tail of a Kite normally shows a distinct fork (C). An abraded tail may, however, appear truncated.

On the whole the Kite is a paler bird which shows greater contrasts in pattern due to the pale tail and the

conspicuous pale wing areas, which on average are larger and paler, showing more contrast with the dark primaries than in the Black Kite. In the Kite the upperparts are rust-red to greyish-yellow as opposed to the Black Kite's mid-brown to grey-brown. The underparts of the Kite are red-brown to pale rust-brown (juveniles), whereas in the Black Kite they are dark brown, the young however having a pale breast. Seen from below an excellent character is that the colour of the Black Kite's tail corresponds with that of the body, whereas the Kite's rust-red tail differs markedly from the rest of the underparts. The young birds of the two species are the most difficult to distinguish from one another. From the viewpoint of contrast they are almost the same, both above and below. Young Black Kites have more conspicuous pale areas on the primaries than the adults. The Kite is basically red-brown, whereas the Black Kite is grey-brown, a difference that is particularly noticeable on the tail.

In the Middle East, Black Kites of the *aegyptius* race are sometimes confused with Kites, because they have a more rust-red body and larger white areas on the underside of the hand.

Kite (w. 175–195 cm)

A ad.

B juv.

5

1

4

2

3

C ad.

6

3

D juv.

E soaring

G gliding

Black Kite
Milvus migrans

General impression: slightly larger than a Buzzard, but smaller than a Kite, with long, very broad wings and a long slightly forked tail (A 1) which is certainly the best field character.

Proportions: smaller than the Kite with relatively shorter, slightly broader and more rounded wings, and giving a more compact impression. The forked tail is clearly seen when folded (A 1). However, when the tail is spread it is only slightly concave or may have a straight rear edge. In certain cases the spread tail may even be slightly rounded (B 1).

Plumage: this is very dark. At a distance it appears almost black, but at closer quarters mainly dark brown. The underparts, however, often show a pale area on the hand (A 2), but this varies in size and intensity from bird to bird and in some may be very slightly marked (B 2). The upperparts are also dark but with a conspicuous pale band on the central wing-coverts (D 3). Seen from below the colour of the tail does not differ from the rest of the underparts. Seen from above it often appears a warmer brown.

Young birds: the basic difference between the juvenile and adult plumages is the same as in the Kite: paler body (C 4), a pale band above and below at the transition between flight feathers and wing-coverts (E 5, C 6) and a broader, paler band on the upperside's central wing-coverts (E 3). In addition, the pale area on the wing's underside is on average larger and paler, the lesser wing-coverts on the upperside have paler edges, and the rump is pale. At about one year old the young birds resemble the adults, but still show a few juvenile feathers. The species acquires the full plumage at an age of two years.

Flight: very similar to that of the Kite (*see* p. 332), but not so elegant in the air. Soars on flat wings whereas the Kite holds them slightly raised.

Characteristic behaviour: sometimes seen hunting in the vicinity of water or flying low, looking out for prey with wavering flight, the wings moving independently in Kite fashion and the tail twisting on its own axis.

Likelihood of confusion: *see* under Kite (p. 332). Like the present species, the Marsh Harrier also flies over open country. The female Marsh Harrier is also dark and this may give rise to confusion. However, it hunts with distinctly raised wings, whereas Kites do so on flat, drooping or arched wings. The dark phase of the Booted Eagle creates a problem as it also flies on flat wings. The tails of the two species are, however, different: slightly forked in the Kite, but slightly rounded in the Booted Eagle. Furthermore, the latter's head is more striking and rounded, with a more powerful beak. The Booted Eagle can generally be identified by the pale area on the innermost primaries. Nevertheless, very dark Black Kites may show exactly the same character (B).

The two species also fly in a different way, the eagle having more rapid, more powerful wing beats.

Black Kite (w. 160–180 cm)

A ad.

2

1

B ad.

1

2

C juv.

4

6

E juv.

3

5

D ad.

3

F soaring

G gliding

Black-winged Kite
Elanus caeruleus

General impression: only a little larger than a Kestrel, with a large head, long wings and a short tail.

Proportions: a large, protruding head gives the bird an almost owl-like appearance (B 1). The long wings, and particularly long arms, are broader than in the falcons, and the short tail, less than the wing breadth, is often slightly forked when folded.

Plumage: the underparts are white in contrast to the black primaries (A 2). The upperparts are blue-grey with the exception of the head (C 3) and outermost tail feathers which are white, and the wing-coverts which are black (C 4). Under good conditions the red eye can also be seen, surrounded by a black streak.

Young birds are darker (brownish) on the breast, head, tail and the upperside of the body. The flight feathers are also darker, so the black wing-coverts on the upperside do not show so much contrast to the rest as in the adults. There is a pale band over the upperside of the wings.

When three months old the bird starts to moult towards the adult plumage, and at six months the brown feathers on the upperside have been replaced by blue-grey. A full plumage is acquired at an age of about one year.

Black-winged Kite on the lookout.
Photo B. Génsbøl/Biofoto.

Flight: flies with soft, rapid wing beats. Often seen flying low, like a harrier, and also with the wings arched but with the hand flat. Or they hover (D) at a height of 10–20 m sometimes with the wings raised high. When soaring the wings are pressed forwards and raised (E). In gliding flight they are almost flat (F).

Likelihood of confusion: unlikely under good conditions for observation. When conditions are bad and the bird is flying over open country it may resemble one of the paler harrier males on account of the colour pattern, particularly the Pallid Harrier. The habit of frequently hovering gives it a superficial resemblance to a Kestrel which is the same size. The proportions are, however, very different including the markedly short tail of the present species. It is also typical of the Black-winged Kite that the wings appear to be placed too far back on the body.

Black-winged Kite (w. 75–87 cm) Black-winged Kite

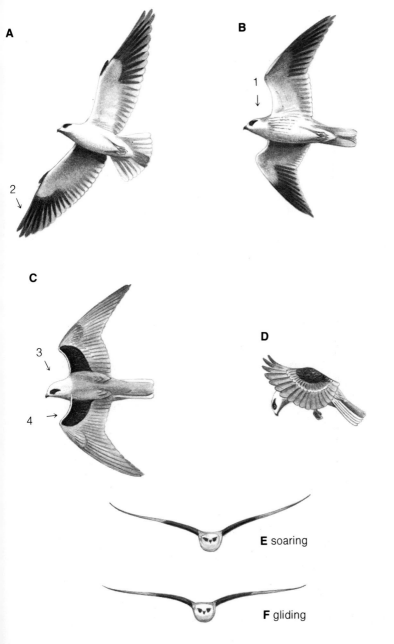

E soaring

F gliding

Marsh Harrier

Circus aeruginosus

General impression: a typical large harrier – very slender, long-winged, with a long tail. In flight the wings are held well raised.

Proportions: the largest of the harriers, about the size of a Buzzard but not so compact. The head and body are more slender, the wings relatively a little longer, more slender and with more parallel front and rear edges. The tail, too, is longer, normally a little more than the greatest wing breadth. Compared with the Hen Harrier, Montagu's Harrier and Pallid Harrier, it is heavier and particularly has more rounded wing tips than the last-named.

Plumage: On the underside adult males have the black wing tips of male harriers (A 1 and B 1), but are much darker than the other species. The head and the front of the breast are greyish with fine longitudinal stripes, the body red-brown, tending to have longitudinal stripes. The wing-coverts may also be red-brown but are often paler grey or white. Flight feathers are mainly greyish-white, except for the black tips to the primaries already mentioned. On the upperside the wing-coverts and back are mainly brownish (D 2), the tail, rump and secondaries pale grey to greyish-white, the tips of the primaries black.

As drawings H and I show the adult female is a much darker bird. It normally has some good field characters in the yellowish-white areas on the forewings (K 3), head (K 4) and throat (I 5). The main impression is a very dark brown bird, and at close quarters the secondaries are greyish and the tail from grey to pale red-brown. Certain individuals also have a pale areas on the breast (I 6).

Variants: The males vary considerably, from dark (C), through intermediate forms (B) to so pale (A) that they are very reminiscent of a Hen Harrier. They are, however, always dark on the belly and vent.

Dark females and young birds (without pale areas on the wings, head and throat) occur frequently. These, however, always have somewhat paler inner primaries and a red-brown to grey-brown tail.

In Eastern Europe, the Western part of Asia and – migrating – in the Middle East – a melanistic form occurs. The old males have an almost one-coloured, dark backside. The underside is also dark, although with a light wingband, formed by light base of the flight feathers. The tail is grey as normal. The melanistic females are also very dark and have a yellow-white spot on the back of the head and a small light field at the base of the outer primaries. The tail is coloured as the normal females.

Young birds: in their first (juvenile) plumage the birds are normally very dark (blackish-brown). As drawing L shows they mostly resemble the female. However, they generally lack the pale fore-wings and are completely dark. In such a plumage they can be distinguished from completely dark adult females because they do not have the pale area on the breast (I 6).

After the first moult both sexes are the same (some males may have slightly grey flight feathers), with a plumage that is intermediate between the juvenile and the adult female. After the second moult, at about two years, there is a clear difference between the sexes. The females then have a full plumage. At this point the grey feathers on the males are scarcely as pale as in the adults and have a brownish tone. When around 3 years old, the young males can no longer be distinguished from the adults.

Flight: typical harrier flight on raised wings when soaring (F) and gliding (G). The wing movements are light and elegant, the beats often seen in series of 5–10 followed by gliding. The Marsh Harrier is clearly larger than, for example, Montagu's Harrier, so its flight will appear relatively heavier.

Characteristic behaviour: searches the terrain in typical harrier fashion, flying low over open country, often over reed-beds or similar damp areas.

Likelihood of confusion: the plumage is normally so characteristic that there should be no problems in identification, particularly when account is taken of the typical harrier behaviour. Completely dark individuals may be difficult. Here the wing posture and behaviour must be noted. These characters will distinguish it from dark Honey Buzzards, Black Kites and dark phase Booted Eagles which all soar on flat wings, and from dark Buzzards partly by the proportions and partly because in gliding (not when soaring) they hold the wings flat.

Marsh Harrier I – ♂ (w. 115–130 cm)

Marsh Harrier

A ad. (pale)   ← 1

1 ↘

B ad. (intermediate)

C ad. (dark)

2 →

D ad.

← 1

E imm. (2 yrs)

15F soaring

G gliding

H ad.

I ad.

5 →
6 →

J ad.

3 →
4 →

K ad.

L juv.

M juv.

Hen Harrier

adult ♀

juvenile,

Like the Pallid Harrier this species has a pale collar but it is narrower

and far less visible as it is spotted and striped. Note juvenile's contrasting head pattern and so possible

confusion with an adult female Pallid Harrier. Unlike the other two species it does not have a pale throat.

Montagu's Harrier

adult ♀

juvenile

Broad superciliary stripe, usually combined with the pale cheek. This species has more white

on the face than the Pallid Harrier. Nevertheless, not all Montagu's and Pallid Harriers have the typical

patterns on the head. Marginal cases may make identification impossible.

Pallid Harrier

ad. ♀

juv.

The best recognition character is the pale collar, which is most

prominent in juveniles. Note that, compared with Montagu's Harrier, the black streak through

the eye separates the very narrow superciliary stripe from the white cheek.

Hen Harrier

Circus cyaneus

General impression: a typical medium-sized harrier which is most often seen flying low over open country with the wings raised high (G).

Proportions: intermediate in size between the Marsh Harrier and Montagu's Harrier, and compared with the first-named, it has a more slender body and hands, slightly narrower, more pointed wings with a distinct curve at the rear edge, and a relatively longer tail.

Plumage: adult males have greyish-white underparts with a dark head and front of the breast in contrast to the black primaries (B 1). The upperparts are slightly darker and here, too, the black wing tips are very striking (F 1). The rump is white (F 2). Adult females have pale yellow-brown underparts with longitudinal stripes both here and on the wing-coverts. The secondaries and the tail have very conspicuous dark bands (A 3). The upperside of the tail is similarly patterned (E 4). The upperparts are mainly a uniform dark brown with the contrasting white marking on the rump (E 2). The central wing-coverts are also paler. In spring the old females may be very bleached.

In their first (juvenile) plumage these can, in most cases, be distinguished from the adult females. They are generally darker with the underside's coverts red-brown, often with the tail bands scarcely so prominent, and most important with darker secondaries (D 5). Furthermore, the white pointed edges to the upperside's greater wing-coverts normally form a pale band over the wing, and pale central coverts provide the upperside with more contrast than is seen in the adult females.

With the first moult which takes place in December–January and until the birds are about one year old the males can be clearly distinguished, for they show the grey feathers, although these still have a brownish sheen. At this stage the secondaries are often very dark and the whole effect may be variegated (C). At this age the young females can often be distinguished by the dark secondaries, but when about two years old they can no longer be distinguished from the adults. However, the males differ until they are around three years old.

Flight: normally in the typical harrier fashion, with wings raised high for both soaring and gliding (G and H). Exceptionally seen gliding on flat or even drooping wings. Active flight resembles that of the Marsh Harrier, but owing to smaller size has slightly lighter and more rapid wing beats.

Likelihood of confusion: the colour patterns of male Hen Harriers, Montagu's Harriers and Pallid Harriers are similar to one another. There are proportional differences between the present species and Montagu's. The latter is a more slenderly-built bird with a longer tail and more slender and more pointed wings. There are differences in the plumages when these are considered in detail. The most important is that Montagu's Harrier is a darker bird with the upperside a more mottled grey in contrast to the Hen Harrier's uniformly pale grey. Montagu's has dark bands at the base of the secondaries and it lacks a white rump, where in rare cases it has a diffuse pale marking here. On the underside the most decisive difference is that Montagu's Harrier has two dark bands on the secondaries and on the innermost primaries. The Pallid Harrier's proportions are almost identical with those of Montagu's Harrier. The plumage of the former differs from that of the Hen Harrier and Montagu's in having much paler, almost white underparts. In the Pallid Harrier the pattern of the black wing tips is completely different from that of the other two species. However, immature males of Hen and Montagu's Harrier may have a primaries pattern resembling that of the Pallid Harrier.

For possible confusion between female Hen Harriers and female Montagu's (and Pallid) Harriers *see* under the latter two species.

Hen Harrier (w. 99–121 cm)

Hen Harrier

B ad. ♂

1 →

A ad. ♀

C imm. ♂ (2 yrs)

E ad. ♀

D juv.

2

4

← 5

F ad. ♂

G soaring

2

H gliding

343

Montagu's Harrier

Circus pygargus

General impression: a typical small harrier, usually seen flying easily and elegantly over open country with the wings raised high (H and I).

Proportions: smaller than the Hen Harrier, more slenderly built, with narrower, more pointed wings, longer hands and a longer tail which is considerably longer than the wing breadth. All in all, a more slender, light and elegant profile.

Plumage: adult males are characterized by their pale grey underparts contrasting with the black primaries (A 2). Compared with the other grey male harriers this species has characteristic bands on the secondaries, both above and below (A 1). Also, the grey upperside of Montagu's Harrier is practically always mottled where the other grey male harriers are uniformly coloured. Furthermore, the black wing tips seen on the upperside (E 2) contrast sharply with the otherwise grey impression. The males may vary considerably in ground colour, from very dark ash-grey to very pale grey.

Adult females are very similar to those of the Hen Harrier, with the underparts basically pale yellow-brown, the belly with longitudinal stripes, the wing-coverts spotted, the greyer flight feathers with distinct bands, two complete ones on the primaries as opposed to the Hen Harrier's three, and a tail with three conspicuous bands. The upperparts are dark brown with white at the root of the tail (F 3) and here

again with three tail bands. The uniform brown impression is somewhat broken by the slightly paler central wing-coverts.

Variants: there is a rare melanistic form in which the male is brownish-black with a black head, the tail grey-brown above, grey below, in some cases banded. The outermost primaries have a silvery-green sheen and the secondaries have pale tips. The females are dark brown (and without a white rump), the undersides sometimes with rust-red spots. The secondaries, primaries and tail are grey, the latter with the typical bands. Occasionally one sees partly melanistic individuals.

Young birds: juvenile plumage resembles the females but with the important difference that the underparts do not have red-brown stripes (D 4) and that the secondaries are so dark (D 5) that the bands, found in old females (B 6), are not visible or almost so. The head pattern also shows more contrast. The upperparts are dark with a distinct pale area on the wing-coverts (G). In a completely fresh, unworn plumage the pale tips to the greater wing-coverts form a pale band over the wings (G 7).

When the juvenile birds come to Europe in the following spring, at an age of about ten months, the young males can usually be distinguished by having a number of greyish-blue feathers on the head and breast. In the course of the summer and autumn the primaries acquire the typical

pattern of the adult males. With its greyish appearance the rest of the plumage now shows that the birds are male. At an age of ten months the young females can be distinguished by their dark juvenile secondaries. When around two years old they can no longer be distinguished from the adults. Young males can be distinguished until they are about three years old.

Flight: as is typical of the harriers, Montagu's flies with distinctly raised wings, both when gliding (I) and particularly when soaring (H). The wing beats are very elegant, and are executed with such power that the bird is often raised. This gives the active flight a hopping, tern-like character. Gliding flight is often rather wavering and slow, interrupted by soft wing beats.

Characteristic behaviour: in true harrier fashion searches the countryside by flying low. Most often seen over cultivated areas, meadows, grassland and the outskirts of wetlands.

Likelihood of confusion: the females of Hen, Montagu's and Pallid Harriers are very similar to one another and the separation of the last two is very difficult, indeed identification may only be possible under optimal conditions. The two species have the same proportions and plumage but differences in head patterns can be used (see p. 341). In addition, Montagu's Harrier has two bars on the

Montagu's Harrier (w. 97–115 cm)

A ad. ♂

← 2

1

← 1

B ad. ♀

← 6

D juv.

← 5

4 →

C im. ♂ (2 yrs)

E ad. ♂

3
↓

G juv.

7

F ad. ♀

← 1

← 2

H soaring

I gliding

345

primaries, the Pallid three. Males of Montagu's and Hen Harrier have different proportions, the former being a more slenderly-built bird with a longer tail, longer and narrower wings and in particular longer and more pointed hands. The last-named character may, however, be of limited value when the primary feathers are worn. The plumage of the two species is similar. Among other things the Hen Harrier has slightly more conspicuous longitudinal stripes on the underside of the body and three bars on the primaries.

Identification is best achieved by comparing the proportions with the mode of flight. Montagu's Harrier will then be seen as a lighter, more slender and elegant bird, with elastic, sometimes tern-like wing beats and often with an almost hopping flight.

The melanistic variant already described may be confused with the considerably larger and more broad-winged females and juveniles of the Marsh Harrier. For possible confusion of male Montagu's with male Hen Harriers and Pallid Harriers *see* under the former, and with immature Pallid Harriers *see* under that species.

Pallid Harrier
Circus macrourus

General impression: a small harrier, resembling Montagu's Harrier in size, appearance and flight.

Proportions: as for the Marsh Harrier, but the females may be rather powerfully built.

Plumage: old males are easily recognizable by the white underparts in contrast to the dark pattern on the second to fifth primaries. This pattern is completely different from that of the Hen and Montagu's Harriers, a difference which is very noticeable in the field (A 1). The upperparts have a similarly clear pattern, but in pale grey contrasting with the dark wing tips (F 1).

Adult females are very similar to female Hen and Montagu's Harriers, but differ from these in the head pattern (*see* under Montagu's Harrier). Furthermore, there is a difference in the number of bands on the secondaries (B 2). Hen and Pallid Harriers have three, Montagu's only two that are complete. But as with the head pattern this is also a character that is difficult to record.

Young birds: in their first plumage they are coloured like the females but with the underside of the body and the wing-coverts rust-brown and unstreaked (G 3) and usually with dark secondaries (G 4). The facial patterns (*see* p. 341) are often prominent in the young birds (E 5 and G 5). Here the pale collar is a particularly useful character. In its second summer, when about a year old, the male will usually show the characteristic wing pattern (D 1) of the definitive plumage. At this time the secondaries are often juvenile in character, so the birds sometimes appear very dark. At one year the females (C) have still not moulted the secondaries and will usually be recognizable because these are dark without the conspicuous bands

normally seen in the definitive female plumage. However, adult females may also have dark secondaries.

The full plumage is acquired at about two years old.

Flight: as in the other harriers, the wings are clearly raised when soaring and gliding (H and I). The flight is very like that of Montagu's Harrier.

Likelihood of confusion: the male with the males of Hen and Montagu's Harriers, *see* under the former, or with female Montagu's, *see* under the latter.

At about a year old, in a transitional plumage, male Pallid Harriers may be very difficult to distinguish from male Montagu's.

At this moulting stage Montagu's Harrier may show a primaries character which is very similar to that of the Pallid Harrier, namely bleaching and abrasion of the juvenile feathers.

Pallid Harrier (w. 99–117 cm)

Pallid Harrier

A ad. ♂

1

B ad. ♀

5

2

C imm. (2 yrs, Apr)

← 1

D imm. (2 yrs, July/Aug)

E juv.

5

G juv.

4

5

3

F ad. ♂

← 1

H soaring

I gliding

Combined with this there may be new greyish feathers forming an indistinct pale collar which is also the Pallid Harrier's best recognition character. Here, Montagu's darker head and front of breast serve as a recognition character, but identification may be very difficult.

There may also be difficulties in distinguishing between female Pallid Harriers and female Hen Harriers, for the latter also has a pale collar, but this is far less conspicuous (see p. 341). There is also a considerable difference in proportions and flight. Separation of the young of the two species is much easier because the Pallid Harrier has no markings on the underparts. However, young Hen Harriers show more contrast in the pattern on the head than adult females.

Dark Chanting Goshawk
Melierax metabates

General impression: medium sized hawk-like raptor, with a trace of the buzzards.

Proportions: short, broad and rounded wings with parallel edges. A long tapering tail, relatively a little shorter than a Goshawk's.

Plumage: Adult: the upperparts are slate-grey to dark brownish-grey, darkest on the head, shoulders and back. The tail-coverts are pale, with conspicuous dark cross-bands (C 1), the central tail feathers black. The primaries above and below are blackish-brown (C 3, A 3). The underparts are very pale. At close quarters the belly, and to a lesser extent the wing-coverts and flight feathers, show red-brown cross-bands. The cheeks, throat and the uppermost part of the breast are slate-grey. The underside of the tail is pale with weakly marked dark cross-bands. The feet, cere and the base of the beak are orange-red.

Young birds: the juvenile plumage is, roughly speaking, a brown edition of the adult's with the following exceptions: the underparts have more prominent cross-bands and only the outermost flight feathers are dark. On the upperside the primaries have conspicuous pale cross-bands, with only the tips dark. The whole of the tail is cross-banded. The feet and cere are yellow.

Flight: similar to that of the hawks, but the wing beats are not so rapid. Soars with raised wings like a Marsh Harrier.

Likelihood of confusion: the adult is so characteristic that there is normally no chance of confusion. Superficially it may resemble a male Hen Harrier. There are, however, differences in plumage and proportions.

The young birds are scarcely so characteristic, and may show resemblances to the buzzards and hawks. However, the long tail, the pale rump and the pattern on the underparts should render identification easy.

Dark Chanting Goshawk (w. 95–110 cm)

A ad.

B juv.

3

C ad.

D juv.

1

2

3

E

Goshawk

Accipiter gentilis

General impression: a typical hawk, with very broad, short, rounded wings and a long tail, considerably longer than the wing breadth.

Proportions: a striking difference in size between the sexes. The female is as large as a Buzzard, the male much smaller.

The species has a characteristically elongated body with a broad breast and a powerfully-built rump area. The head is pointed, elongated and protruding (B 1), the tail broad and when spread distinctly fan-shaped with rounded corners (in the Sparrowhawk these are sharp). The wings are relatively longer than in the Sparrowhawk, and in particular the hand is longer and more pointed.

Plumage: Adult: the underside has close transverse stripes on the belly and wing-coverts, with bands on the flight feathers and tail. The basic coloration is pale so that at a distance the bird appears greyish. The transverse stripes are only seen at close quarters. The under tail-coverts are more clearly marked with white, but this is of doubtful value as a field character.

The upperparts are uniformly brown, the male's with a blue-grey sheen. The cross-bands on the tail are conspicuous. Under good conditions for observation the head pattern may be a good field character: dark ear-coverts and dark crown (E 1 and B 1). The superciliary stripe is particularly noticeable in the female (E 1). The beak is more powerful than in the Sparrowhawk.

Young birds: in the first plumage the underparts are yellowish with longitudinally arranged markings on the belly and wing-coverts (D 3), while the flight feathers have prominent transverse bands. The upperparts are dark brown with rust-coloured edges to the feathers and with a contrast between flight feathers and wing-coverts (F).

In its second spring, when about a year old, the bird starts to moult into its definitive plumage. This moult is mainly complete in the autumn of the same year. However, even after this young birds can be recognized in the field because the dark head pattern is not fully developed. The birds have a full plumage at an age of about two years.

Flight: usually a series of very rapid wing beats followed by gliding with the wings held flat (H). In soaring the female has the wings distinctly raised, whereas in the male they are only slightly raised. In soaring the tail is usually spread.

Likelihood of confusion: the large female will usually not be difficult to identify, as it appears as a large hawk. Even for experienced observers, however, it is difficult to distinguish a male Goshawk from a female Sparrowhawk as they are close to one another in size. There are, however, differences in proportions. The male Goshawk is a more powerfully-built bird. This is seen most clearly in the belly which appears to be more elongated with a broader breast, and with the rump also broader than in the Sparrowhawk. Furthermore, the head is larger and far more protruding, appearing almost triangular, whereas the Sparrowhawk's is rounded. The Goshawk's tail is also broader. The distinction is most easily seen in soaring flight. The Goshawk is then very much like a large falcon, the wings being more pointed than in the Sparrowhawk. The tail is also distinctly rounded and fan-shaped, while in the Sparrowhawk it is more truncated and almost triangular. When soaring the Goshawk appears to be heavier, circling in larger arcs, with more regular, slightly stiff and not particularly deep wing beats. In the same situation the Sparrowhawk executes 4–5 rapid and energetic wing beats. At close quarters the head pattern on adult Goshawks is more conspicuous, as the ear-coverts are darker.

Goshawk (w. 96–127 cm)

A ad. ♀

B ad. ♂
1
2

C ad. ♂

F juv.
3

E ad. ♀
1

F juv. ♀

F ♀ soaring

H gliding

Sparrowhawk

Accipiter nisus

General impression: a typical small hawk with short, broad, rounded wings, a relatively small head and long tail, considerably longer than the wing breadth.

Proportions: the male is about the size of a Kestrel, the female somewhat larger. Compared with a Goshawk, the body is less powerfully built, particularly the breast and rump, the head is scarcely so prominent and is more rounded. The tail is more slender and almost truncated, in soaring flight almost triangular, and the wings are relatively broader and slightly more rounded.

Plumage: Adult: underparts with the typical hawk stripes. Ground colour pale greyish, the stripes on the belly reddish, on the rest of the underparts brown, giving the impression at a distance of a uniform red-brown underside. The upperparts vary from blue-grey to dark slate-grey, appearing uniform at a distance apart from the 4–5 prominent tail bands, which also appear distinctly on the underparts (E 1).

The adult female resembles the male, except that the belly stripes are brown. The upperparts are dark brown often with a slate-grey sheen. In addition the female has a distinct pale stripe over the eye (A 2). This is usually lacking in the male.

Young birds: in the first plumage the ground colour of the underparts varies between white, cream-coloured and (rarely) reddish-beige. The transverse stripes are broader and more irregular. The cheeks are dark brown (F 3), the throat greyish, and there are longitudinal stripes on the front part of the neck (E 4). The upperparts are dark brown with rust-coloured feather edges. After the first moult the young cannot usually be distinguished from the adults, but the full plumage is not acquired until they are about two years old.

Flight: typically hawk-like, with a few rapid wing-beats followed by gliding, with the wings almost flat (H). Also seen soaring, mostly on migration, often with the tail only slightly spread, in contrast to the Goshawk. The wings are held slightly raised or flat (G).

Characteristic behaviour: sometimes seen hunting low over the ground or in winter around houses or in gardens, trying surprise attacks on small birds.

Likelihood of confusion: *see* under Goshawk and Levant Sparrowhawk. On account of the very similar size can be confused with a Kestrel, particularly in a strong wind and in poor light when the colours cannot be seen. In a strong wind the Sparrowhawk bends the wings backwards and appears sharp-winged like a falcon. In soaring flight the tail is more truncated. *See* also under Merlin (p. 374).

A ad. ♀

2 ↓

B ad. ♀

C ad. ♂

D ad. ♂

1 ↑

E juv.

4 ↓

1 ↑

F juv.

3

G soaring

H gliding

Levant Sparrowhawk
Accipiter brevipes

General impression: a typical small hawk, more falcon-like than a Sparrowhawk.

Proportions: similar in size and proportions to the Sparrowhawk. The body is, however, more slender, the hand longer and more pointed, giving the falcon-like impression.

Plumage: in the adult male the wing undersides are white or cream-coloured with prominent black wing tips (B 1). The belly is pale with rust-red transverse stripes and the tail has 5–6 bands, thus more than the Sparrowhawk. The upperparts are blue-grey with darker wing tips and a paler colour on the rump. The central two tail feathers are unstriped.

With its prominent transverse belly stripes and bands on the flight feathers the adult female is far more like a Sparrowhawk. However, it also has prominent dark wing tips (A 1), a good field character,

and like the male more bands on the tail (A 2). The upperparts are brown with a grey sheen, and the head pattern is darker than in the Sparrowhawk. Also the eye stripe is lacking. At close quarters a dark streak on the throat can be seen.

Young birds: best recognized by the belly having drop-like markings arranged longitudinally (C 4) and the throat having a distinct dark streak (C 3); this is only indistinct in the adult female. As in other hawks the young have rust-coloured feather edges on the upperside. There is a striking pale marking on the front of the back.

In the second summer, when about a year old, the young birds have most of the adult plumage, but still with a few juvenile feathers above and below.

Flight: very similar to the Sparrowhawk.

Characteristic behaviour: more often seen soaring

than the Sparrowhawk, using thermals, and sometimes in large flocks.

Likelihood of confusion: compared with the Sparrowhawk the present species is more slender, with more pointed wings and above all with dark wing tips, the latter being less prominent in young birds (C). The tail bands are more difficult to see; the present species has 5–6 visible, the Sparrowhawk 4–5. The very pale male can, on account of the species' more falcon-like appearance, be confused with a male Lesser Kestrel, which is also very pale. The latter, however, has a prominent distal tail band.

The young Goshawk also has longitudinal stripes.

The underside of the Goshawk is more distinctly marked, and again the tail bands can be used. The Goshawk also appears heavier in flight. *See* also under Goshawk p. 350.

Shikra
Accipiter baduis

General impression: a small pale hawk.

Proportions: very like a Sparrowhawk.

Plumage: Adult: the upperside is pale blue-grey, the 4–5 longest primaries with almost black tips and the outermost tail feathers with weakly marked dark bands (B 2). The underparts

are very pale with the wing tips a little darker (A 1). At close quarters a dark band can be seen on the throat (A 3). The tail is very dark with prominent cross bands (A 4). Also at close quarters the weakly-marked transverse red-brown stripes can be seen.

The adult female resembles the male, but is slightly darker on the

upperside (more brown). The underside has weakly marked transverse red-brown stripes.

Young birds: in the juvenile plumage the upperside is dark brown with rust-red feather edges, paler head and tail-coverts and a tail with 5–8 prominent bands. On the underside the belly has

Levant Sparrowhawk (w. 64–80 cm)   Levant Sparrowhawk/Shikra

1 →   **A** ad. ♀   1 →   **B** ad.   **C** juv.

2

D ad. ♀

1

3 4

F juv.

E ad. ♂

G soaring

H gliding

Shikra (w. 60–70 cm)

B ad. ♂

A ad. ♂

C juv.

4

2

large, brownish, drop-shaped markings, while the wing-coverts and flight feathers have more prominent spots and bands than the adults.

Flight: resembles the Sparrowhawk.

Likelihood of confusion: the colour pattern is like that of the Levant Sparrowhawk which is, however, more falcon-like with more pointed wings and darker wing tips. In the field, young birds of the two species will be difficult to distinguish

from one another by their plumage. As mentioned there are, however, differences in the proportions.

Gyrfalcon
Falco rusticolus

General impression: a very large falcon, the wingspan as in the Buzzard, and therefore considerably larger than, e.g., the Peregrine.

Proportions: the wings are long and particularly broad at the base. The hand is very rounded for a falcon. The belly is large, the tail broad and long. The head is large, with a powerful beak.

Plumage: Fenno-Scandinavian birds all belong to the dark phase in which the adults have a white underside with dark drop-like or arrow-like markings varying in extent. The flight feathers, however, are dark brown with paler bands (A). The upperparts are mainly slate-grey, usually with paler bands particularly on the tail (H). In the field the crown appears a uniform slate-grey. The cheeks have some dark feathers (D 1).

Variants: in addition to the dark phase there is a grey and a white phase. The *grey phase* (M) is like the dark on the underparts, sometimes with a rather weaker pattern. The upperparts are noticeably paler. At a

distance the dark phase appears uniformly dark, whereas the grey phase appears grey with distinctly pale bands. The head is mainly white with dark feather shafts, but its appearance may vary considerably. *White phase:* a white bird with black wing tips (L). However, the plumage above and below shows many dark spots, often more than in drawing L. There are transitional forms between the phases. In Greenland about nine per cent are between grey and white. Birds from the European mainland (dark phase) also vary (*see* drawings A, B, C and D).

Young birds: *dark phase:* distinctly darker on the underside on account of the belly's dark longitudinal stripes and the dark wing-coverts (F and G). The upperside is also darker (I), being dark brown in contrast to the slate-grey of the adults. The crown is also darker so that the pale nape marking appears more distinctly.

From its second summer the young bird resembles the adults. However, it is still darker with more prominent markings. Thus, in many cases the wing-coverts will

be darker and the innermost secondaries with no cross bands, while the underparts are more strongly spotted than in the adults.

Grey phase: the upperside has larger pale spots and feather edges, giving a more mottled appearance.

White phase: the dark markings are drop-shaped but not arranged in cross bands as happens in certain of the adults (K).

Flight: on account of its size this species has very slow wing movements for a falcon. It is also characteristic that these are not very deep and almost appear to be executed by the hands alone. When soaring the wings are slightly upturned (N) and the tail widely spread and fan-shaped.

Characteristic behaviour: in contrast to the Peregrine most often hunts low over the ground. Two birds sometimes work together.

Likelihood of confusion: nearest in appearance to the Peregrine Falcon, but normally much larger with slightly longer arms, broader and more rounded wings. The

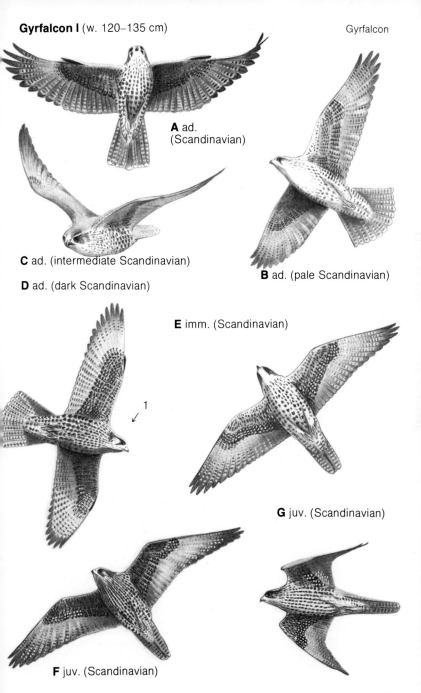

Gyrfalcon I (w. 120–135 cm)

A ad. (Scandinavian)

C ad. (intermediate Scandinavian)

D ad. (dark Scandinavian)

B ad. (pale Scandinavian)

E imm. (Scandinavian)

1

G juv. (Scandinavian)

F juv. (Scandinavian)

underparts are often paler and normally without the transverse striping of the Peregrine. The upperparts are somewhat paler. The head has less contrast than the Peregrine's in which the moustachial streak contrasts clearly with pale cheeks. Young Gyrfalcons are more similar to young Peregrines. Birds of the grey and white phases have such pale upperparts that they cannot be confused with other large falcons.

The dark phase might be confused with the Saker Falcon. The two species have almost the same silhouette. The Saker is normally smaller but the difference in size is difficult to perceive. In general, the head of adult Gyrfalcons is darker, the upperparts paler and the tail has less prominent bands. In the Gyrfalcon the darker colours on the upperside are greyish while in the Saker they are various shades of brown. In young Sakers the primaries on the upperside are darker. The head pattern of the Gyrfalcon is clearly darker. Under good conditions the moustachial streak of the Saker can also be used in identification. In practice the two species will very rarely be seen in the same area so there should not normally be any problem in separating them.

Gyrfalcon – Scandinavian. *Photo J-M. Breider*

H ad./imm. (Scandinavian)

I juv. (Scandinavian)

K juv. (white Greenland)

J juv. (white Greenland)

M (grey phase)

L ad. (Greenland)

N soaring

Saker Falcon

Falco cherrug

General impression: a very large falcon, the wingspan about the same as a Buzzard's.

Proportions: very similar to the Gyrfalcon, so with long, often somewhat rounded and broad wings and a long tail. There are evidently variations in the proportions.

Plumage: adults may be very pale on the underside (cream-coloured) with only a few dark spots on the belly and wing-coverts, weakly patterned transverse markings on the flight feathers and slightly dark on the wing tips (B). Apparently it is the males which are so pale. The females sometimes have more spots on the belly and wing-coverts (A), particularly the greater wing-coverts which at a distance appear to form a dark wing band.

The upperside varies from dark brown, red-brown or yellow-brown to grey-brown with the flight feathers darker and therefore contrasting with the rest (F 1). The tail pattern is very striking. The central tail feathers are often uniformly coloured. The others have oval, yellowish-brown markings on both the inner and outer vanes (F 2), so that the tail appears either cross-banded or with spots on the sides. At a distance the pale head contrasts with the otherwise dark upperside (F 3). At close

quarters the head pattern may be useful in identification. It is basically cream-coloured with a few brown feathers. A black streak extends back from the eye and there is usually but not always a weak longitudinal moustachial streak. The cheeks are almost without markings and therefore appear pale. Above the eye and backwards to the nape there is a whitish superciliary stripe (seen under extremely good conditions for observation).

Variants: the plumage described is valid for Europe. Other races in Asia are darker or paler. In Europe birds are seen with a blue-grey or cross-banded rump.

Young birds: in general these are darker in colour and pattern. The underparts are often clearly marked with dark longitudinal stripes rather than spots (D 5). The wing-coverts are normally still darker (D 6). The pale feather edges on the upperside are narrower so this also appears darker. The same is the case with the head where the black backward-directed streak from the eye is broader and the moustachial streak more distinctly marked. In certain cases the age can only be determined by comparing the characters mentioned here. At an age of about one year the young bird resembles the adult. Usually, however, it can still

be distinguished, primarily by the underside's long dark stripes, and by the fact that the greater wing-coverts on the underside have not been moulted. They will appear as a distinct dark band (C 7). At two years the bird has a full plumage.

Flight: on account of its size this species flies with very slow wing beats. These do not go very deep and appear almost as though executed by the hand alone. When hunting, the rate of wing beats increases and the movement becomes deeper. Small males can fly very rapidly. When soaring the wings are slightly upturned (H) and the tail widely spread.

Characteristic behaviour: hovers now and again. Most of the prey is killed on the ground. Normally uses a surprise attack. Dramatic chases of birds over long distances are not often seen.

Likelihood of confusion: regarding Gyrfalcons and Lanner Falcons *see* under these species. Compared with the Peregrine the Saker appears considerably larger, usually with broader, more rounded wings and a longer tail. Also the head is larger and more rounded.

The Peregrine has blue-grey to slate-grey upperparts, the Saker brown. The head patterns also differ, the Peregrine's being distinctly darker and always with a prominently marked moustachial streak.

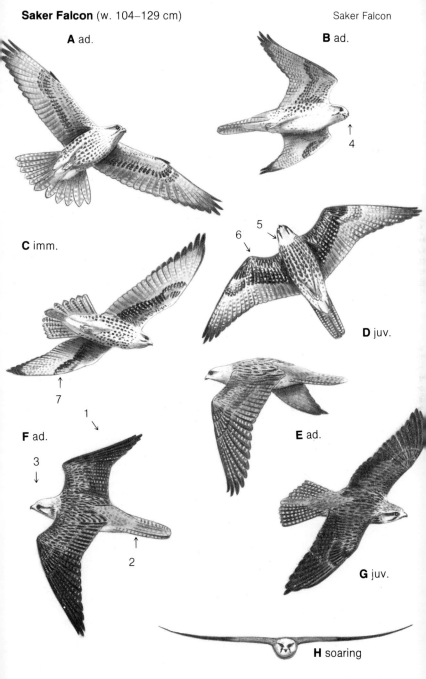

Saker Falcon (w. 104–129 cm)

A ad.

B ad.

↑
4

C imm.

6 5

D juv.

7

1

F ad.

3
↓

2

E ad.

G juv.

H soaring

Lanner Falcon

Falco biarmicus

General impression: a large falcon although smaller than the other two large species: Gyrfalcon and Saker.

Proportions: an elongated, relatively slender falcon with long wings. These have a very broad arm and a pointed hand although this may be rounded when soaring. Compared with the Saker the body is more slender and the head smaller. With its long tail the Lanner may resemble a giant Kestrel.

Plumage: the adult bird often has very pale underparts, beige or with a tinge of rust, with only a few dark spots (B) usually placed on the sides of the body and on the wing-coverts. The wing feathers have weakly marked cross bands (A). Darker birds are seen including some with spots on the breast. There are also birds (males) with no spots on the underparts.

The upperside is darker or paler slate-grey. At close quarters the paler feather edges can be seen, but at a distance the bird normally appears uniformly coloured, although paler towards the rump (E). The upperside and tail may have pale cross-bands. The head is rust-coloured (E 1) with its front almost black. A broad dark stripe extends back from the eye (A 2) and a moustachial streak is usually seen contrasting with the pale cheek (A 3). Individual birds may only have a trace of moustachial streak.

Races: *erlangeri* (B) in Tunisia-Morocco and *tanypteris* Libya-Middle East are paler above and below (fewer spots).

Young birds: most easily recognized by the more or less distinct longitudinal stripes on the underside (D 4) and darker wing-coverts (D 5). Owing to narrower pale feather edges the upperside appears darker and has a brown sheen. The head is similarly darker. Some birds seem to moult directly into the adult plumage. Others at about a year are still recognizable as young because of dark stripes on the breast. Also the greater wing-coverts on the underside have not been moulted and are therefore seen as a dark band (C 6).

Flight: an elegant bird in the air. In ordinary flight the wing beats are slow and not particularly deep. The speed is much increased and the beats are deeper during hunting. Compared with the Peregrine, flight is heavier and slower with less powerful beats. In soaring the wings are slightly upturned (H).

Likelihood of confusion: compared with the Peregrine the Lanner has slightly longer wings, especially the arms, and they are more rounded when soaring. Also the tail is longer. Adult Peregrines have a dark head. The problem is greater in the young birds. Both species then have dark heads, the Peregrine distinctly darker. In the Lanner the contrast on the underside between wing-coverts and primaries is however a rather good recognition character.

There are considerable problems when comparing the Lanner with the Saker. Adult Lanners have a more slender body and smaller head than Sakers, which often appear broad-breasted with a more tapering tail. In many cases Lanners have narrower wings, and an overall more slender impression. The proportional differences are shown in the drawings. Normally the Lanner has a red-brown head in contrast to the Saker's whitish. The upperside is also grey whereas the Saker's is brown in various shades, most often red-brown.

There are also differences in the pattern and colour of the tail. The Lanner's is ash-grey with close stripes, the Saker's pale brown with oval pale markings on the outermost feathers.

At close quarters the head pattern may be a valuable recognition character. The Lanner has a typical, clearly marked black streak extending back from the eye and there is usually a distinct narrow moustachial streak. These characters are weaker in the Saker which has a pale stripe over the eye.

At a distance it is often impossible to distinguish young Lanners from young Sakers. The proportions however provide a clue. At close quarters one sees the contrast on the Saker's upperside between the brown body and wing-coverts and the almost black hue of the flight feathers. Here the Lanner is uniformly dark. The head pattern is also different, the Lanner's being darkest above.

Lanner Falcon (w. 95–115 cm)

a ad.

C imm.

2

3

E ad.

B ad. (*erlangeri*)

1

4

5

D juv.

F ad. (*erlangeri*)

H soaring

G juv.

Peregrine Falcon

Falco peregrinus

General impression: a medium-sized to large falcon with powerful flight.

Proportions: a considerable size difference between the sexes. On account of the stout body and, for a falcon, very short tail this bird appears compact. The wings are long and pointed with a very short, broad arm and a long narrow hand. The proportions may vary from a broad-winged Gyrfalcon type to a slender-winged bird like a Hobby.

Plumage: Adult: a pale underside with distinct dark transverse stripes. The males often have a larger unstriped or unspotted area on the breast (B) than the females (A). The upperside is very dark with the head and front of the back black and the rest blue-grey or slate-grey, the tail with conspicuous bands. The very striking broad moustachial streak (B 1 and F 1) is a good field character, combined with the dark crown (B 2 and F 2) and the white cheeks.

Races: the northern race *calidus* (C) is larger, paler on the underside and pale grey to grey-blue on the upperside. The Mediterranean race *brookei* is smaller, darker with distinct rust-coloured nape feathers and a rust-coloured sheen on the underside.

Young birds: the underparts are yellow-brown with distinct brown longitudinal stripes (E 3) and clearly marked wing patterns. The upperparts are blackish-brown. On account of the dark patterns on the neck the moustachial streak is scarcely so prominent. In their second summer the young normally retain some juvenile feathers.

Flight: active flight is rather slow and powerful with somewhat stiff and not particularly deep wing beats. The speed, power and depth increase during hunting. When soaring the wings are held slightly upturned (H).

Likelihood of confusion: in relation to the three large falcon species (Gyrfalcon, Saker and Lanner) the Peregrine is easily recognized by differences in proportions: the wings are normally more slender, the body scarcely so elongated and the tail is a little shorter. When soaring the wings appear to be more pointed. Large Peregrine females and small males of the other species may overlap in size and proportions. There is only a small difference in size between the Peregrine and Lanner.

As regards plumage, it is important to mention that in adult Peregrines only the front of the breast is pale, while the adults of the three large species are very pale on the whole of the underside. The Peregrine is most easily distinguished from these by its dark head and broad, prominently marked moustachial streak contrasting sharply with the white cheeks.

Differences between the young of the four species are discussed under each of the three larger species. There is also a chance of confusion with the Hobby, particularly in relation to the young Peregrine. Usually, however, there is a difference in the proportions. The Hobby is also darker with a narrower and pointed moustachial streak.

On account of a similarity in size there may also be confusion with Eleanora's Falcon. Normally, however, the proportions are very different. Eleanora's is distinctly more slender, with longer and narrower wings and a longer tail which is very similar in proportions to that of the Hobby. Furthermore, Eleanora's underparts are darker, but this does not apply to the young which are pale with dark under the wings.

Normally the Peregrine Falcon, particularly the larger female, is very characteristic. The small males may be difficult to identify, especially at a distance and in bad light, so there may be confusion with the Hobby and Merlin. In good light, however, and at a distance, it should be possible to see the pale breast of an adult Peregrine, a character lacking in the small falcons.

Peregrine Falcon (w. 80–117 cm)

A ad. ♀

B ad. ♂

2

1

D imm. ♂

C ad. ♂

E juv. ♀

3

F ad. ♀

2

1

G juv. ♀

H soaring

Barbary Falcon
Falco pelegrinoides

General impression: very similar to the Peregrine.

Proportions: similar to the Peregrine but more slender so a little less compact. Often about the size of the smallest Peregrine.

Plumage: Adult: upperparts pale grey-blue with grey-black primaries. Crown and nape are red-brown, the forehead and moustachial streak blackish. The underparts appear uniformly pale, at close quarters yellow-brown with only a few dark spots or transverse stripes.

Races: the eastern race *babylonicus*, from Iraq and eastwards, has even paler upperparts, pale brown crown and nape and only a weak moustachial stripe.

Young birds: very similar to those of the Peregrine but more brown and also with paler upperparts (pale feather edges), paler head with a larger and more red-brown band at the nape, narrower moustachial streak and narrower stripes on the underparts.

Flight: as for the Peregrine, often very temperamental.

Likelihood of confusion: underparts distinctly paler than Peregrine, although the front of the breast is paler in the latter. Upperparts also paler. Under good conditions of observation the rust-coloured crown and nape are excellent recognition characters. Also the moustachial streak is not so conspicuous as in the Peregrine.

The coloration somewhat resembles that of the Lanner Falcon which, however, has a longer tail with several bands, whereas the Barbary only has one conspicuous dark distal band.

Sooty Falcon
Falco concolor

General impression: very similar to Eleanora's Falcon.

Proportions: a little smaller than Eleanora's Falcon, with a more wedge-shaped tail.

Plumage: Adult: dark phase (A) is very like Eleanora's dark phase. The more common pale phase is a slate-grey bird with somewhat darker primaries (B). In both phases the yellow cere and yellow feet are very striking.

Young birds: a more brown upperside with a pale marking on the nape. The underparts are yellow-brown with conspicuous longitudinal stripes. There is a narrow moustachial streak.

Flight: very similar to Eleanora's Falcon but often with the hand more angled.

Characteristic behaviour: in the winter quarters often seen in small flocks hunting for insects. On the breeding grounds likes to hunt morning and evening.

Likelihood of confusion: at a distance the plumage of Sooty and Eleanora's Falcons will appear identical. At close quarters it can be seen that the underside of the Sooty Falcon lacks the pale bases to the flight feathers present in Eleanora's. As already mentioned the Sooty has a more wedge-shaped tail, and it also has a more slender beak. Under good conditions of observation the pale slate-grey phase will appear as a clearly paler bird than a dark Eleanora's. It also has a dark marking between the eye and the pale throat. The young of both species are very similar. At close quarters, however, the young Sooty can be distinguished because it lacks the pale red-brown on the body and under wing-coverts of Eleanora's.

Barbary Falcon (w. 80–100 cm)

Barbary Falcon/Sooty Falcon

A ad.

B juv.

C ad.

D juv.

Sooty Falcon (w. 85 cm)

B ad. (pale phase)

A ad. (dark phase)

D juv.

C ad.

E soaring

Eleanora's Falcon
Falco eleanorae

General impression: a medium-sized falcon with a strikingly long tail and very long wings.

Proportions: resembles the Hobby, but is larger with relatively longer and narrower wings and in particular a much longer tail.

Plumage: Adult: in the pale phase the underside is cream-coloured to red-brown with prominent stripes. The wing-coverts are dark brown, contrasting with the grey flight feathers (A 1). The throat and cheeks appear very pale against the dark brown crown and conspicuous moustachial streak (A 2). The upperside is uniformly dark, brownish-black to bluish-black. At close quarters it will be seen that the rear of the back is paler. In some birds the under tail-coverts are red-brown. In the dark phase (about 25 per cent) the plumage is almost uniformly slate-grey, but here again with the flight feathers somewhat paler (B 1).

It is not yet clear whether there are intermediate forms. Birds appearing darker than the pale phase may be one-year-olds of the dark phase.

Young birds: in the first plumage the bird is distinctly paler and rather like the young of the Red-footed Falcon. The underparts are greyish with longitudinal stripes, the flight feathers have narrow dark transverse bands and the wings a dark rear edge (D 3). The wing-coverts have dark spots (D 4). The difference from the adult plumage is seen most clearly on the upperside where the tail shows narrow pale bands.

It is not known when the full plumage is acquired.

Flight: a very good flier which often stoops impressively, even when not hunting. In active flight the wing beats are soft, relaxed, not particularly deep and very slow. When hunting they are more rapid and more powerful.

Characteristic behaviour: sometimes hunts in small flocks. Most often seen in the colonies on islands in the Mediterranean.

Likelihood of confusion: on account of its profile and colour pattern the pale phase is closest to a Hobby. However, Eleanora's Falcon is larger and more powerfully built with somewhat broader arms and a longer tail. Adults are also separated by the underwing patterns and darker body. Young birds of the two species are more similar to one another but in Eleanora's the dark under wing-coverts contrasting with the flight feathers are characteristic.

Dark phase birds may be confused with adult male Red-footed Falcons. The latter are, however, smaller, more slender and move in a different way (often like a Kestrel), and there are also plumage differences, including a distinct contrast on the upperside between wing-coverts and flight feathers.

Confusion with a Peregrine Falcon is also possible, but it usually has a very compact silhouette and transverse stripes on the underparts. However, young Peregrines are very dark and have longitudinal stripes, so small, very slender young males may be tricky. A reliable difference, however, is the distinctly shorter tail of the Peregrine.

For possible confusion with the Sooty Falcon *see* under that species.

A ad.   ← 1   ↗ 2

B ad.   ↖ 1

C imm.

D juv.   3 →   ← 4

E ad.

F juv.

G soaring

Hobby
Falco subbuteo

General impression: a small to medium-sized, very powerfully-built falcon with very long, slender and pointed wings and a very short tail. In flight it has often been compared with a giant Swift.

Proportions: the size of a Kestrel but with completely different proportions. The wings are more slender and more pointed, with the arm very short and the hand long and narrow. The tail is normally very short.

Plumage: the underparts are pale, often with a rust-coloured sheen, and marked with conspicuous longitudinal stripes. The rust-red under tail-coverts and tibial feathers are also striking. The wing-coverts are spotted and the flight feathers are distinctly banded. The wing tips are slightly darker. The upperparts are a uniform dark blue-grey, but paler on the rump, the female with a tinge of brown. The head (C 1) is dark like the back, with a particularly prominent moustachial streak (A 2). The throat is pale.

Young birds: very similar to the adults, but can be distinguished by the underside having the area around the tail-coverts cream-coloured, not rust-coloured as in the adults. On the upperside there is a good recognition character in the contrast between the dark flight feathers and the paler wing-coverts.

There is also a pale band at the transition between wing-coverts and flight feathers, although this disappears fairly soon. The paler colour of the wing-coverts is also continued on the head which is therefore browner than in the adults.

Flight: marvellously adept in the air, reflected in its ability to hunt swallows and swifts. This requires both speed and the ability to manoeuvre. In active flight the wing beats are very slow, not particularly deep and rather stiff. When hunting the movement is faster, deeper and more elastic. Active flight is interspersed with periods of gliding.

Characteristic behaviour: apart from the dramatic bird-catching the species is often seen hunting insects in the evening over damp terrain.

Likelihood of confusion: possibly with the Red-footed Falcon which, however, has a slightly longer tail but not such long wings.

There is a characteristic difference in behaviour, for the Red-footed Falcon frequently hovers whereas the Hobby rarely does so. In most cases the plumages differ. Adult male Red-footed Falcons are so dark that they are easily distinguished in reasonably good light. Females and young birds have a distinctly pale head in contrast to the dark-headed Hobby. There are difficulties in distinguishing the Hobby from one-year-old male Red-footed Falcons. At some distance the Hobby often shows a uniform underside where the pale throat may be difficult to discern. On the underparts the male Red-footed is warm red-brown with darker longitudinal stripes, where the Hobby is pale with distinct longitudinal stripes. In fact, however, identification is often impossible in less favourable conditions.

Comparison with Eleanora's Falcon is discussed under that species.

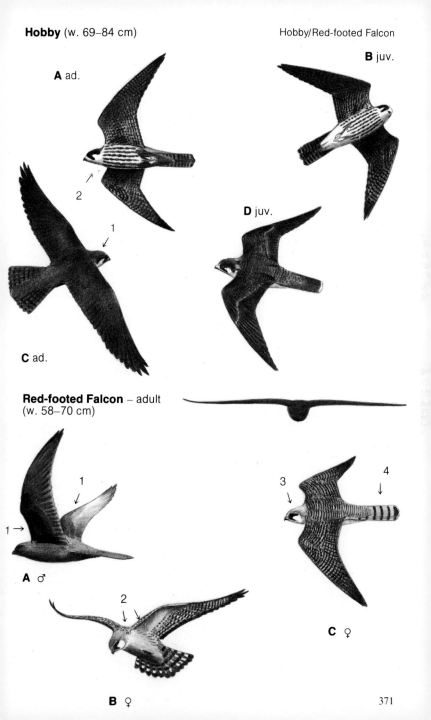

Hobby (w. 69–84 cm)   Hobby/Red-footed Falcon

A ad.

B juv.

2

1

D juv.

C ad.

Red-footed Falcon – adult
(w. 58–70 cm)

1

1

3   4

A ♂

2

B ♀

C ♀

371

Red-footed Falcon

Falco vespertinus

General impression: a small falcon, slightly smaller than a Hobby, which it much resembles in silhouette.

Proportions: slender body, long, narrow and pointed wings, in relation to the Hobby scarcely so long-winged and with a slightly broader arm. The tail is normally longer than in the Hobby, in certain cases almost as long as the Kestrel's.

Plumage: the adult male is very characteristic with its grey-black plumage, the only striking contrast being the red under tail-coverts and tibial feathers. Both above and below the dark wing-coverts contrast strongly with the somewhat paler flight feathers (A 1).

The adult female has a slightly rust-coloured or yellowish underside with the body and wing-coverts mainly unspotted (B 2), the flight feathers with close transverse bands. The upperside is mostly blue-grey with close transverse bands and with the tips of the primaries contrasting slightly with their darker grey-black colour. The pale, usually rust-red head (C 3) and the cross-banded tail (C 4) are conspicuous. A distinct dark pattern around the eye and a narrow moustachial streak can also be noted.

Young birds: in the first or juvenile plumage the bird resembles a young Hobby. The body has conspicuous longitudinal stripes (L 5),

the wing-coverts have dark spots (L 6) and the rear edge of the wing is very dark. The upperparts are mainly brown with a very dark hand. Certain of the wing-covert tips have pale edges, producing a pair of pale bands, but these soon disappear. The head is pale, like the female's, and there is often a pale collar which extends on to the nape (L 7). When the birds arrive in Europe during the next spring the sexes can usually be distinguished. Very few still have the juvenile plumage.

The young immature male (D–J) may in May–June be more or less like the adult. The underside of the body may be grey-black with red tibial feathers, the undersides of the wings as in the juvenile (H) and the upperparts a very uniform dark slate-grey. Other birds are not so far advanced in the moult (D) and are more like the juvenile. The throat is pale and the remainder of the underside darker without conspicuous markings, while the top of the head is dark. It is fairly typical for remains of the juvenile collar still to be seen on the sides of the neck (F). There are all sorts of intermediate forms between the extremes D and J. By the autumn the changes are far advanced towards the adult plumage. The young male may still be distinguished as some of the flight feathers are of the juvenile type (I).

In the next spring (at

about one year old) the young female cannot always be distinguished from the adult. The underside of the body often has some of the young bird's dark stripes or fine, drop-shaped spots. The wing-coverts on the underside are spotted as in the young bird. Under good conditions a brown sheen can also be detected on the upperside, while the crown is whitish, not yellow-brown. The full plumage is acquired at an age of two years.

Flight: when actively chasing insects the flight much resembles that of a Hobby. With rapid, elastic and not particularly deep beats the bird flies low over the terrain. At other times the flight may be more like that of a Kestrel, especially when the bird is hovering and not chasing insects.

Characteristic behaviour: as already mentioned this species frequently hovers. Insects are usually hunted from one or two favourite perches to which the bird returns after chasing a particular insect. This is a rather shy falcon.

Likelihood of confusion: *see* under Hobby and Eleanora's Falcon. Every small hovering falcon may not be a Kestrel. There are, however, considerable plumage differences but in spite of this there may be confusion when the light conditions are poor and the view is only superficial.

Red-footed Falcon II – juv. imm.

Red-footed Falcon

D imm. ♂
(1–2 yrs)

E imm. ♂
(1–2 yrs)

F imm. ♂ (1–2 yrs)

H imm. ♂ (2 yrs)

G imm. ♂ (2 yrs)

I imm. ♂ (2 yrs, Sept)

J imm. ♂ (2 yrs)

K imm. ♀

6

7

5

L juv.

373

Merlin

Falco columbarius

General impression: a small, compact falcon with pointed wings, mostly seen flying at lightning speed.

Proportions: much resembles a miniature Peregrine Falcon. The wings have a very short broad arm and a long pointed hand. The body is powerfully built with a broad breast and the tail is generally medium-long. The male is Europe's smallest raptor. The largest females may be larger than the other small falcons but in most cases they are smaller than these.

Plumage: the adult male has beige-coloured underparts, often with a rusty sheen and with fine, dark longitudinal stripes. These, however, are only seen at close quarters (A 1). On the underside the wing-coverts have fine dark spots closely arranged and the flight feathers have close cross-banding. The upperparts are blue-grey, paler to the rear and on the tail, while the primaries are dark in contrast to the rest (D 2). The tail is blue-grey above and below, with a broad dark distal band (D 3).

The adult female has a paler ground colour on the underside and the longitudinal stripes are more conspicuous (B 4). The tail has several pale bands both above and below (E 5). The female can also be recognized by the mainly brown upperside with a grey sheen on the back and rump.

Young birds: are difficult to distinguish from the females. However, they often lack the grey sheen on the back and rump, and have a darker brown ground colour on the underparts.

Flight: often seen flying very rapidly and purposefully, more markedly so than other raptor species. To do this such a small bird must have very rapid wing beats. Active flight is interspersed with short periods of gliding.

Characteristic behaviour: often seen flying low and rapidly over open country.

Likelihood of confusion: the small size usually separates this from other species. This applies particularly to the males and the smaller females. The compact, powerfully built body, the short very broad wings and the relatively short tail distinguish it from the other small falcons, which are usually not so fast in the air.

There is a possibility of confusion with the Sparrowhawk particularly when this bird is hunting low over open country, as for instance during migration, and when the hand is folded so that it appears pointed and falcon-like. However, the Merlin has more slender wings and a considerably shorter tail than the Sparrowhawk, and the Kestrel-like contrasts on the upperside will also help in identification.

There is also a chance of confusion with the Peregrine Falcon when the birds are seen in silhouette against the sky while soaring or gliding and when it is not possible to assess the size. In such cases identification may be impossible.

Merlin (w. 52–69 cm)

A ad. ♂

1

B ad. ♂

4

C juv.

D ad. ♂

3

2

E ad. ♀

5

F juv.

G soaring

Kestrel
Falco tinnunculus

General impression: a small to medium-sized falcon with long, narrow, pointed wings and a very long tail.

Proportions: about the size of a Hobby, but with different proportions and completely different behaviour. The wings are a little broader and more rounded and the hand is scarcely as long. The tail is longer and relatively the longest among the small falcons, apart from the Lesser Kestrel.

Plumage: the adult male is pale on the underside with a brownish-yellow tinge, particularly on the body. Both the body and wing-coverts are spotted, the latter appearing very pale. The flight feathers have weakly defined bands. The tail is pale grey to blue-grey above and below with a very conspicuous black distal band (A 1). The upperside is very characteristic with its red-brown colour on the body and most of the wing-coverts (D 2), both marked with black spots. In contrast are the mainly black flight feathers (D 3). The crown is blue-grey.

The adult female is considerably more spotted, with more subdued coloration. This is most marked on the upperside which is not a warm red-brown but more brown, with numerous transverse bands on the coverts. The flight feathers are not as dark as in the male. The tail is brownish and striped (E 4) and the crown is brownish. So there is distinct sexual dimorphism.

Young birds: very like the adult female, but often with a more yellowish underside. The spots on belly and sides of the body being long but rather diffuse.

In the field the juveniles can be recognized by the fact that the large upper wing-coverts are light in colour, forming a band along the wings. Furthermore the legs and feet are greenish yellow compared to the adult females, which have yellow legs and feet.

The juvenile birds can often be distinguished as to their sex. The juvenile female having brown, striped tail feathers and upper tail-coverts, where the juvenile male often has become grey, sometimes also with a grey head.

In the course of the first winter *the juvenile male* moults a large part of its body feathers, whereafter it can be recognized without difficulty. Its back is now brownish red with black spots. The juvenile tail feathers are moulted in August-September (2K).

In spring *the juvenile female* is very difficult to distinguish from the adult female.

Flight: for a falcon the Kestrel is not a particularly powerful flier. It often uses a somewhat fluttering mode of flight, almost throwing itself from side to side. The wing beats are rapid, slightly stiff and not particularly deep. Active flight is frequently interrupted by gliding. When hovering the wing beats are rapid and whirring with the tail spread and depressed. Particularly during migrations Kestrels have a rapid, gliding and elegant mode of flight.

Characteristic behaviour: mostly seen hovering over open country.

Likelihood of confusion: *see* under Lesser Kestrel and Red-footed Falcon.

Kestrel (w. 68–82 cm)

A ad. ♂

1 →

B ad. ♀

C juv.

D ad. ♂

E ad. ♀

2 →

4 →

→

F soaring

Lesser Kestrel
Falco naumanni

General impression: very like a Kestrel in silhouette.

Proportions: a little smaller than a Kestrel, a touch more slender with slightly narrower and more pointed hands and usually with a more pointed tail (A 1 and D 1). However, the use of these characters requires much experience.

Plumage: the adult male has characteristic pale underparts with a yellowish body and grey under the wings. As shown (A) this may be almost unspotted. There are usually dark spots on the wing-coverts (B). The dark tips to the primaries (A 2 and B 2) are typical of the species. The dark distal band on the blue-grey tail (A 1) is also distinctive. As in the Kestrel the upperside is rust-red, contrasting with the dark primaries. But unlike the Kestrel the present species has unspotted underparts (D 3). The greater wing-coverts are blue-grey but this is difficult to see. On the whole has stronger colours than the male

Kestrel. The head, for instance, is a brighter blue-grey colour. Unlike the Kestrel there is only a trace of moustachial streak.

The adult female is very like a female Kestrel, and the two cannot always be distinguished (*see* under Likelihood of confusion).

Young birds: in their first plumage are difficult to distinguish from the adult females. In some cases the upperside has a more reddish ground colour. As moulting proceeds the young males will show a transitional plumage between juvenile and adult.

Flight: very similar to the Kestrel. The flight may be faster and more whirring. The Kestrel's tendency to flutter and move from side to side is not so pronounced in the Lesser Kestrel. The bird often hovers but again not so much as the Kestrel.

Characteristic behaviour: nests in colonies, often in towns, more commonly than the Kestrel.

Likelihood of confusion: in spite of the plumage differences between the males of this species and the Kestrel, the two are similar in general appearance, flight and behaviour and so are often difficult to distinguish. However, when conditions are good the Lesser Kestrel can be recognized by its pale underside without or almost without spots, and by its own spotted back. The blue-grey greater wing-coverts may be difficult to see in flight. The elongated tail feathers are an excellent recognition character when they are present. In practice it will be impossible to distinguish the females from those of the Kestrel. The Lesser Kestrel is a slightly more slender bird, often with a more pointed tail, and it is faster in flight than a Kestrel. All in all, the identification of these two species is one of the most serious problems among European raptors.

Lesser Kestrel

A ad. ♂

B ad. ♂

D ad. ♂

C ad. ♀

E

F soaring

379

Bibliography

1. Cramp, S. & Simmons, K.E.L.: Handbook of the Birds of Europe, the Middle East and North Africa, Vol. II, 1980.
2. Parslow, J.L.F. & Everett, M.J.: Birds in need of special protection in Europe. Council of Europe, 1981.
3. Bijleveld, M.: Birds of prey in Europe, 1974.
4. Flint, P.R. & Stewart, P.F.: The birds of Cyprus. London (Brit. Orn. Union), 1983.
5. Theide, W.: Persönliche Beobachtungen und Informationen.
6. Galushin, V.M. & Pereva, V.I.: Status of rare raptors in USSR. Bul. 1. WWGBP.
7. Randla, T. & Oun, A.: Annual Status Report., 1982 Halieaetus albicilla. Bul. 1. WWGBP.
8. Thomsen, Jørgen B.: Projekt Havørn. Fugle 1982: 3.
9. Nilsson, Sven G.: De svenska rovfågelbeståndens storlek. V.F. 1981: 249–62.
10. Saurola, P. (1985): Finnish birds of prey: status and population changes Orn. Fenn. 62: 64–72.
11. Randla, T.: Estii röövlinnud, Tallin 1976.
12. Glutz, N. et al.: Handbuch der Vögel Mitteleuropas, Band 4, Falconiformes, 1971.
13. Naurois, R. de (1982): Remarques à propos des Buses (Buteo buteo ssp.) observés en Afrique occidentale. Malimbus 4: 5–8.
14. Thibault, J.C.: Status et effectifs des rapaces de Corce. Courier du Parc de la Corce, 1978.
15. Thomsen, Jørgen B.: pers. comments. +3. verdenskongres om rovfugle. DOFT 1982: 153–4.
16. Helander, B. (1983): Reproduction of the White-tailed Sea Eagle in Sweden – Dep. of Zoology, Univ. of Stockholm.
17. Rüger, A. & Neumann, T. (1982): Das Projekt Seeadlerschutz in Schleswig-Holstein. Min. f. Landwirt. u. Forsten.
18. British Birds 1988: 1, 1988: 3, 1988: 9.
19. Meyburg, B.-U. (1984): Present status . . . countries bordering the Mediterranean. IV. Int. Conf. on Med. Birds of Prey.
20. Sylvén, M.: Projekt Glada verksamhetsrap. f. perioden 1981–2. V.F. 1983: 106–14.
21. Sveriges Natur 1986:1, 1987: 6.
22. Rheinwald, G.: Brutvogelatlas der Bundesrepublik Deutschland – DDA. 1982.
23. Fischer, W.: Zur Situation des Rotmilans – Der Falke 1980: 86–7.
24. DOFT 1986: 75.
25. Schifferli, A. et al.: Atlas des Oiseaux de Suisse. 1980.
26. Chiavatta, M.: Status of Italian Breeding Population. World Conf. on Birds of Prey, 1977.
27. Garzon, J.: Birds of prey in Spain, the Present Situation. World Conf. on Birds of Prey, 1977.
28. Tjernberg, M.: Breeding ecology of the Golden Eagle. Aquila chrysaetos, in Sweden (1983).
29. Horner, K.O. et al.: Density of Black-shouldered Kites in Egypt. The Ostrich 1982: 249–51.
30. British Birds 1982: 249–51.
31. Meyburg, B.U.: Distribution and Present Status of the Black Vulture. Bul 1. WWGBP, 1983.
32. Cortes, J.E. et al.: The birds of Gibraltar (1980).
33. British Birds 1981: 260.
34. Viksne, J.: Birds of Latvia, 1983.
35. Nørreevang, A. & Hartog, J.C. den (1984): Birds obs. in the Cape Verde Islands. Cour. Forsch.-Inst. Senckenberg 68: 107–34.
36. Rutschke, E.: Die Vogelwelt Brandenburgs, 1983.
37. Richford, A.S. (1984): The . . . status of Black Vulture in Mallorca. Bull. Brit. Orn. Cl. 104: 117–18.
38. Opdam, P. (1980): Roofvogels en mens: een geslande combinatie? Limosa 53: 139–40.
39. Clouet, M.: L'Aigle royal (Aquila chrysaetos) dans les Pyrenees françaises. L'oiseau et la Revue Française d'ornit 1981: 89–90.
40. Haraszthy, L. and Bagyura, F.: Greifvögel daten von Ungarn. Pers. letter (1988).
41. Schenk, H.: Status and Conservation of Birds of Prey in Sardinia. World Conf. on Birds of Prey, 1977.
42. Puscariu, V. & Filipascu, A.: The Situation of Birds of Prey in Rumania 1970–4. World Conf. on Birds of Prey, 1977.
43. Danko, S.: Number of breeding pairs of birds of prey in Czechoslovakia. Pers. letter (1988).
44. Hartog, J.C. den, Lavaleye, M.S.S. (1981): Birds Obs. in the Azores – Bocagiana 56.
45. WWGBP, Newsletter 5, 7 and 8.
46. Massa, B.: The Situation of the Falconiformes in Sicily. World Conf. on Birds of Prey, 1977.
47. Sharrock, J.T.R.: The Atlas of Breeding Birds of Britain and Ireland (1976).
48. Bauer, K.: Present Status of Birds of Prey in Austria. World Conf. on Birds of Prey, 1977.
49. Willgohs, J.F.: Birds of Prey in Norway. World Conf. on Birds of Prey, 1977.
50. Vår Fågelvärld 1987: 387.
51. Bomholt, P.: Population trends in Danish raptors since 1970. Proc. of the Third Nordic Congress of Orn., 1981.
52. Klafs, G. & Stübs, J.: Die Vogelwelt Mecklenburgs (1979).
53. Teixeira, R.N.: Atlas van de Nederlandse Broedvogels (1979).
54. British Birds 1982: 570.
55. Irish Birds 1988.
56. Jørgensen, H.E.: Rørhøg og Hedehøg. Fugle 1983: 2.

57. Risberg, L.: Årsrapport 1982. V.F. 1983: 301–32.
58. Enemar, A. & Unger, U.: Hur mange sparvhökar häckar im Sverige? Anser 1977: 107–12.
59. Looft, V. & Busche, G.: Vogelwelt Schleswig-Holsteins, Band 2. Greifvögel (1981).
60. Kenward & Lindsay: Understanding the Goshawk (1983).
61. Hagen, Y.: Loddenbenet musvåge. Norden Fugle i Farver, bind 5 (1961).
62. Haftorn, S.: Norges Fugler (1971).
63. Acar, B. et al.: Status and Migration of Birds of Prey in Turkey. World Conf. on Birds of Prey, 1977.
64. Vär Fuglefauna 1981: 205–8.
65. Cade, Tom J.: The Falcons of the World (1982).
66. British Birds 1980: 575.
67. Accipiter 1986: 4.
68. The Peregrine Fund. Newsletter No. 10: 1–4.
69. BTO New No. 120: 3.
70. Ornis-Consult. Nyt 1988: 3.
71. British Birds 1981: 261.
72. Kjøller, F.: pers. comments.
73. Benoit, F. (1981): La distribution de Faucon hobereau, Falco subbuteo, en Suisse – Nos Oiseaux 36: 21–4.
74. Dybbro, T.: Oversigt over Danmarks Fugle (1978).
75. Sveriges Natur 1988: 1.
76. Kesteloot, E.J.J.: Present Situation of Birds of Prey in Belgium. World Conf. on Birds of Prey, 1977.
77. Meyburg, B.-U. (1985): . . . Die Situation des Wanderfalken in Deutschland. WWGBP 2: 4–5.
78. Bloch, D.: Fugeltællinger på Færøerne sommeren 1981. DOFT 1981: 1–6.
79. British Birds 1987: 1, 1987: 7.
80. Król, W.: pers. medd.
81. DOFT 1980: 81.
82. Bruun, B.: The Lappet-faced Vulture in the Middle East. Sandgrouse No. 5: 91–2, 1983.
83. Peltzer, R. (1981): Zur Brutveerbreitung des Rotmilans (Milvus milvus) in Luxemburg – Regulus 14: 72–7.
84. Handrinos, G. & Demetropoulos, A.: Birds of Prey of Greece. Athens 1983.
85. Berthon, D. & Compte, S.: Rendu de l'expedition . . . du Maroc. L'oiseau et la Revue Française d'ornit, 1984.
86. Folkestad, A.V.: Situasjonen for havørna, Haliaeetus albicilla i Norge. Vår Fuglefauna 1984: 209–14.
87. Dornbusch, M.: Bestand und Schutz der Greifvögel und Eulen in der DDR. Der Falke 1986: 12.
88. Berrgo, G.: Projekt hønsehauk. Vår Fuglefauna, 1984.
89. Robel, D. & Königstedt, D.: Der Adlerbuzard in Bulgarien. Der Falke 1984: 258–65.
90. Schrei, P.J.: Siste nytt on vandrefalken. Vår Fuglefauna 1984: 224–6.
91. Lindberg, P.: Projekt Pilgrimsfalk. Sveriges Natur 1984: 1.
92. Thiollay, J.-M. & Terrace, J.-F. (ed.) (1984). Estimation des effectifs de rapaces nicheurs diurnes et non rupestres en France. Enquete FIR/UN-AO 1979–82 X + 178 S.
93. Dennis, R.H. et al. (1984): The status of the Golden Eagle in Britain. Brit. Birds 77: 592–607.
94. Weiss, J. (1981): Baumfalkenvorkommen in Luxemburg. Regulus 14: 108–10.
95. Lelov, E. (1984): The Golden Eagle in South-West Estonia. Eesti Loodus 27: 774–5.
96. Newsletter No. 4 (Aug. 1984) WWGBP.
97. Benny Génsbøl: Inform. from III World Conf. on birds of prey in Elat 1987.
98. Sylvén, M.: Förekomst af större och mindre skrigörn i Sverige V.F. 1975: 27–36.

General bibliography

Arroyo, B. et al.: Biologia de reproduccion de una pareja de Hieraaetus fasciatus en España central. Doñana Acta Vert. 3: 1976: 33–45.

Backhurst G. C. & Pearson, D.J.: Southward migration at Ngulia, Tsavo, Kenya 1978/79. Scopus 3: 1979: 19–25.

Balfour, E.: Obs. on breeding biology of the Hen Harrier in Orkney. Bird notes 1957. 177–83 & 216–24.

–: The nests and the eggs of the Hen Harrier in Orkney. Bird notes 1962: 69–73.

–: The Hen Harrier in Orkney. Bird notes 1962–3: 145–53.

–: & Macdonald, M.: Food and feeding behaviour of the Hen Harrier in Orkney. Scot. Birds 1970: 157–66.

Baumgart, W.: Steht der Schreiadler unter Zeitdruck? Falke 27: 1980: 6–17.

Bednarek, W. et al: Über die Auswirkungen der chemischen Umweltbelastung auf Greifvögel in zwei Probeflächen Westfalens. J. Orn 1975: 181–94.

Bertel, B.: Feltbestemmelse af Laerke- og Aftenfalk. Felt. 1976: 101–106.

Brown, L.: Birds of Prey. London 1976.

–: British Birds of Prey. London 1976.

Brüll, H.: Das Leben europäischer Greifvögel. Stuttgart 1977.

Bylin, K.: Bruna kärrhöken, Circus aeruginosus i Sverige år 1979. V.F. 1981: 455–60.

Calderon, J.: El papel de la Perdiz roja (Alectoris rufa) en la dicta de los predadores ibéricos. Doñana Acta Vert. 4: 1977: 61–126.

Cant, G.: Eleonora's Falcon wintering in the Southern Aegean. Nature – Hellenic Soc. f. Prot. of Nature. 1978: 28–9.

Christensen, S.: Feltbestemmelse af ung Aftenfalk. Felt. 1970: 154–5.

–: Feltbestemmelse af overgangsdragten af hanner af Hedehøg og Steppehøg. DOFT 1977: 11–27.

–: et al.: The spring migration of raptors in Southern Israel and Sinai. Sandgrouse 1981: 1–42.

Cheylan, G.: La place ..phique de l'Aigle de Bonelli Hieraaetus fasciatus dans les biocénoses méditerranéennes. Alauda 45: 1977: 1–15.

Cronert, H.: Lärkfalkens förekomst i Skåne. Anser 1978: 101–108.

Dyck, J.: Miljøgifte og bestandsaendringer hos fugle (i "Status over den danske dyreverden", Zool. Museum, København, 1972).

Ferdinand, J.: Nogle danske Dagrofugles føde: DOFT: 1923: 97–112.

–: & Paludan, K.: Fortsatte undersøgelser over danske rovfugles og uglers føde: DOFT: 1931: 89–103.

Fischer, W.: Der Wanderfalke. Wittenberg-Lutherstadt 1967.

Franco, A. & Andrada, J.: Alimentacion y seleccion de presa en Falco naumanni. Ardeola 23: 1977: 137–87.

Frey, F.: Darf der Bartgeier wieder fliegen? Natursch. heute 17:2: 1985: 11.

Galushin, V.M.: Synchronous fluctuations in populations of some raptors and their prey. The Ibis 1974: 128–34.

Goslow, G.E.: The attack and strike of some North American raptors. The Auk 1971; 816–27.

Göransson, L.: Duvhökens betydelse för vinterdödligheten hos fasaner. Anser 1975: 11–22.

Haller, H.: Raumorganisation und Dynamik einer Population des Steinadlers Aquila chrysaetos in den Zentralalpen. Orn. Beob. 79: 1982: 163–211.

Hantge, E.: Untersuchungen über den Jagderfolg mehrere europäischer Greifvögel. J. Orn. 1980: 200–207.

Hogg, P.: On the Barbary Falcon Falco pelegrinoides in North Eastern Africa. Malimbus 5: 1983: 90.

Holstein, V.: Duehøgen. København 1942.

–: Hvepsevågen. København 1944.

–: Spurvehøgen. København 1950.

–: Musvågen. København 1956.

Höglund, N.: Der Habicht in Fennoskandia . . . Viltrevy 1964: 195–270.

–: Über die Ernährung des Habichts in Schweden. Viltrevy 1964: 271–328.

Högstedt, G.: Födosökstek-nik hos bivråken. Anser 1976: 150–51.

Hård, I. & Enemar, A.: Stenfalkens, Falco columbarius, byteval och matning under ungarnas botid. V.F. 1980: 25–34.

Tribarren, J. J.: Biologia del Aguila Calzada (Hieraaetus pennatus) durante el periodo de nidificacion en Navarra. Ardeola 21: 1975: 305–20.

Jordano, P.: Relaciones interespecificas y coexistencia entre el Aguila Real (Aquila chrysaetos) y el Aguila Perdicera (Hieraaetus fasciatus) en Sierra Morena central. Ardeola 28: 1981: 67–87.

Jørgensen, H. E. et al: Ynglebestanden af Rørhøg, Circus aeruginosus i Danmark 1979–81. DOFT. 1982: 3–14.

Kalchreuter, H.: Habicht, Mench und Beutetier. Wildforsch. Baden-Württ. Nr. 1, 1980.

Kenward, R.E.: Predation on released Pheasants (Phasianus colchicus) by Goshawks (Accipiter gentilis) in central Sweden. Viltrevy 1977: 79–112.

–: Hawks and Doves: Factors effecting success and selection in Goshawk attacks on Woodpigeons. J. of Animal Ecology 1978: 449–60.

–: Goshawk hunting behaviour, and range size as a function of food and habitat availability. J. of Animal Ecology 1982: 69–80.

–: et al: Goshawk winter ecology in Swedish Pheasant habitats. J. Wildl. Manage 1981: 397–408.

Lindberg, P.: Forsök med "dubbla äggkullar" för pilgrimsfalk. V.F. 1981: 273–7.

–: Första falkarne utplanterade. Sveriges Natur 1982: 7:1–5.

Marcström, V. & Kenward, R.E.: Movements of wintering Goshawks in Sweden. Viltrevy 1981: 3.35.

Mebs, T.: Zur Biologi und Populationsdynamik des Mäusebussards. J. Orn. 1964: 247–306.

Meyburg, B-U.: Studies of

. . . Lesser Spotted Eagle. Br. Birds 1973: 439–47.

Moll. T.: Pilgrimsfalken i Finland. Sv. Natur 1979: 73–5.

Møller, A. Pape: Nordjyllands Fugle. Klampenborg 1978.

Newton, I.: Population Ecology of Raptors. Berkhamsted 1979.

–: **& Marquis, S.:** Effects of additional food on laying dates and clutch sizes of Sparrowhawks. Orn Scan. 1981: 224–9.

Nielsen, B. Pors: Danske Musvågers, *Buteo buteo*, trækforhold og spredning. DOFT. 1977: 1–10.

–: Danske tårnfalkes, *Falco tinnunculus*, trækforhold og spredning. DOFT. 1983: 1–12.

Norderhaug, M.: Report from WWF symposium on the White-tailed Eagle. WWF Norge 1977.

Norriss, D.W. & Wilson, H.J.: Survey of the Peregrine in Ireland 1981: Bird Study 1983: 91–101.

Odsjö, T. & Sondell, J.: Populationsutveckling och häckningsresultat hos brun kärrhök, *Circus aeruginosus*, i relation til förekomsten af DDT, PCB och kviksilver. V.F. 1977: 152–60.

–: Fiskgjusen – inventering. 1978. Sv. Natur: 1979: 16–18.

Olsen, S.F.: Artsbestemmelse av vandrefalk og jaktfalk. Vår Fuglefauna 1983,1: 15–19.

Olsson, V.: Revir, biotop och boplatsval hos svenska havsörnar. V.F. 1972: 89–95.

Österlöf, S.: Fiskgjusen i Sverige 1971. V.F. 1973: 100–106.

–: Migration, wintering areas and site tenacity of the European Osprey, *Pandion haliaëtus*. Orn. Scan. 1977: 61–78.

Ornithologische Arbeitsgem. Bodensee: Die Vögel des Bodenseegebietes. Konstanz (Selbstv).: 1983.

Palästhy, J. & Meyburg, B.-U.: Zur Ernährung des Schreiadlers (Aquila pomarina) in der Ostslowakei unter atypischen klimatischen Bedingungen. Orn. Mitt. 25:

1973: 63–72.

Pearson, D. J. & Meadows, B.S.: Lesser Spotted Eagles Aquila pomarina in Kenya during 1978/79, with comments on the identification of the species. Scopus 3: 1979: 48–53.

Pedersen, K.: Rovfulgenes forårstræk over Skagen. Fugle 1983,1: 12–13 & 30.

Perrins, C.M. & Geer, T.A.: The effect of Sparrowhawks on tit populations. Ardea 1980: 133–42.

Porter, R.F. *et al*: Flight Identification of European Raptors, 3. udgave. Berkhamsted 1981.

Ratcliffe, D.: The Peregrine Falcon. Calton (Poyser).

Rebecca, G.: Status and breeding ecology of Merlin in Grampian. Scott. Birds 12: 1983: 195–6.

Ritzel, L.: Der Durchzug von Greifvögel . . . über Bosporus im Frühjahr 1978. Die Vogelwarte 1980: 149–62.

Rüppel, G.: Analyse des Beutefanges des Fischadler (Pandion haliaëtus). J. Orn. 1981: 285–305.

Rudebeck, G.: The choice of prey . . . Contribution No. 75 from Falsterbo Bird Station. 1976.

Rust, R. & Kechele, W.: Ergebnisse langjähriger Bestandskontrollen beim Habicht (Accipiter gentilis) auf zwei südbayerischen Kontrollflächen. Garmisch. Vogelk. Ber. 11: 1982: 10–26.

Schelde, O.: Danske spurvehøges trækforhold. DOFT. 1960: 88–102.

Schilling, F. & König, C.: Die Biozidbelastung des Wanderfalkes J. Orn. 1980: 1–35.

Suetens, W. & Groenendael, P. van: Sobre Ecologia y reproductore del Buitre Negro (*Aegypius monachus*). Ardeola 1966: 19–50.

–: La indigestión du Vautour moine, *Aegypius monachus*. Gerfaut 1967: 93–118.

Svensson, Lars: Större skrigörn *Aquila clanga* och mindre skrigörn *Aquila pomarina* - problemet att artsbestämma dem. V.F. 1975: 1–26.

–: *et al*: Sveriges Fåglar. Stockholm 1978.

–: Om bestämning i fält av bivråk. V.F. 1981: 1–12.

–: Fjällvråkdräkter. Fåglar i Stockholmstragten 1982: 136–41.

Sylvén, M.: Ålderskriterier hos glada och brun glada. V.F. 1977: 33–7.

–: Reproduction and survival in Common Buzzards (*Buteo buteo*). 1983.

Thiollay, J.M.: Migration de printemps au Cap Bon. Nos Oiseau 1975: 109–21.

Tjernberg, M.: Presentation av Projekt kungsörn. Anser suppl. 3, 1978: 235–8.

–: Diet of the Golden Eagle, *Aquila chrysaëtos*, during the breeding season in Sweden. Orn. Scan. 1981: 139.

–: Breeding ecology of the Golden Eagle, *Aquila chrysaëtos* in Sweden. Uppsala 1983.

Uttendörfer, C.: Neue Ergebnisse uber die Ernahrung der Greifvögel und Eulen. Stuttgart (Ulmer): 1952.

Voigt, A.: Exkursionsbuch zum Studium der Vogelstimmen. 9. Aufl. (Quelle & Meyer): 1921.

Walther, H.: Eleonora's Falcon. Adaptation to Prey and Habitat in a Social Raptor. Univ. of Chicago Press, 1979.

Westernhagen, W. v.: Zuggeselligkeit bei Greifvögeln. Vogelwarte 18: 1955: 15–19.

Wiklund, Ch. G.: Increased breeding success for Merlins Falco columbarius nesting among colonies of Fieldfares Turdus pilaris. Ibis 121: 1979: 109–11.

Williams, G.A.: The Merlin in Wales: breeding numbers, habitat and success. Brit. Birds 74: 1981: 205–14.

Willgous, J.: The White-tailed Eagle in Norway. Bergen 1961.

Wonneberger, G.: Brutbestand und Zug der Weihen im Rheinland seit 1947. Charadrius 11: 1975: 85–91.

Ziesemer, F.: Untersuchungen zum Einfluß des Habichts (Accipiter gentilis) auf Populationen seiner Beutetiere. Beitre. Wildbiol 2 (Hartmann V., Kronshagen): 1983.

Index